Handbook for Research Students
in the Social Sciences

Handbook for Research Students in the Social Sciences

Edited by

Graham Allan and Chris Skinner

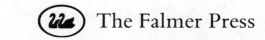 The Falmer Press

(A member of the Taylor & Francis Group)
London · New York · Philadelphia

UK   The Falmer Press, 4 John St., London, WC1N 2ET
USA   The Falmer Press, Taylor & Francis Inc., 1900 Frost Road, Suite 101,
      Bristol, PA 19007

First published 1991

**British Library Cataloguing in Publication Data
A catalogue record for this book is available from the British
Library**

**Library of Congress Cataloging-in-Publication Data is available
on request**

Typeset in 10/12.5 pt Bembo by
Graphicraft Typesetters Ltd., Hong Kong

*Printed in Great Britain by Burgess Science Press, Basingstoke on paper
which has a specified pH value on final paper manufacture of not less than 7.5
and is therefore 'acid free'.*

Contents

Contents

Foreword

Howard Newby

I write from the unique perspective of someone who was a research student funded by the ESRC (then SSRC), but who is at present Chairman of the Council responsible for postgraduate training in the social sciences in the UK. For both reasons I take a personal interest in the evolution of the ESRC's training policy and in ensuring, wherever possible, that both the ESRC and the students themselves receive value for money from the investment which we, and they, make during the period of our studentships.

In recent years the public debate about research studentships has tended to be dominated by management and procedural issues — submission rates, stipend levels, supervision arrangements, and the like. As a result, it has often been overlooked how great a substantive contribution to the social sciences is made by research students, whose theses will never be merely a training, but, in the phrase employed by many PhD regulations, an original contribution to knowledge. Students not only acquire research skills; they also contribute very substantially to the development of their chosen disciplines. A flourishing social science research community therefore requires a constant stream of high-quality research students in order to guarantee its future well-being.

In this regard we are commencing a crucial decade. For largely demographic reasons, we face a major turnover in personnel in universities and polytechnics towards the end of the 1990s. The cohort which entered academic social science during the rapid expansion of the 1960s will, by then, be approaching retirement. The recent lack of recruitment and the encouragement of early retirement has created a very narrow age band which will produce commensurate difficulties when it comes to recruiting their replacements.

These concerns are not, of course, limited to the academic sector alone. There is now a growing recognition that in Britain we must pay more attention to human resources if we are to maintain an internationally competitive edge. Properly trained research students will contribute the requisite skills to society as a whole, particularly as we move further towards a 'post-industrial' era in which the information economy will continue to grow in significance.

To contribute fully, however, students must be properly trained in research skills. This may sound a truism, but, observed from an ESRC standpoint, we must do our best to ensure that the renewal of the social science research community is based upon a sound training in skills that are appropriate to the 1990s and not the 1960s. The ESRC is not a degree-awarding body (nor would it wish to become one) and so we can only cajole, encourage and enable supervisors and students to employ good practice.

For this reason I regard this book as both welcome and timely. Good practice needs to be disseminated as widely as possible — but so, too, does information about the experience of being a research student, which has tended to be an isolated existence at the best of times. On certain matters students need good, hard advice — of a kind many supervisors too often take for granted. The skills required by research students are not just those relating to the finer points of hermeneutic epistemology, but practical matters to do with word-processing, access to libraries, writing skills, research ethics and choosing a supervisor. Half the battle in accomplishing a research degree is to recognize that it is a process which needs to be actively managed: the enemy of successful completion is lack of organization, intellectual drift and existential *ennui*.

The precise package of appropriate skills will clearly vary according to the needs of a particular student. However, there are certain basic skills which should be the prerequisite of any proper research training. Most of them are to be found in the following pages. They are the kinds of skills which will be a necessary, but not a sufficient, condition of research excellence. Perhaps they are best summarized by the phrase 'technical competence', which is not to be confused with intellectual contribution, but without which researchers will be stunted in their personal development and run the risk, at the very least, of intellectual impoverishment. The social sciences in the UK have gained an enviable international reputation. If it is to be sustained into the next century, our students will need to be adequately trained.

There are a number of students whose motivation to undertake a research degree is compellingly personal. The selection of a topic and the desire to research it is often guided by biographical, political and vocational reasons as much as intellectual or careerist ones. To these students research training can seem an irksome obstacle to their impatient desire to 'get on' with the 'real' research. I hope the sound advice offered in this book is sufficient demonstration of the folly of this approach. Certainly, the acquisition of research skills must never quench the initial personal enthusiasm. Indeed, it should complement, rather than interfere with, a student's motivation. But the notion that students can set out on a field of intellectual enquiry and simply pick up the requisite skills as they go along by some kind of *ad hoc* accretion, is becoming outmoded by developments in modern social science. A brief chat with a supervisor, followed by a couple of glasses of warm sherry at the end of each term, is not a research training.

Properly managed and organized, a research student's life can be an enormously rewarding and emancipatory period. For many the freedom it offers is unlikely to recur again during their subsequent careers. The frustrations are many and varied, finance is a constant concern; but on completion the sense of achievement is a real one and the frustrations will be forgotten. The contribution — to social science *and* personal development — will have been secured.

Howard Newby
Chairman
ESRC

Preface

This book is aimed primarily at social sciences research students in the United Kingdom. A research student is taken here to mean any student registered on a degree, whether at master's or doctoral level, which is conducted by research. Thus we exclude students on instructional courses, whether undergraduate or postgraduate. We should like to stress that our concern is with both part-time and full-time students since in our experience part-time students can feel somewhat marginalized and may have a particular need for a book such as this. While we focus on the needs of social sciences students, much of the book, in particular Parts 1 and 2, should also be of relevance to research students in other disciplines. Similarly, while aimed mainly at students studying at universities and polytechnics in the UK, we would expect that much of the book will be of relevance to research students elsewhere.

This book's origins lie in a scheme of training offered to research students at the University of Southampton. While being involved with this scheme, we have developed the impression that research students often experience a need for advice and information beyond that available from their supervisor or supervisory group; furthermore there is only a limited amount of relevant literature available to guide a social science student new to postgraduate research. The book's contents reflect what we and the contributors (almost all of whom have also been involved with the scheme) judge to be of most potential value to research students. Perhaps we should add here, given the current controversy surrounding research training, that we view books and training schemes as serving quite different functions and we are certainly not advocating the contents of this book as a curriculum for a training scheme. We view the book as a source of reference rather than as a course text.

The training scheme at Southampton involves contributions from a large number of individuals from many departments. In this way students can become acquainted with a wide variety of aspects of research in the social sciences and are able to follow up topics they find of particular interest with an individual staff member who has specific experience in that topic. The same style of presentation is employed here with diverse and short contributions, almost all of which provide suggestions for further reading in greater depth. The potential disadvantage of this style of presentation is that the coherence and consistency possible with a smaller number of contributors is harder to achieve. We have attempted as editors to create a coherent text but equally we hope that readers will find the concord, disagreement and variations in approach between chapters a source of interest rather than a problem.

We are very grateful to colleagues and students at the University of Southampton for their help and encouragement with this book; and to those who contributed to the volume our thanks for being so ready to meet deadlines and accept unreasonable word limits. Cathie Marsh made a number of very useful suggestions at an early stage, not all of which we were able to incorporate. Our special thanks too to Glynis Evans and Anne Owens who typed and corrected a number of the chapters in the book with great efficiency.

Graham Allan
Chris Skinner
University of Southampton
January, 1991

Notes on Contributors

Graham Allan is Senior Lecturer in Sociology at the University of South-ampton. His main teaching and research interests are in informal social relations and domestic life. His publications include *Family Life*; *Friendship: Developing A Sociological Perspective*; and, edited jointly with Graham Crow, *Home and Family*.

Begoña Arregui comes from the Basque Country, Spain. She was a full-time PhD student in demography, completing her thesis on 'The Evolution of Fertility in the Basque Country: 1950–1985' in 1989. Before registering for a PhD, she completed a first degree in Sociology and an MSc in Demography. In between degrees she undertook a variety of miscellaneous jobs, until she settled down for three years in an Employment Agency. She is currently involved in several demographic projects and lectures on Popula-tion at the University of the Basque Country.

Nick Axford is in his third year as a full-time PhD student. He is research-ing the role of development associations in local economic development. He became a research student directly after finishing his first degree in Geo-graphy, which he also took at Southampton University. Upon completion of his PhD he will be joining the research department of Gerald Eve Chartered Surveyors in London.

Ann Buchanan completed her PhD thesis in March 1990. While registered as a part-time student, she was working full-time as a senior social worker in a child and family guidance clinic. Before qualifying as a social worker, she undertook research into the causes of mental handicap. She is now a Lecturer in Social Studies at Bracknell College.

Stephanie Cadbury has been registered for three years as a part-time MPhil/PhD student, researching psychological aspects of depression and dependency in women. She works part-time (three days per week) as, a principal clinical psychologist, employed by the National Health Service. She is 36 years old and completed her first degree thirteen years ago.

Peter Calvert is Professor of Comparative and International Politics at the University of Southampton. His research and teaching interests focus international and comparative politics with special reference to Latin America and the USA. He has published widely, his most recent book being *Revolution and Counter-Revolution*.

Gordon Causer is Lecturer in Sociology at the University of Southampton. He has published papers on aspects of class structure and business organization and is editor of *Inside British Society*. His current research is concerned with the employment of scientific and technical personnel in high technology firms.

Jon Clark is Professor of Industrial Relations at the University of Southampton. He has published extensively in the fields of labour law and industrial relations. He is co-author of *The Process of Technological Change* and *Technological Change at Work*. He is also principal editor of the Falmer Sociology Series, and has recently published volumes on the work of Robert K. Merton, Anthony Giddens and John H. Goldthorpe in the series.

Chris Colbourn is Lecturer in Psychology at the University of Southampton. His major areas of research and teaching interest are in cognition and educational computing. He has published a number of papers in these fields.

Ian Forbes is Lecturer in Politics at the University of Southampton. His teaching includes political theory and British government, and the MSc in Equal Opportunities Studies. He has published on equality of opportunity, rights, Nietzsche, and international relations, has written *Marx and the New Individual* and co-edited *Politics and Human Nature*.

Tony Gale is Professor of Psychology at the University of Southampton. He has considerable experience of successful (and unsuccessful) PhD supervision in several universities. His research includes both experimental and qualitative work. He is series editor of the Wiley Psychophysiology Handbooks and his recent publications include *Ecological Studies of Family Life* (with Arlene Vetere) and *Smoking and Human Behaviour* (edited with Tara Ney).

Bryan Glastonbury is Professor in the Department of Social Work Studies at the University of Southampton. He is also Director of the CTI Centre for

Human Services at the University. His main teaching and research interests are the uses of computers in human services, the management of social services and social survey methods. His publications include *Computers in Social Work, Managing People in the Personal Social Services* and *Information Technology in the Human Services.*

Andy Hinde is Lecturer in Population Studies at the University of Southampton. He has analyzed data from a number of large national surveys, in particular the Women and Employment Survey, and has also published several papers based on the analysis of data from the nineteenth-century censuses of England and Wales.

Tim Holt is Leverhulme Professor of Social Statistics at the University of Southampton. He has published extensively on the properties of statistical methods of analysis when applied to sample survey data.

Carol Jones is Senior Lecturer in Employee Relations in the Department of Organization Studies in the Lancashire Business School at Lancashire Polytechnic. Prior to this she was a Research Fellow at the New Technology Research Group at the University of Southampton. Her research and teaching interests include gender in employment, women in engineering and women managers.

Robin Lovelock is Fellow in Applied Social Studies in the Department of Social Work Studies at the University of Southampton. He is also Director of that Department's Centre for Evaluative and Developmental Research (CEDR). His main interests are in applied research methodology, quantitative and qualitative evaluative research and the interface between social and health care services.

Diana Marshallsay retired from the post of Sub-Librarian at Southampton University Library at the end of 1990, having specialized in official publications for thirty-six years. She is joint editor of two volumes in the Southampton University Studies in Parliamentary Papers series and was closely involved with several others. She has indexed over fifty books for staff in the Faculty of Social Sciences and is the author of a number of articles and book reviews.

Haydn Mathias is Senior Lecturer in Academic Staff Development in the Department of Teaching Media, University of Southampton. He is responsible for coordinating the University's Academic Staff Development Programme and organizes seminars and workshops on a variety of educational topics, including lecturing and presentation skills, small group teaching, research supervision, study skills, evaluation of teaching and the use of audio-visual aids.

Jill MacKean has spent five years as Senior Experimental Officer in the Department of Social Statistics at the University of Southampton. Prior to this she was involved in the practical aspects of organizing surveys. Her main interests are survey research, design and analysis. She has now left the University in order to devote her time to consultancy work.

Joan Orme is a Lecturer in Social Work Studies at the University of Southampton. She is a consultant to the Home Office National Probation Service. Her main teaching and research interests include women in social services, women in management, work load management and equal opportunities. Her publications include *Managing People in the Personal Social Services* (with Bryan Glastonbury and Richard Bradley). She is also Director of the Personal Research Programme in the Department of Social Work Studies.

Chris Parker is an Information Officer working at the University of Southampton Library, specializing in information technology, enquiry services and user education.

Jackie Powell is Lecturer in the Department of Social Work Studies at the University of Southampton. She is Associate Director of the Department's Centre for Evaluative and Developmental Research (CEDR). Her main research and teaching interests include quantitative and qualitative evaluative research, developing mental health services and the impact on professional practice, and users' views of health and social services.

Tony Rees is Senior Lecturer in Social Policy at the University of Southampton. His interests include social theory, policy analysis, nineteenth and twentieth-century social history, housing and social security. He is the author (with Eric Briggs) of *Supplementary Benefits and the Consumer* and of a completely revised fifth edition of *T.H. Marshall's Social Policy* and is currently editing (with James Connolly) a book of essays on 'Citizenship and Welfare'.

Howard Rose is a Senior Lecturer in Management Studies at Southampton Institute of Higher Education. Previously he was a Research Fellow at the New Technology Research Group at the University of Southampton, a unit with which he is still associated. His research interests are in the area of new technology and organizational change. He is co-author of *The Process of Technological Change*.

Chris Skinner is Senior Lecturer in Social Statistics at the University of Southampton. His main teaching and research interests include sample surveys and statistical theory. He was the first course tutor of the Faculty of Social Sciences Postgraduate Research Training Scheme at the University of Southampton.

John H. Smith is Professor of Sociology at the University of Southampton. He has published widely on sociological aspects of management, and is currently completing a long-term study of the pioneering work of Elton Mayo.

Chapter 1

Introduction

Graham Allan and Chris Skinner

Being a research student is a quite different experience to being a student on an instructional programme. The latter will comprise a number of separate courses, each with their own objectives defined by given syllabuses, examinations and course-work requirements. Basic resources for following each course are supplied to the student in the form of lectures, seminars and reading lists. With a research degree, on the other hand, you have the opportunity to investigate a single topic in considerable depth but without the guidance and signposting of taught courses. Being a research student can thus be quite a lonely experience. Apart from library and computing services and perhaps various forms of research training, your main 'resource' will be the individual guidance provided by your supervisor or supervisory group, supplemented by the support and friendship of other research students.

This book is not intended to compete with the advice offered by your supervisor. Rather it is meant to provide one further resource to assist you in your research by acting as a source of reference. It contains discussions of a wide range of topics which have been selected to be of most direct value to research students in the social sciences. Different parts of the book may be of greater relevance at different stages of your research. Because the book does not involve the linear development of a single theme, it is not expected that chapters be read in sequence. Rather we hope that you will find it useful to dip into different chapters when you find them most appropriate. Because of the obvious impossibility of including everything of relevance to a social science research student in a book of this length, most of the chapters are intended to act only as introductions, signposting you to further sources where you can read about the subject in greater depth.

The broad contents of the different parts of the book are as follows:

Part 1: The Nature of a Research Degree

This part of the book provides some orientation towards what a research degree entails and how it differs from an instructional course. The aim is to give you a flavour of what you can expect from a research degree as a personal experience and to offer some suggestions as to how to make the most of that experience. While the various rewards of research study are mentioned, there is inevitably an emphasis on the possible pitfalls and difficulties that may arise, since it is mainly in relation to these aspects that advice is relevant. We hope that such a focus on problems will not in any way dampen the enthusiasm with which you embark on research study!

Chapter 2 provides an introduction to the nature of a research degree. It draws on research on the experiences of research students and emphasizes, in particular, the importance of the student–supervisor relationship. Chapter 3 includes a number of personal accounts of postgraduate research by both students and supervisors. The students reflect on their own experiences and the strategies they have found most useful in research study. We have deliberately included accounts from students with a diversity of experiences, for example two are full-time and two are part-time. Following these accounts, the chapter includes advice from two experienced supervisors who use their knowledge of supervising research students to offer useful hints and guidance.

The final chapter in this section, Chapter 4, discusses what examiners are looking for in a thesis. While this chapter may seem most relevant nearer the time of submission, it should also be of interest to new students attempting to understand what a research degree entails in terms of the expected final product.

Part 2: Study Skills and the Management of Research

One factor which emerges from Part 1 as being vitally important in the success of research study is the effective management of the research. Clearly management concerns the strategy and design of your specific project (matters considered in Part 3), but it also involves the way you handle the different tasks and demands which any prolonged piece of academic research entails. It is these which are the focus of Part 2. In particular, this section includes discussions of a variety of the skills and crafts which will prove useful in carrying out your research.

Chapter 5 provides an introduction to the broad range of skills which you will need to develop in managing and organizing your project. Included in this is a discussion of the use of computing and information technology, such as word-processing and the compilation of bibliographies.

It is followed by two chapters on the use of libraries — obviously a significant component in most students' research. Chapter 6 deals with computer-based methods of literature search and is likely to be of particular relevance in the early stages of your research when you are carrying out a literature review and trying to ensure familiarity with previous studies. Chapter 7 is a little more specialized. It provides a guide to official publications in Britain, which constitute a complex body of materials, though one which is of particular relevance to a good number of research students in the social sciences.

Next come two chapters concerned with the skills required in communicating your ideas to others. The focus of Chapter 8 is on writing skills. These are of course of major importance in the actual production of your thesis. However, as the personal views in Chapter 3 indicate, they will be essential throughout your time as a student for you will need to be able to express your ideas clearly at all stages of your work. The presentation and communication skills discussed in Chapter 9, while not quite so fundamental, can nevertheless be very helpful in order to communicate your work to persons other than your supervisor and hence achieve broader feedback on your research.

Chapter 10 is concerned with using documentary sources in the social sciences. Different projects will rely to a greater or lesser extent on such sources, but nearly all research makes some use of them, at least in the context of reviewing previous approaches. The aim of this chapter is to highlight some of the more important issues you need to address in using documentary material.

The following three chapters are more directly concerned with the management and conduct of research than with specific skills. Much empirical research conducted by students in the social sciences takes place within the setting of an organization or agency, such as a business or the health or probation service. To gain access to such agencies and to achieve cooperation with individuals within the agency requires considerable care. This is the subject matter of Chapter 11. Chapter 12 is concerned with the sorts of ethical issues that are likely to confront research students. As is pointed out, much research in social science involves ethical questions, the answers to which are not always straightforward. Finally, the related issue of the relevance of equal opportunity considerations to research in the social sciences is discussed in Chapter 12. Again the point is made that these matters are of concern to all research students and not just those conducting research into discrimination and disadvantage.

Part 3: Research Strategies in the Social Sciences

It would be virtually impossible to provide a general discussion of research strategies which would be of value to all research students in the social sciences because the differences between the kinds of research undertaken are so great. For example, what advice would be relevant to both a laboratory-based study in experimental psychology, a theoretical study of the political philosophy of Hegel, an ethnographic study of 'acid-house' parties and a computer-based study of the statistical properties of an econometric procedure? To make our task more manageable we restrict our attention in Part 3 to different forms of empirical research because of the great difficulty in offering general advice on theoretical research which would be relevant across disciplines.

Even within the restricted area of empirical research, there are very wide variations in research strategies. These variations are reflected by the range of books available on research methodology in the social sciences. You might ask whether our brief discussions in Part 3 can add anything useful to this literature. In reply we would point out that much existing research methods literature is addressed to the generic 'researcher', who often does not work under the same time and resource constraints as a research student. For example, texts on survey methods may discuss strategies which would be feasible for a government survey agency or a large organization but not for an individual research student. Thus the feature of Part 3 which is intended to distinguish it from more general methodology texts is that it specifically addresses the needs of research students. This has implications for our selection of topics. For example, a whole chapter is devoted to secondary analysis (Chapter 20) since this is a form of research which is particularly feasible for a research student. As a further example, there is some emphasis on interviewing skills (Chapters 17 and 19) since research students are themselves often involved in interviewing, but we include little discussion of issues related to the use of teams of interviewers since this is seldom an option for research students.

Even with a focus on the needs of research students conducting empirical research, we stress that the chapters in Part 3 can only provide brief introductions and that in this part of the book, even more than in Part 2, an important role of each chapter is to point to further literature where topics are considered in more depth.

Let us then turn to the contents of Part 3. Chapter 14 provides an introduction to the elements of the research process and to the strategic choices facing the research student. This is an important chapter for all students but especially for those who are currently involved in developing the research strategy they are going to pursue in their study.

The following chapters are separated into two broad groups concerning qualitative and quantitative research. While this distinction can be over-emphasized, we hope it provides some loose structuring of the chapters for the benefit of the reader. Chapter 15 provides an introduction to qualitative research and offers an overview of some of the major issues raised by this type of research. The two chapters that follow are concerned more with specific approaches. Chapter 16 examines the nature and use of case studies, while Chapter 17 discusses qualitative interviewing and offers useful advice to research students undertaking this form of data collection.

Chapter 18 provides an overview of quantitative methods and introduces different types of quantitative research design. It also refers to some criteria by which these designs might be evaluated. It is followed by a chapter on survey methods which discusses the issues that need to be considered by research students collecting their own quantitative data by this means. Chapter 20 is concerned with secondary analysis. It outlines the different secondary sources of quantitative data available to research students and the considerations which should govern their use. Finally, Chapter 21 focuses on methods of statistical analysis of both primary and secondary quantitative data and again offers advice and guidance that should prove particularly useful to research students.

1

Part 1

The Nature of a Research Degree

Chapter 2

Undertaking a Research Degree

Haydn Mathias and Tony Gale

Introduction

In this chapter we present a broad overview of some of the main features of postgraduate research in the social sciences. We appreciate that our account is bound to be general while your experience of research work will be unique and special to you. Indeed, the concept of a social sciences research degree is something of a myth as the field comprises a wide variety of disciplines and even within each discipline a diversity of research traditions and methodologies exist. Nevertheless, what we have attempted to do is to draw upon both research and our own personal experience in order to offer some observations and insights which might help you to prepare for your role as a research student and to enable you to take more responsibility and control over the process of undertaking postgraduate research.

The New Research Student

Postgraduate research is different from undergraduate study. The undergraduate is one of many following a set of common paths. The undergraduate degree operates within a set structure in which there are identifiable and bounded units of learning, entitled courses, seminars and classes. The student occupies a shared world in which there are others, following a similar path, ahead of and behind them. Each year is seen as part of the whole and as a natural progression, from broader generalities to more specific interests and focuses of concern. Courses are bounded not only by time but by examinations and assessments; these landmarks in turn provide feedback about personal competence and performance. At the end of each year the undergraduate is aware of being classified within a particular category and of the classification tag they are likely to end up with when the course is over. They can compare themselves with others. Landmarks and feedback provide emotional security and remove ambiguity and doubt. The undergraduate degree is thus a shared experience in which other students are subject to common pressures and common concerns.

In contrast, postgraduate research can be seen as a period of uncertainty, ambiguity and lack of structure. The task is not really complete until the oral examination is over and the examiners' verdict is given. It may make sense to talk in terms of years, but calendar years are unlikely to coincide with particularly important personal landmarks or stages. The future is therefore uncertain until it has become a fact of the past. You will rarely attend lectures or courses in which what is required of you is defined by someone in authority. Rather, you are largely dependent on your own resources and willpower. You create your own curriculum. In exchange for such uncertainties, however, you derive certain intellectual and personal pleasures which the undergraduate would be lucky to encounter. You pursue your own academic interests; you no longer need to carry out work or follow aspects of the discipline which do not appeal to you; you acquire a sense of expertise, which very quickly becomes authoritative. Indeed within six months a postgraduate researcher could have more grip on the literature relating to their topic of choice than most people in the world. Given a good problem, you could well become an expert very quickly.

Analyses of working life (Jahoda, 1979) indicate that it is structure, the sharing of common experience, the identification with group goals and the exposition of personal skills, which are some of the latent properties which provide a major part of psychological satisfaction with work. It is hard to impose structure on postgraduate research; you are lucky to share experience, and group goals may or may not be present in your working environment. Personal skill may take time to develop and you may experience long periods of frustration when little seems to be happening and time seems to be running away.

An important aspect of the notion of a critical mass of research students within a department or faculty is that experience can be shared. The first-year postgraduate can discuss problems of research with second and third-year students. There is access to past theses. There are members of the academic staff with whom intellectual exchange is fruitful. The group can offer collegiality, conviviality and the informal set of networks which make living in a community of common purpose so satisfying and supportive. In such an environment it is more likely that others will have had problems similar to those you are encountering and survived them. Advice is available on coping strategies. Thus a large postgraduate cohort can offer some of the psychological supports that undergraduates enjoy by virtue of common shared experience. It is difficult to see how such supports can be enjoyed by the single, sometimes socially isolated, postgraduate student.

Finally there is role ambiguity. As a postgraduate the individual is a student and a learner. But if the person also acts as a tutor or demonstrator to undergraduates, they are also a teacher, a mentor and a model. Such mixed roles are often hard to handle, particularly if the organizational ethos of the department is one in which status, privilege and differential resource allocation are part of the process of social control.

The problems of transition and adjustment are accentuated in the case of the part-time research student. If you are such a student it is likely that you have not been in full-time education for some time and are having to hold down a demanding job while pursuing a higher degree. Your motivation might be exceptionally high as a result of a very deliberate and considered decision to become a research student, but you will be involved in travelling for supervisions and to use facilities, and it will take you considerably longer to feel part of your host institution. It is particularly important, therefore, to establish regular mechanisms for maintaining contact not only with your supervisor but also with other researchers.

Research into Postgraduate Study

There has been remarkably little research into the process and experience of postgraduate study in comparison to that into undergraduate study. Cuts in government funding of the Research Councils and the need for accountability in the expenditure of public money have put the spotlight on postgraduate research. Until very recently there has been no impetus to study the research process. However from the work which has been undertaken over the past thirty years or so we can gain some useful insights which might better prepare you for your task.

Postgraduate wastage and completion rates have been of concern not only to students but also to those who provide funding for them. Research students in the social sciences have not fared very well in these respects in comparison to their science colleagues. In one early study, for instance, the overall non-completion rate for a sample of 2,000 students was around 30 per cent but within subject areas the wastage rate for arts doctoral students was around 50 per cent in comparison to 15 per cent for scientists (Rudd and Hatch, 1968). Moreover for part-time students around 41 per cent had still to gain their degree after nine years.

In the 1980s the Economic and Social Research Council (ESRC) became concerned about the length of time it was taking doctoral students to submit their work and took steps to improve submission rates. Institutions were encouraged to introduce research training programmes and those which failed to achieve acceptable rates of submission within a given period had studentships withdrawn. The Committee of Vice-Chancellors and Principals (CVCP) also took steps to ensure that systematic arrangements were in place for the supervision of research students and for making more explicit the procedures for dealing with appeals against the academic judgment of the examiners on the grounds of prejudice, bias or inadequate assessment. It issued a code of practice on Postgraduate Training and Research (CVCP, 1985a) and a code of practice on Academic Appeals Procedures at Postgraduate Degree Level (CVCP, 1985b) by which universities were expected to abide. You will find it instructive to read both documents.

Such external pressures on institutions have had the effect of shifting the balance of power towards the research student who has now become a precious resource in departments. In particular, there has been a much more explicit prescription of the rights of the research student and the propriety of the procedures employed to make decisions about them, for example, in relation to transfer from MPhil to PhD or, indeed, in relation to appeals against negative decisions. Departments recognize that they must provide appropriate levels of facilities and support to ensure that completion is achieved within the specified period.

The impetus for these changes partly stemmed from research in the 1970s which indicated areas of postgraduate student dissatisfaction with aspects of instruction and supervision, as well as with the research facilities available in institutions. Such research typically indicated that arts and social sciences postgraduates tended to be less satisfied than science postgraduates with the supervision they received and had fewer opportunities to attend supporting instructional programmes and seminars. They were also less satisfied with facilities for study, such as places to work and computing and library services.

A number of studies have focused specifically on the experience of undertaking a research degree, utilizing data from personal interviews with students over a period of time. One interesting study by Welsh (1979) followed a group of postgraduates in one university over their first year. She found the early optimism of many students was gradually replaced by the more practical realism of the demands of the research undertaking. By the end of their first year a significant minority of students expressed dissatisfaction with their progress and around a half declared problems with their supervision.

Welsh's study illustrated a process of adjustment which, after the event, is easy to recognize and appreciate, but which is probably a source of discomfort when you are actually in the throes of it. For example 'floundering' was not uncommon as students sought the standards expected of them and struggled with developing the direction of their research. There were also problems of intellectual isolation, loneliness and other personal difficulties associated with the individual pursuit of knowledge in a new and unfamiliar situation. Many students felt that supervisor feedback and support were crucial in these early stages, a view not confined to social sciences postgraduates.

Studies have also highlighted differences in the way that postgraduate research is undertaken in different disciplines. If you are a science postgraduate, for example, you will probably find yourself placed in the laboratory quite early on, perhaps familiarizing yourself with a particular technique or repeating familiar experiments set by your supervisor. As scientific research is usually undertaken by groups working on different aspects of a broad problem, you will have others working around you who are available for advice and assistance. There will probably also be an instructional programme which you are required to attend. Your reading is likely to be directed towards the immediate practical tasks at hand, broadening out and becoming more intensive later on as you begin to delimit your specific area of enquiry.

In contrast, if you are a social sciences postgraduate your early work is likely to involve a good deal of reading around the subject with the aims of familiarizing yourself with the relevant literature and delimiting your research topic and methodological approach. You may also be required by your supervisor to submit written work on your reading which will form the basis of discussion for defining your research project. Although you are likely to be attending some kind of research training programme where you will meet other postgraduates in your department or faculty, you will for the most part be working on your own on a problem area which is not being worked upon by your fellow students. You may not find yourself engaging in any empirical work until well into your research degree programme.

In the natural sciences knowledge is organized within coherent theory, whereas in the social sciences knowledge is typically an aggregation of different theories, methods and data sets. Such characteristics may make it easier for the science research student to be quicker off the mark than you. However they are likely to experience similar problems with defining a research problem for investigation. If the worst that can happen to you is trying to see an elusive supervisor to help you to guide the formulation of your research topic, the worst that can happen to your science colleague is that he or she is being used as a 'pair of hands' by his or her supervisor.

The above portraits are very general stereotypes. We appreciate that within the social sciences there will be different types of experience. In reality your precise circumstances are going to be unique and will depend on the department you are in, your supervisor, your research area and the extent to which your research problem has been formulated in advance or needs to be developed from a wide range of possibilities.

Your Supervisor

No discussion of postgraduate research can avoid considering the role of the supervisor. He or she plays such an important part in all you do, from advising on the content of your work to giving you encouragement when you feel that things are going from bad to worse. But this is not a one-way process. You have to ensure that you get the best from your supervisor during the course of your work and take the initiative when you feel it is required.

Your professional working relationship with your supervisor is undoubtedly important but so is your personal relationship. After all, this is the one person who will be your main point of guidance and contact throughout your postgraduate degree. 'Getting on with your supervisor' therefore takes on a real meaning once you embark on your project. Welsh's (1979) study reflected both professional and personal dimensions of the supervisor-student relationship when she identified students' expectations of the supervisor as someone who possessed expertise in the area under study, provided guidance and advice on the choice of topic and the conduct and direction of the research, gave constructive criticism and possessed certain personal qualities which allowed him or her readily to show interest and enthusiasm for the student's work.

In another study McAleese and Welsh (1983) found the four characteristics of the 'ideal' supervisor rated most highly by students were: knowledgeable, available, helpful and stimulating. What was interesting was the close correspondence of these characteristics to desirable supervisor characteristics given by supervisors in the same study: helpfulness, subject expertise, personal experience and availability. It is worth noting, however, that students placed a higher priority on 'availability' than did supervisors.

Styles of supervision can vary enormously. Welsh (1979) identified four from her study: a) initially highly directive; b) highly directive throughout; c) directive in the early and final stages of the research; and d) non–directive throughout. Brown and Atkins (1988) provided a neat conceptual summary of the variation of supervisor style a student might expect, using a two-fold classification: cold/warm and structured/free. Using this two–by–two grid they summarized the research on student style preference as follows. The least preferred style was the cold and free approach. A warm, friendly manner combined with too little structuring was not popular either and typified the supervisor who was a 'nice' person but 'no good' as a supervisor. More preferable was the somewhat aloof supervisor who, nevertheless, provided direction and kept the student on track. Not surprisingly, the most popular style was that represented by the supervisor who expressed personal warmth with professional guidance.

The frequency of contact between supervisor and student has also emerged from research as a concern of students. In general, social sciences postgraduates are likely to have less frequent contact with their supervisors than science postgraduates probably because the latter tend to be based in the supervisor's laboratory. What most students appear to want, however, is more contact with their supervisors in the early stages as the project is being defined and delimited. This is also a period where good personal relationships are highly valued as the student adjusts to a new and unfamiliar way of working and a new social context. However expectations change over time. Once the research is underway, supervisor expertise, as well as regular contact, becomes a more important consideration. This is carried through to the final writing-up stage where regular feedback on submitted thesis drafts becomes a major concern.

Models of the Postgraduate Student

Explicitly or implicitly, supervisors hold a model of the postgraduate student and act accordingly. The model determines the behaviour of the supervisor and in turn fashions the supervisor-student relationship. For example, the '*chuck 'em in the deep end*' model implies a minimum of support and guidance; after all a bright person ought to know what to do, right? The *apprenticeship* model is one of learning by example, hand in hand with the supervisor, learning how to manipulate the tools of the trade; this is a craft model in which experience is shared. Apprenticeship models can, of course, be exploited and deteriorate into the *dogsbody* model, in which the postgraduate does the work of the supervisor as a low-paid research assistant, often learning by error rather than design. Unlike the apprenticeship model the work done tends to be not the attractive and desirable work but the hard graft. Apprenticeship has its attractions, particularly in the early stages of research work, particularly if it provides structure and a set of achievable goals.

But some supervisors might be reluctant to enforce such structure on research students, considering it a breach of the student's intellectual rights as an original mind with a new approach to a problem. There is something to be said for such a view, but it does have implications for our notion of what a thesis should be. In some social sciences disciplines a thesis can be a masterpiece by being a sound, competent piece of work, without major flaws, and capable of publication. It need not be outstandingly original or earth-shaking. Set against such a criterion, the notion of *the original mind*, which challenges all that has gone before, and which offers the discipline a completely new viewpoint, is unrealistic and unachieveable for the majority.

A model which draws upon the *deep-end, apprentice, dogsbody,* and *original mind* approaches, is the *evolving intellect* model. This sees the student as following a developmental path or voyage of personal and intellectual discovery. Hopefully, and over time, initial structure, guidance and modelling are replaced by intellectual independence, personal competence and a tolerance for uncertainty. In this model the research student may stumble and stutter at early attempts at writing; but by the end of the thesis, writing is smooth, structured and controlled, and the text is read without a distracting thought. The supervisor who sustains an evolving intellect model also sees the postgraduate as a budding peer, just a short step below on the academic ladder and passing through a series of transitional stages each involving its own characteristic form of initiation.

Roles of the Postgraduate

Role ambiguity has already been mentioned. Within the symbolic interactionist tradition, role ambiguity is a source of psychological stress. Attempts are made by the display of appropriate signs and the development of role-prescribed behaviours to reassure both the individual actor and others that the new role has been acquired. The postgraduate student has a variety of roles or social selves which have to be reconciled: the student and learner; the tutor or demonstrator and/or counsellor to undergraduates; the apprentice learning the craft; the scholar; the empirical researcher; the expert; the colleague; the original thinker; the writer. The development and integration of these roles over time leads ultimately to the creation of the professional academic and job applicant.

Essentially what is displayed by the postgraduate is a transition from anxiety to competence, from uncertainty to confidence, from mixed identity to predictable and accepted social role. Within some period of time the person is aware of having graduated, of becoming a research student, of being accepted by others as a teacher, as behaving 'as if' certain roles are possessed, and then, as possessing those roles and being a new, yet recognizable person. 'They are academics; I sound like an academic; I am behaving like an academic; I am an academic'.

Establishing Communication

Communication is a primary purpose of the practice of supervision. Good communication presupposes a number of elementary precautions. Channels of communication need to be clearly defined from the outset. Regular and scheduled meetings are essential; and meetings can be wasted without an agenda. The student must know how, where and when the supervisor can be contacted, and correspondingly, the supervisor must be in possession of similar information about the research student. Such clarity ensures that channels of communication are clear and free of noise.

Second, the messages which are transmitted must also be clear. Thus, at the end of the meeting, it should be clear what has been achieved, when the next meeting is to be, and what is to be done or attempted in the meanwhile. The student may, for example, have text to write, or the supervisor may have text to read and annotate. Both student and supervisor need to sense an obligation to transmit clear messages and to dispose themselves to receive them. The transmission of messages within a communication system is essential for feedback or the exchange of information about information.

It is inevitable, even with the best will in the world, and for unpredictable reasons, that communications can break down. To ensure that the system is working effectively, it is on occasion worthwhile to engage in a discussion of the system itself, to ensure system maintenance or to change the system.

The pattern of meetings may alter as the student's work progresses. Many more meetings might be necessary at the beginning and end of the process than are required or wanted in the middle. For example once the task has been defined and is on course, there may be little but encouragement to offer; but as the task comes to its latter stages, a great deal of practical support and feedback is likely to be essential.

Meetings benefit if there is cross–fertilization of goodwill from other meetings. Thus a postgraduate student and supervisor who teach others together, design a course together, attend conferences together or write together, can bring to the supervisory relationship extra levels of interpersonal understanding. For example teachers share a common sense of group identity *vis-à-vis* undergraduate students. They share common tasks, such as marking essays or practical reports. Thus communication within the supervisory relationship benefits from the existence of parallel contexts for communication.

Problems and Difficulties

It is all too easy to dwell on the problems and difficulties of postgraduate research and forget about the tremendous sense of personal achievement and satisfaction that is gained from completing a piece of research and submitting a thesis. However problems and difficulties with postgraduate work tend to have a habit of draining your intellectual and emotional energy and prevent you from seeing them in the context of the overall process. If you can appreciate the problems and difficulties which you might encounter, at least you can place them in some kind of perspective and be better prepared to deal with them.

We have already referred to Welsh's (1979) longitudinal study of first-year postgraduates in which she highlighted the problems of adjustment and floundering. A more recent study by Rudd (1985), this time of postgraduate failure, revealed at least six common problem areas faced by students. These were: a) poor planning and management; b) methodological difficulties; c) writing-up; d) isolation; e) personal problems outside the research; and f) inadequate or negligent supervision. Let us examine each of these areas in more detail.

Careful *planning and organization* are key factors in completing your research within a reasonable time-scale, and preferably before your financial support runs out! The technical skills of good management go hand in hand with the creative process of research. This is equally true in other creative walks of life such as film-making and drama. In both cases the person has to create their own structure. That is not to say you will have one plan to work to throughout your project. Your plans are likely to change as the research proceeds, but the important point is that you should have a plan or timetable of work, otherwise you are likely to run into problems.

In the social sciences a great deal of emphasis is placed on conceptualizing the research and defining and delimiting the research problem and methodology. However too long spent on this stage can quite easily prejudice data collection and writing up. Collecting and analyzing data usually take more time than is initially anticipated. Problems invariably arise with empirical work which cannot be predicted. In turn, this puts pressure on writing up the thesis. Although you are likely to be drafting chapters as the research proceeds, putting everything together into a coherent written piece of work can take longer than you think.

The above planning problems are related to time management. There are also problems to do with the failure to organize the intellectual elements of your research so that they are coherently integrated. For example, poor definition of the project problem may lead to irrelevant data collection. If little thought has been given to the analysis of the data and how it illuminates the main problem, you can quite easily end up with a daunting mass of data whose relevance has to be assessed. An over-concentration on interesting but not entirely relevant data may distort the research and leave gaps which may need to be plugged by further empirical work at the time when you are trying to draw the research together.

The latter is an example of side-tracking. In one sense, getting side-tracked on a particular aspect of the research is all part of the open-ended and creative nature of research. It might lead to exciting new lines of investigation or new conceptual insights which are more significant than the original definition of the research problem. In another sense, it can sap valuable time and energy and distort the project. What is important in all this creative effort is maintaining a view of the research as a whole. This means continually referring back to your current research plan and assessing the implications of pursuing a particular line in terms of the direction and goal of the project, the overall time-scale and your deadline for submission. Howard and Sharp (1983) provide a detailed account of various ways of planning and managing student research projects.

The second problem area of *methodological difficulties* in the research is related, in many ways, to the first. There is an inherent problem in designing research in ensuring that it is manageable within the time-scale available, contains scope for original work and will also lead to some solution or conclusion. By its very nature research is not predictable so changes in design and direction may be necessary to ensure a satisfactory outcome. These changes may involve reconceptualizing the methodology and acquiring new methodological skills. Quite often the student produces too much material and then has to face the challenge of what to cut out, particularly when the institution has regulations about the length of theses.

Acquiring relevant methodological skills in order to carry out and analyze empirical work can create its own problems. Apart from the time it may take to become familiar with relevant research methods, there may not be the support and experience available in your particular area of study especially if you are working in a new or esoteric field. All this has implications for time management and the need to keep the overall project in mind. In this respect it is also important to be aware of the temptation of being side-tracked by computers. The power and speed of computers have transformed the conduct of many types of research but they can also be great consumers of time. There is a danger of the student being sucked into becoming a programmer, when that is not the purpose of their thesis.

The third area of difficulty, *writing*, is not unique to postgraduates. Academic writing presents problems for lecturers also. The two main difficulties are bringing the material into coherent shape and the actual process of getting down to the business of writing. Part of the solution is to undertake regular pieces of writing throughout your research and to get feedback and constructive criticism from your supervisor. Some supervisors will expect this as a matter of course. Others may not and it is worth discussing this aspect of your work with him or her. Without regular writing practice and feedback, and the preparation of draft chapters as you move through your research, it is all too easy to be overwhelmed and demoralized by the apparently insurmountable task of preparing the thesis in one go in the final stages.

In some disciplines research students may be encouraged to submit their work for publication prior to the submission of the thesis. This has several advantages: the need to clarify ideas and express them succinctly; the feedback from external and independent referees; the sense of achievement which comes from publication; and the confirmation that one's work is along the right lines. Presentation of papers at conferences not only provides the opportunity and incentive to prepare written work but enables you to participate actively in the scholarly community associated with your discipline.

The fourth problem area of *isolation* is characteristic of the early stages of adjustment and may present particular difficulties for part-time and overseas students. The lack of external pressure and deadlines, and the essentially individual activity of research can lead to drifting, floundering and lack of motivation. You can take at least two steps to combat the feeling of isolation. The first is to develop a research plan quite early on to give your work direction and structure, and a tangible time-scale to work to. The second is to seek opportunities for discussion and debate about your research with others. One obvious source is your supervisor but there are also fellow students with whom you can talk both informally and in the context of instructional programmes and research seminars. The more you take advantage of such opportunities for interaction, the less socially and intellectually isolated you will feel and the more likely your own ideas will be refined and developed.

The fifth area of *personal problems* outside the research will vary from individual to individual. There are some fairly common personal problems which arise and can deflect energy from research, for example, finance, accommodation, illness and family commitments. Others are more complex. It is important to resolve such problems as soon as possible before they begin to impinge seriously on the progress of your research. You should discuss such problems with your supervisor. Most institutions also have a variety of student welfare services which can offer help and advice on a wide range of personal matters.

The final problem area of *inadequate or negligent supervision* has already been touched upon. As your supervisor is probably the most important influence on the success of your research, it is not surprising to find many student comments directed at the nature, style and quality of supervision. In such a close working relationship there are bound to be tensions and misunderstandings. Problems with supervision can range from those which are probably resolvable through discussion to those which are more serious and suggest a serious breakdown in the personal and professional relationship. Such problems include: lack of interest in the student or topic; infrequent meetings; lack of help with planning and direction; holding on to written work too long; *laissez-faire* attitude to supervision; absense or departure from the department; and lack of relevant knowledge or research experience.

For the student, tackling some of these problems can be difficult if the personal and professional relationship with the supervisor is not to be seriously damaged. However students have rights too, and being assertive about these rights through being open and through clarifying the 'ground rules' in the relationship, is an important aspect of developing a proper professional relationship with a supervisor. In fact most institutions now have more explicit procedures for monitoring postgraduate training which should, in principle, reveal problems at a much earlier stage than was the case previously. These procedures should be well documented and should be made available to you on request.

The mutual expectations of postgraduate and supervisor are summarized by Phillips and Pugh (1987) in the following way. Students expect their supervisors to: read their work well in advance; be available when needed; be friendly, open and supportive; be constructively critical; have a good knowledge of the research area; structure the situation so that it is relatively easy to exchange ideas; have the courtesy not to conduct a telephone conversation during a tutorial; have sufficient interest in their research to put more information in the student's path; and be sufficiently involved in their success to help them get a good job at the end of it all!

On the other hand, supervisors expect students to: be independent; produce legible written work; seek advice and comments on their work from others; have regular meetings; be honest when reporting on their progress; follow the advice that they give, when it has been given at the request of the postgraduate; be excited about their work; be able to surprise them; and be fun to be with!

Conclusion

The two aspects of the postgraduate research process which come through much of the research are the importance of good organization and planning, and the development of a good personal and working relationship with your supervisor. Furthermore if you are to get the most from the opportunity of studying for a higher degree then you need to take the initiative in managing the process. After all, this is all part and parcel of becoming a professional.

Within higher education there can be no task so challenging yet so satisfying as supervising a keen, well-motivated and committed research student. It is likely that the student has talents in excess of those of the supervisor and is clearly on an upward trajectory. This makes the process of supervision a privilege. In a lifetime of supervisory experience, the supervisor will be lucky to enjoy the challenge of having to think again about intellectual issues thought previously to be closed and resolved. Each research student is unique, or rather, the particular combination of personal strengths and possible weaknesses will vary from student to student.

Within an academic career, there can hardly be a time as challenging and rewarding as being a research student. The privilege of organizing one's own time, allocating one's intellectual resources to things which are exciting and intrinsically attractive, far outweighs the anxiety of uncertainty, frustrations over lack of progress, and the sheer dogged commitment needed to get the thesis actually finished.

However, as relationships go, the postgraduate-supervisor relationship is potentially as hazardous as is any other personal relationship. What is needed is an explicit working contract about now the relationship should be managed. For the supervisor, of course, experienced in supervision, the way ahead and the potential pitfalls should be clear. For the research student the experience is novel and the way ahead is clouded. But both share a responsibility to ensure that the relationship works.

Suggestions for Further Reading

Two books, already mentioned, are worth looking at for further information about the business of undertaking a postgraduate research degree. The first by Howard and Sharp (1983) on *The Management of a Student Research Project* focuses on the planning, organization and conduct of research degree work. It is fairly task-centred and provides advice on the mechanics of research work at both undergraduate and postgraduate level. The second book by Phillips and Pugh (1987) on *How to Get a PhD* is more broadly based and considers the personal and social aspects of the research process, including relationships with the supervisor, as well as the conduct of research.

References

Brown, G. and Atkins, M. (1988) *Effective Teaching in Higher Education*, London, Methuen.

Committee of Vice-Chancellors and Principals (1985a) *Postgraduate Training and Research*, London, CVCP.

Committee of Vice-Chancellors and Principals (1985b) *Academic Appeals Procedures at Postgraduate Research Degree Level*, London, CVCP.

Howard, K. and Sharp, J.A. (1983) *The Management of a Student Research Project*, Aldershot, Gower.

Jahoda, M. (1979) 'The impact of unemployment in the thirties and seventies', *Bulletin of the British Psychological Society*, **32**, pp. 309–14.

McAleese, R. and Welsh, J. (1983) 'The supervision of postgraduate research students', in Eggleston, J.F. and Delamont, S. (Eds) *Supervision of Students for Research Degrees*, BERA.

Phillips, E.M. and Pugh, D.S. (1987) *How to Get a PhD*, Milton Keynes, Open University Press.

RUDD, E. (1985) *A New Look at Postgraduate Failure*, Guildford, SRHE/NFER-Nelson.

RUDD, E. and HATCH, S. (1968) *Graduate Study and After*, London, Weidenfeld and Nicolson.

WELSH, J.M. (1979) *The First Year of Postgraduate Research Study*, Guildford, Society for Research into Higher Education.

Chapter 3

Personal Views

Students: 1

I am currently in the final stages of writing up my thesis, and so this is possibly not the best time to write a balanced view of my experiences because my mood varies from simple pessimism to abject despair! Nevertheless, in looking back over my time as a research student I have come to the conclusion that it was all worthwhile, that the good times far outweighed the bad, and that most importantly I have enjoyed it.

Looking back, my main impressions and the lessons I have learned (most of them the hard way) seem to fall into a number of broad categories relating to reading, writing, talking and surviving. However, at a more general level two factors inevitably tend to dominate the way in which a research project develops: the topic and the supervisor(s). Both need to be handled with extreme care, particularly if you wish to retain any control over your own destiny! Fortunately, the topic which I chose to study has proved interesting and worthwhile, and both of my supervisors have been extremely helpful and supportive. I can only hope that you have the same good fortune. More detailed discussion of the relationship between student and supervisor can be found elsewhere in this publication. The only observation which I would make is that students have to compete with other interests for their supervisor's time, and so the more enthusiastic you are about your own work the more attention and assistance you will get. An exceptionally useful reference on these and other issues is Phillips and Pugh (1987), while Wilson (1980) provides some interesting and entertaining tips for research students.

Beyond these two issues, as someone undertaking serious research for the first time there were a number of other aspects which I initially found difficult to come to terms with. One of the most important of these was the organization of my reading. The early stages of most research involves the infamous 'literature review'. An appreciation of previous work in your research field is an essential requirement, but the initial excitement of preparing oneself for the task ahead can soon degenerate into a boring slog through seemingly endless piles of books and journals. The ability to 'skim-read' is one which most students soon develop, as it is important to be able to distinguish material which needs only cursory attention from that which requires more detailed study. This is a skill which can only be gained through practice, and initially I caused myself many problems by spending either too much or too little time on particular areas of the literature. However, a number of things can be done to maximize the benefit and effectiveness of the literature review.

First, the search for information should be well planned and carefully organized — simply plucking likely looking titles off library shelves is not recommended as a general policy, although it can sometimes turn up surprisingly useful material. The search should be organized according to defined areas of interest. The references from a few key articles or previous theses on similar subjects can obviously provide a way into the topic, as can abstracts and computer searches. It is important not to view the latter as an easy shortcut, as you will need to be well informed about the topics involved before you can gain much benefit from a computer reference database. Consequently, computer searches might be more appropriate after 'conventional' sources have already been followed up. But whatever methods are used, achieving an organized and effective search requires that reading is conducted in relation to some outline plan of the research to be undertaken. Your supervisor should be able to assist in this process by helping you to draw up such a plan and by guiding your early reading.

In addition, it is important to ensure that you keep some record of everything that you read. While you will not make detailed notes on everything that you come across, it is vital to develop a system that allows you to return to particular pieces of work at a future date. It may seem obvious, but it is crucial to make an accurate note of a reference when it is first read, and inclusion of page numbers relating to specific passages or quotations can also save a lot of time and frustration should you need to refer back to a piece of work. It is also amazing how often something which was read during the early months (and disregarded as irrelevant) suddenly becomes very important later in the research. Developing a reference system that works is not easy and it takes time to keep it up to date, but it is essential to do so. Take advice from other members of your department on the system that they use, and bear in mind that there are several computer catalogue packages available which make sorting and producing reference lists for papers and the final thesis much easier.

Third, the whole process of reading should be balanced. It is important that literature searches should have some purpose and direction, but there must also be room to explore topics which may initially seem peripheral to the main focus of the research. It is worth bearing in mind that few projects end up examining precisely the issues which they set out to investigate. Balance is also important when planning your daily schedule. Where possible you should try to integrate periods of reading during the day with other activities, as it is easy to miss important information when the senses are dulled through hours of 'book-bashing'. In addition to this, it is important to integrate reading into your work throughout your research, as keeping up to date with new journal issues and books is essential.

Another common problem among research students is deciding how much to read. Particularly in the early stages of the project, there is a tendency to feel that you have to read everything. At some point, you must stop reading and get on with something else, be that fieldwork or writing. It is very difficult to determine when that stage has been reached, and more often than not you will feel that you have not read enough. The purpose of the initial literature search is to familiarize yourself with the general topic. Further detailed reading should be related to specific issues thrown up by your own research, and can therefore only be done at a later stage. Working to a timetable is useful in this respect as it provides a means of deciding when to move on to something else.

Overall, I found that reading could be very stimulating at any stage of the research, engendering enthusiasm in the project and reviving interest in work which had come to seem mundane and boring. However, it can also be a depressing chore unless it is undertaken in the right context and with some purpose. That purpose should be to generate ideas. Whether engaged in reading, writing or 'doing' I found it important to set aside time for stepping back from the tasks in hand and just thinking. Needless to say, good ideas always seemed to come while cleaning my teeth or washing my hair and never while sitting at a desk — so always keep a notebook handy, and preferably a waterproof one!

The second major topic which always seems to crop up whenever students talk about their research is writing. Most of us seem to fear putting pen to paper (or these days, finger to keyboard) above all other activities. However, writing up is an essential step in ensuring the progression of a project, and should not be viewed simply as an end product. Throughout my research I have been encouraged by my supervisors to write as often as possible, and this has been exceptionally helpful in clarifying my thoughts, highlighting gaps in my knowledge and guiding further reading and fieldwork. Only a small proportion of what I wrote in the early stages will ultimately end up as part of my thesis, but the *process* of writing has been critical in developing my own ideas. It has the added advantages of keeping your supervisor up to date with what you are doing (and thinking), and it does provide some raw material for the thesis. Each piece of research that I did was written up in some form, so that actually 'writing' the thesis is more a process of fitting together, editing and rewriting previous work.

I have also been fortunate in that my supervisors have been prepared to read and comment on whatever I have given to them, and they have encouraged me not to be afraid of imperfect (as opposed to bad) work. A useful tip is to double-space anything which you pass on to other people, as this allows them to make comments and corrections much more easily. With regard to such comments, be prepared to develop a fairly thick skin and recognize that criticisms are made to help you improve your work, not to highlight your personal shortcomings. Several of my fellow students have told me that their supervisors hate to leave any piece of paper untouched by a red pen and would gladly correct their weekly shopping list given the chance, so it is important to accept comments in the spirit in which they are given — that is, as a positive input to your research. A final point in this respect is that it does take time to develop a style of writing which is suited to presenting academic work, and obviously the more often you write work up the better you will become at doing so. Deadlines (and in some cases word limits) are an excellent way of disciplining yourself to write clearly and succinctly, and they can also help to keep your research on course for thesis completion within the ever more important time constraints.

On the practical side, writing in this way has been made immeasurably easier through the widespread availability of wordprocessors. Not only do they make redrafting and correcting much easier, they also allow discrete sections of work to be integrated in the final thesis. It is important to find out what facilities are available for your use, and you should choose a word-processing package with care as they are not all the same by any means. The ability to import data from other sources and to combine text, tables, graphs and diagrams varies enormously from one system to another. Think carefully about your likely needs and if possible obtain some expert advice. You should also consider a basic course in typing and keyboard skills, as this could save you a considerable amount of time in the long run.

A third research activity worthy of consideration is talking. It is very easy to become isolated by being totally absorbed in your own work, and this should be avoided at all costs. It is always helpful if there are other postgraduates researching similar topics within your department, but even in these situations it is vital to develop contacts with students and staff in other departments and institutions. Conferences and courses can be at least as helpful in providing such contacts as they are from an academic viewpoint, if not more so. Also worthy of investigation are any postgraduate organizations which may operate within your subject area, or postgraduate groups within the larger professional associations. It is worth remembering that talking to researchers in other disciplines can be especially useful in giving a new angle to your work, and can open up whole new areas of interest. Developing a range of academic contacts is important not only to help your work, but also to preserve your sanity! There is nothing quite so refreshing as having someone else show an interest in your work, and when things are not going well it can be a great relief to talk to other research students about your problems — particularly as you will usually find at least one person who is in a far worse position than you are.

In presenting my own experiences in this way, I may have given the impression that research is a series of distinct activities. However, the various aspects discussed above are in fact all closely interlinked, and in my case formed a rapidly revolving cycle. Reading, writing and discussion with other people (not least my supervisors) were all essential in forming my conclusions about the work I have done, and all three had a significant impact on the direction which my research took at various stages. However, combining all of these activities while actually generating some results is far from easy, and it is essential to be as organized as possible. Not only does this involve the efficient use of time at work, it also means that life outside the department has to be fitted around your preferred work patterns.

In conclusion, the most valuable piece of advice which was given to me was to keep a sense of perspective about my work. I was reminded that although the research would take up most of my time it should not occupy my whole life, and so it was important for me to retain interests outside academia. This was helpful in ensuring that on the whole I was in control of the research and not vice-versa — there is life outside a PhD! A research degree is certainly not an easy way to avoid getting a 'real job'. When things are going well, it just seems easy. When they go badly you feel incredibly stupid and helpless. Research is nearly always very hard work, and the 'ivory towers and dreaming spires' of academia which people keep referring to are conspicuous only by their absence. After talking to many other research students, I have come to the conclusion that the crucial thing is not to worry yourself into a nervous breakdown, but just to keep going — your difficulties are not unique. From my own experience, coming to terms with the practical and academic problems involved and working through them is the key to successful completion. The hardest battles that I have had to fight have been coping with my own feelings of inadequacy and keeping myself motivated, not with academic issues related to the topic which I have been studying.

Nick Axford, Full-time Geography Research Student

Students: 2

PhD Snakes and Ladders: Take Your Chance . . .

A game of snakes and ladders is a game of perseverance, chance and discovery. You roll the dice; you move a few squares, and then with luck, you land on a ladder — you are on your way. Right across the board in the far corner is Nirvana — the end of the great journey, but in between there are not only ladders but snakes. Just as you are making progress, you land on a monster and go slithering backwards. Determined as ever you continue rolling the dice and very slowly with a little bit of luck and a lot of perseverance you reach the end. What has snakes and ladders to do with doctoral research? When I started my thesis I had a funny idea that good research was related to intelligence. People with PhDs were clever people. All I had to do to achieve honour was to prove I was equally intelligent. Looking back now at the end of my journey, I am certainly wiser but not, I think, particularly clever. What snakes and ladders could have taught me is that the skill is not in rolling the dice; a good study supervisor can teach you that. The skill is knowing how to take your chances when you meet a ladder and how, when you run into a snake, to resist throwing over the board — 'Well I never wanted a PhD anyway!'. Six years later I know I only achieved my doctorate by good luck, much dogged determination, and a supervisor who kept me to the task.

An Idea

All research begins with an idea. I was working full-time in a child-guidance clinic. I was interested in the interrelationship between physical and psychological symptoms in children. The question was: how could I develop this idea into a research project? I wanted to demonstrate that treating the whole child, that is treating both the emotional and the physical symptoms was more effective than single focus therapy. Along with the initial idea often comes what at first sight appears to be the absurd. In my practice I was treating a number of children with soiling problems — a distressed group of children who are unable to sustain bowel control. I had been treating these children with some success. Could I set up a multidisciplinary treatment study of soiling children to test out my ideas? But a thesis about faeces — would anyone take that seriously? In a way this was my first 'ladder'. First I had access to a population of children with this problem. Second (and this is of interest to other part-time research students), I could legitimately undertake much of the treatment of these children in my work time. But third, when I started a literature search, I found that there was surprisingly little research, much controversy, poor treatment success rates, and a very distressing problem which affected over one in every hundred children in primary school. Even at this early stage it occurred to me that my subject could be PhD material. Suddenly the idea was not so absurd. I had stepped on to my first ladder.

Do I Care Enough to Bother?

This is the first snake, for any potential research candidate. There is no disgrace in deciding that maybe you do not care enough to undertake a research project which may take several years. And however hard you work it will take several years. When I started I thought the University of Southampton was offering a two-year part-time MPhil programme. An MPhil in two years — the thought was quite seductive, but that was only the taught element of the course. This is the second snake. It is exceptional for an MPhil to be completed in three years. If you think that you might like to convert your MPhil to a PhD, you need to double the time. Potential students may justifiably feel that their time would be put to better use developing their careers in other directions. It is important to get your thinking straight before you start, because throughout a long research project, the biggest snake is losing your motivation. There is often a great temptation to throw the whole blessed PhD in the bin at various fraught moments. I placed myself in a situation where it was very difficult to drop out. There is nothing like the mother-in-law who asks in a piercing voice across a crowded room 'Now when are you going to complete your PhD?', to spur you on. But that apart, the greatest force for me were the children and families in the treatment programme. I shared in their distress and genuinely sought a resolution of their difficulties.

Getting Started

You have your idea; you have got your motivation right. It is all very exciting. You are beginning to dream, but where do you get started? I started with a small pilot study. This highlighted some of the potential problems and saved much time later. The other side of getting started is of course the literature search. If you are a social worker, your first thought is to go to the social work section of the library where the familiarity of the surroundings has a nice homely feel. Home however may not be the best starting-point. The most up-to-date and relevant literature may well be housed in other sections. I became quite brazen in using a variety of medical, psychological and educational libraries and I photostatted everything I could lay my hands on. Nothing is more frustrating when you are writing up than to have an abstract of a research paper rather than the original. Another tip is to identify the key words from the various research indices. Soiling may have been my subject but you would be surprised at the number of key words that describe the intricacies of the intestinal tract! Very quickly too you discover the key researchers. You then find the dates of their most recent publication and follow up their references. A shortcut is then to write to them directly asking if they have published anything further. Experts around the world are end-lessly flattered by letters from humble researchers.

Planning Research — Methodology — The Value of a Good Supervisor

The planning of your research and developing the appropriate methodology can lead to nasty snakes. It is here that a good supervisor can be of unlimited help. It is tempting to choose a supervisor who is already an expert in your subject. In a doctoral thesis I am doubtful of this rationality. Although a study supervisor needs to have an understanding of your topic area and research setting, I feel it is more important they are experts in methodology and practical research implementation. My supervisor was such a person. But all study supervision can lead to arguments and frustrations. What keeps the relationship going is a mutual respect and trust. Deep down, I knew that my supervisor was usually right, and I respected her for the interest she took, her skills in keeping me on the right track and, more importantly, for keeping me to the task.

A dilemma in planning research is matching what is desirable from research methodology and what is possible. You quickly realize there is not an ideal world. Carefully matched controls are desirable in a treatment study, but ethically in my case it was difficult to elicit referrals and then refuse to help families and children who were in distress in order to establish non-treatment controls. I had to look elsewhere. My supervisor was a great assistance in sorting out early difficulties. I was also helped by examining the methodology used in other projects. If your research is going to be of value to others, your findings need to be comparable and preferably based on the same criteria.

Implementing Your Research

You are creeping up the snakes and ladders board. You have overcome your methodological problems. Referrals are coming in. You are in the 'action' mode. What I had not anticipated in my naivety is that research is not a static process. During your period of study findings are also coming in from other research workers. After several months spent on my literature search, I felt I had completed that part of the work. It was not to be. Every so often I would creep back to the libraries and be infuriated to find that yet another paper of importance had been published. By this time I was beginning to see indicators from my study. I grew quite jealous of these, my early findings, and feared the big snake, the publication of a paper which might duplicate my results. There was indeed a great big snake ahead. I was well into writing up before it showed its ugly face.

Computing the Results

I always knew that I would find computing the data difficult. Two days 'hands-on' practice had not made me computer literate. Happily Jenny came to my rescue. She looked at my data and her face grew furrowed. It was obviously too late to tell me to redesign my schedules. 'Leave it with me', she said. A week later, with consummate ingenuity, Jenny had designed some tracing paper mock-ups which could be placed over the data giving the necessary coding. Together we tapped in the data. And then the excitement one Saturday morning when she said 'I think we will just see what it looks like'. She pushed a knob or two, and suddenly the great machines started rolling. Once they started rolling there seemed no stopping them. Out came the data, sheet after sheet — frequencies, percentages, totals. It was miraculous!

What Does it All Mean?: Sharing and Discussing the Findings

I came out of the University that Saturday evening with a huge box of paper. This was my research project. And then I examined the data. It was a mass of figures and symbols. What on earth did it all mean? Several weeks later and after several more visits to the beloved Jenny, and her mainframes, I slowly made sense of it. But these were exciting times. I had in the early stages of the study formulated hypotheses. The answers, some surprising, were there in the print-out. Gradually these evolved into concrete findings. It was at this stage I felt I needed to share my interpretations. Rather nervously I submitted an abstract of my preliminary findings to the Association of Child Psychology and Psychiatry for their 'Submitted Paper' meeting. I was asked to present my paper and it was well received by a multi-disciplinary audience. More important however was the constructive help I was given at the meeting. 'Had I looked at X factor?'; 'How very interesting . . . I wonder what the relationship is between. . .'. The feed-back from this and other presentations was enormously valuable.

The Big Snake or is it a Ladder?

Research is full of surprises, but I could not have predicted the unexpected child abuse crisis in Cleveland in 1987. One of the issues that Cleveland raised was the possibility that sexual abuse had been a major cause of defecation disorders. Luckily I was not a total innocent in this field. Grabbing the snake by the neck I was able to turn him into a ladder. I undertook some further analyses and published a paper on the relationship between soiling and sexual abuse (Buchanan 1989). But it took months of extra work. The lesson from this experience is that the unexpected, far from being a disaster, can serve to make your research more interesting and topical.

Writing up — Dreaded Meetings with Supervisor — What More Work?

In effect, with my supervisor's encouragement, I had started writing up some years before my research was completed. With wordprocessors, text can always be changed. The final writing up is however a daunting task. The tables take for ever to get right, the statistics ever longer, and then the analyses and interpretation of the findings — it seems to be unending. I found it a comfort, as I toiled on, to know that at least the literature review and the boring details of the methodology were nearly complete.

One of my supervisor's strengths — I can say this with hindsight — was her refusal to accept second best. In the final stages of writing up, I dreaded our meetings. She always had a constructive suggestion. 'What about looking into that aspect?', 'It really would be most interesting...'. And the sting in the tail: 'I think for a PhD you really need to follow that up'. The only problem about her suggestions was that they involved six months more work! But she was right. The results were important.

Where do I Stop?

A few years into your study, you and your research become like friends. You have had the ups and downs contingent on any 'special relationship'. But like old friends, you take constant delight in each new day. When there is turmoil in your life, you retreat into a secret world and communicate with your best friend. It is a rewarding relationship. 'Maybe if we roll the dice once more, who knows what we will find?' Eventually a decision had to be made to sever the relationship. There has to be an ending; a sudden divorce with both partners going their separate ways. Endings are not natural in research, because there is always somewhere else to go, and always the excitement that new truths will be discovered. But at the end — as you scrabble to find page 503 which appears to have gone missing, as you collate the hundreds of pages for the printer, as you sit outside the bindery slipping in the last fold-out sheets, and finally as you hand the collected works over the counter — there is a sense of loss that the partnership has ended. Endings are indeed unnatural in research. But there is always the hope that your ending will be someone else's beginning — a big ladder that will set them off on another game of perseverance, chance, and discovery. And of course there is still the book you are going to write and all those other papers you hope to publish!

Ann Buchanan, Part-time Social Work Research Student

Students: 3

Research is rather like a journey for me. I am not sure what my destination will be, but I have an idea of some of the places I shall visit en route. I would like to describe three aspects of this journey — the nature of postgraduate research, being a part-time student, and being a woman researcher. I shall conclude by sharing some 'survival tips' which have helped me on my journey.

The Experience of Being a Research Student: What is it Really Like?

Postgraduate research is an individual experience, and depends on you, your supervisor, the nature and stage of the research. I have found it very satisfying, although at times frustrating and anxiety-provoking. At first, I had doubts as to whether I was sufficiently academic to do a PhD. However, I soon realized that I had the necessary qualities such as single-mindedness, determination and a strong interest in my subject. I became aware that what was required was the ability to develop the appropriate skills such as literature searching, critical analysis, writing, and to work hard. My second concern, which is common, was that I felt that I should complete the literature review and design the research quickly in order to start the fieldwork which would be 'real research'. There are two issues here. First, 'real research' can consist solely of theoretical contributions; and second, feeling under constant pressure to move on to the next stage can actually impede progress. My research has a sounder base for having carefully analyzed conceptual problems.

Initially, I was particularly dependent on my supervisor for guidance because I could not at that stage anticipate in which direction the research journey would lead. I also began with grandiose ambitions — my research on depression and dependency in women was going to challenge a traditional paradigm and 'shake up' conventional psychiatry! I still have such inclinations but these help to motivate me. I realized that the more theories or 'facts' that I wanted to 'prove', the more difficult the task. I became aware that there are no 'right' answers or absolutely 'true' theories but different competing truths. I discovered this because through questioning the assumptions of other authors I came to see that science was partial. The traditional and popular views of dependency which I had previously accepted as 'true' and 'scientific' appeared very limited when analyzed carefully. I am critical of the 'traditional' concept of dependency which is poorly defined, trait-oriented, negatively value-laden and has limited methods of assessment.

Postgraduate research requires learning to think creatively and express ideas clearly. These skills improve with practice over the years and with helpful feedback. For me an expression of these skills has been achieving a publication. This helped me clarify conceptual confusions in my research and I became more aware of my own skills such as use of logic and ability to organize an argument. It is also rewarding to have my name in print!

Carrying out research has its highs and lows. There is the thrill of feeling that I have found something new or mastered a complex problem. There are also the common frustrations of insufficient time and difficulty in narrowing the area of study. Research is essentially solitary — although important sources of support have been my supervisor, the research community, work colleagues and my partner.

Conducting postgraduate research is really a cyclical process which is disguised by the linear style of most journals and theses. The familiar sequence of 'introduction, methods, results, discussion, conclusion' is not an accurate description of the research process, particularly in non-traditional research. Thus, I have worked in cycles on the following five tasks: review literature, clarify thesis, identify questions, outline proposals and conduct pilot work. In practice, I work on different parts of the research process simultaneously and I alternate between clarifying concepts in the literature, and designing the methodology.

I have become aware that reason is a powerful force within science yet I have already mentioned several *feelings* which are characteristic of conducting research, such as satisfaction, anxiety, dependency, ambition, pride, excitement and frustration. I believe that emotions and values influence the nature of questions asked and the methods used and their impact can be underestimated. For example, I *feel* strongly about my research which is about interpersonal dependency and its link with depression. These feelings, particularly anger (which I regard as appropriate) have influenced my research design and helped motivate me to spend the necessary time. I also keep a diary of my thoughts and feelings in order to clarify issues and remind me of progress. This diary may become part of my research data but in any case is a valuable record of my journey.

Being a Part-Time Research Student

The art of juggling commitments is essential because the non-completion rate of part-time social science students is high. One way to manage the juggling act is to design your research to fit closely with the rest of your job, the benefits being that it can more easily be justified as relevant and meaningful, and you may be able to spend more time on it. My research interest arose through my work as a psychologist over several years, stemming from the knowledge that twice as many women as men are diagnosed as depressed. Some benefits of part-time research are that it complements the rest of my work as a psychologist. It meets intellectual needs not met in my job, for example by enabling analysis of theories and concepts in depth. It improves what I bring to my work, for example it has helped me clarify which psychological therapies have stronger theoretical bases. It has also improved my evaluation skills which are useful at this time of National Health Service change, with the increasing need to evaluate and improve services. Being part-time, the 'pace' of the research is slower than in being full-time. One benefit of this is that the research 'grows' as I grow. This has the advantage that I look back and see how my ideas and skills have developed. However, a feature of part-time work and the consequent slower pace is that I need to be disciplined to keep up the quality and quantity of research work. The quality of my research suffers if it becomes intermittent as my thinking and writing become fragmented. However, on balance, I feel that the benefits of part-time research outweigh the disadvantages.

What is it Like for Women Research Students?

At this point, reader, if you are a man, don't stop reading, because these issues are also pertinent for you. Research raises three issues for me which can be broadly described as 1) motherhood and research, 2) domestic responsibilities and 3) conceptual issues concerning gender and scientific method.

Two years into my research, I had a baby boy who is now a year old. Having a baby is not easy to reconcile with studying for a PhD, as both require a great commitment of time, energy and money. Indeed I have heard it said that doing a PhD is like having a baby! For some women like myself, the two experiences may occur together if you start a thesis in your thirties and then plan to have a baby before you are too old! Combining a thesis and early motherhood is not easy at times, but I find the two experiences can enhance each other: my research includes concerns about the effect on women of their roles as wife/mother and I can therefore draw on my own experiences of dependency in these roles. Fortunately, the University was flexible in enabling me to suspend registration for six months for maternity leave — which also enabled a saving on tuition fees! I find it is sometimes possible to think about research while doing chores, although not when my son Christopher is around. I continually reassess my priorities, and allocate time to satisfy my different roles.

Second, domestic responsibilities are an issue because they take time which competes with research. If you have a partner or family, who does most of the domestic work? If your research intrudes into your 'leisure', how will it co-exist with other demands — having time with your partner/relaxing/cooking and childcare? Fortunately, my partner likes to cook, shop and do housework. I also find that it helps that my partner has a major interest — he likes to record music, so that our need to spend time with each other is roughly balanced.

Third, in conducting research on women, I have become aware of conceptual difficulties in relation to social science theory and method. Eichler (1988) and Harding (1987) argue that much social science suffers from the problem of 'androcentric bias'. By this term I mean that scientific theories and observations are still heavily influenced by the male viewpoint, so that culture-wide biased theoretical assumptions can lead to distorted and incomplete social analyses. It has been argued that this limits the reliability and validity of science, and that theories and models fit women poorly (Shaver and Hendrick, 1987; Wilkinson, 1986).

At first I was quite surprised at the extent of this problem and its implications. Dealing with androcentrism can be confusing and contradictory if you are a woman researcher. For example, it is not easy to find in the research literature descriptions of what it feels like to be dependent from a woman's viewpoint. Women's experience and views can seem to be invisible, and this creates in me a sense of contradiction between myself as a social scientist and as a woman. The concepts and framework on dependency developed largely by men do not accord with my own experience and the questions asked arise out of mainly male experience. I try to integrate my experience as a woman *and* a social scientist and this has made my research more complex but satisfying. Becoming aware of androcentrism has led me towards exploratory and qualitative research. I wish to replace the traditional concept of dependency with new concepts, which will require new methods so that I can explore dependence within its socio-cultural context. I shall focus particularly on dependency as a product of interpersonal interaction between spouses. I have found the 'messy' area of dependency to be best understood by qualitative approaches which enable a focus on depth and richness. I am developing the relevant (non-androcentric) concepts with due regard for the complexity of the socio-cultural context and different gender roles.

Some Survival Tips — How to Keep Your Sanity!

There are many ways to cope, some described elsewhere in this book. Coping strategies may be broadly categorized as the tasks of creating the *practical* and *emotional* resources necessary to conduct research.

Creating practical resources.   Money is an important resource, as it buys time. (Both time and money are particularly precious after having a baby!) I depend on my employer for finance, so I keep my employer and colleagues informed of progress and keep the research 'visible' e.g. by setting up research groups and giving talks. I also acknowledge my employer in publications where appropriate.

The university is an essential resource. I found its training scheme in research methods very helpful. It familiarized me with computers/libraries and so on and enabled me to meet other students. It also gave me an overview of research methods so that I could see their limitations and thus felt more confident. Although I am part-time it is useful to have access to a desk in the university department, partly because this confirms my status as a departmental member. I also have a study area at home. An efficient storage and filing system are a necessity — mine has scope for improvement! Creating space for my research also requires time management. I regularly recorded my hours worked and graphed this so that I had a visual record to spur me on. (Well, what else would you expect from a psychologist!) You also need your own wordprocessor — the more user-friendly you can afford the better. I have an Apple Mac. However as well as these practical resources I also need emotional resources for research.

Creating emotional resources.   *You* are the most important emotional resource for yourself. Hence you need to be aware of and accept your motives for doing research, and the fact that motives can change. For example it is acceptable to admit to yourself 'I want an MPhil or PhD as an end in itself' or 'as the highest academic level I can reach' or to say 'I want an MPhil/PhD as a means to an end, that is to obtain it as quickly as possible in order to advance my career.' Incidentally I no longer see a PhD as necessarily the highest level of academic achievement, but more as a preparation and training for professional research.

Other sources of support for me are my supervisor and other researchers. I try to have realistic expectations, communicate assertively, and take the initiative in maintaining contact. I think about my supervisor's advice and thank him for his help. I particularly value his experience and encouragement. It is important to negotiate your expectations of the supervision process with your supervisor early on, and then whenever necessary. I have also found research support groups useful in reducing potential isolation — both a group organized in the university, and one that I set up informally with other students.

Stephanie Cadbury, Part-time Psychology Research Student

Students: 4

When I was asked to write a piece on the life of an overseas research student, I never thought that it would become a full-time job. Well, I thought, it is just pen and pencil. Sit down, put memories in order and write. In the end it has not turned out to be quite like that.

Of course I was aware — dimly, though — that my life as a research student had not been just a bed of roses, but before I sat down and reorganized my thoughts I would have been ready to explain this period of my life as incentive laden, fruitful and creative, however difficult it might have been sometimes. After a particularly hectic year on my return home, I realized that many of my recollections had faded away and that what I remembered was far too general for words. What I needed was a new 'perspective' and this implied doing some 'research' into the past. I am lucky that I have the sentimental sort of friends and family who dislike throwing things away, so most of my letters were still around. Rereading them, many forgotten memories, people, feelings, anecdotes returned to me. I could now place events, fears, good times and attach faces and names to many experiences.

In a very general way, I could classify my research days in two very different stages: the adapting stage and the adapted stage. During the first stage, it seems that I just worried, persistently, universally, all the time. I worried about everything one can think of: adapting to the place, monotony, loneliness, lack of friends, being homesick, work (though not about the food, or the weather — an earlier stay in Birmingham and London had made me familiar with those). My way out of this general confusion now sounds simple enough although at the time it was not. I concentrated on working, which in the end was the reason for my being in Southampton, and gave it priority over everything else. I tried to be systematic in keeping to a time-table both at work in my office as well as in other activities, and it helped me to keep going at a constant pace. Obviously we all pay a price for rationalizing too much. In my case I developed this 'thing' for vitamins (with iron). I took them religiously every day, with the conviction that the world would fall apart unless I did. Of course this included ginseng for the perfectly horrible days.

Already protected with timetables and vitamins A, B and C, I gradually moved into my adapted stage where I stopped worrying about everything to become more selective. I concentrated on worrying almost exclusively about my research and related matters. I could hear myself thinking: 'Once I manage to settle down to work, it is just a question of time...'. But whatever I did, it never looked or felt nearly enough. I was burdened with the workload, full of insecurity about its quality and anxious that 'more was never enough'. I was also terrified at introducing unfamiliar aspects or methods of analysis into my research and had a persistent fear of not making it in the end. I kept wondering if it was good, deep or long enough, or if it was making me look like a fool, or if I'd ever make it, or if there was perhaps a Catch 22 somewhere? By the middle of my second year I started scheduling my work over and over again. According to my letters I continually set myself time limits for everything I did: this section next week, the chapter in another two weeks.... I was very keen to finish quickly and tried hard for it but then, just like everybody else around, I was forced to deal with delays. I learned to face the fact that meeting my own time limits was in reality almost impossible, and I could expect everything to take longer than planned, sometimes twice as long. I didn't take these delays happily, in fact they depressed me no end. But what could one do besides worrying? Friends resignedly suggested that I exaggerated whenever I tried to explain that everything was a disaster, and sometimes I just could not understand how they could be so blind to my fate. They were probably right though because they could also see that worrying did not keep me from meeting people, pubs, birthday parties, films or trips home.

I believe this feeling of insecurity is common to a greater or lesser extent to all research students. We worried continuously. It could be about lack of inspiration or willingness to work, supervisor moods, being stuck in the middle of a chapter, or bored to tears through brooding over and over again on the same subject. We complained of similar problems, but we were also contented with similar things (recognition of our work efforts), and were made nervous in similar ways (when trying to figure out what the next step was, or speaking in public, or meeting deadlines). We felt an enormous pity for ourselves: 'Oh God, why am I doing this to myself, what's it all for anyway...'.

As students on instructional courses we are somehow protected with syllabuses, papers to write and articles to read, deadlines to meet and final exams to prepare for. The limits, the levels, the aims of a course are by definition clear from the start. It is also a shared experience which allows for integration with other students. As research students, on the other hand, we embark on quite a different journey. To start with, the aim of the research is blurred and the numerous ways open for analysis only add more confusion to our daily experience. Research does not allow the security of a syllabus, of text books and course limits. One has to find enough resolution to move behind the obvious and to read in unknown quarters, maintaining a certain amount of optimism.

However, obvious reasons make the experience of overseas students different from the rest. We are faced with extra difficulties, both of a personal and academic nature, which imply further pressures in the process of adaptation and integration. Initially, in many cases, we depend on our ability to deal with a language not our own: the mastering of a new grammar and syntax together with the knowledge of how to put across one's ideas and intentions without hurting people's sensibilities. Still, most overseas students I have met, mainly those with previous experience of a British degree like myself, have not had much trouble at this point, although not having reached a certain level of proficiency for communication and writing may have been a continuous source of stress for some.

As students we feel alone with our work as much as too deeply involved in it. We are rightly proud of our progress and ideas and, sometimes, far too narrowly set in them. Diverging opinions in supervision may give way to uneasy relationships, even more so when people are expressing themselves in a language not their own. However, I believe that misunderstandings can be clarified and even avoided and communication improved given a relaxed environment between supervisor and student; but this atmosphere can only develop if desired and worked for by both sides.

I would say that the real problem affecting us as foreigners in Britain may not necessarily be related to becoming proficient in the language but to mastering the cultural logic. That implies coming closer to the semantics of words and behaviour in another culture without creating misunderstandings, coming closer to the reasons behind action and reaction, grasping the hidden meanings of words and intentions, not having to wonder at all the different possibilities implied by the meaning of a word, an opinion, a piece of advice or criticism, because, let's face it, overseas students are as foreign to British people as the latter are to them.

In my case, on top of being an overseas student and, no doubt, a foreigner, I was also a mature student. Whatever one thinks of oneself, and leaving aside theorizing about the very interesting interplay between life experience and higher education, for a full-time student the fact of having a 'mature' age can be a great nuisance. I could never get away from the fact that I was on average a good ten to fifteen years older than anybody else around. Trying hard to think positively and not to classify myself in age terms brought me into peculiar and sometimes ridiculous situations. But what can one do when personal experiences and memories are considered history?

As overseas students the cost of a PhD can be high both financially, in relation to gambling current working positions against expected future opportunities, and psychologically. In consequence, we carry around the fear of failure like an unconscious second skin. This makes standard difficulties appear larger than they really are, the isolating nature of research enhancing disorientation and giving a level of stress which is sometimes not easy to bear. Failure is then perceived as a total catastrophe, because it is felt that it could not be redressed.

But this account of my experience reads worse than it was. There are always rewards, and many: the pleasure of being able to carry out research;

of mastering each step; of satisfying our curiosity; of learning about new worlds; the letters and encouragement from home; the sympathy, solidarity and companionship of fellow students; the daily support and protection of the group of friends and family that we all create. In the end, at a personal level everything comes down, as always, to understanding and adapting oneself so as to become recognizable, understood and loved, in a word, to belonging. In this environment, problems are less insurmountable, and fears are controlled. And on our return home, once everything is past and done with, we will be ready to explain that doing a PhD is sort of being in heaven and there will only be old letters to remind you of the difficulties, the fears and the insecurities. Because, returning home, my friends, is another story. . . .

Begoña Arregui, Full-time Demography Research Student

Supervisors: 1

This contribution contains a personal view of some important elements in completing a higher degree. It is addressed to research students, but hopefully contains points of interest for supervisors too.

The Strengths and Limits of the Supervisor/Student Relationship

The relationship of student to supervisor involves a potential or actual degree of dependency on one member of academic staff of a kind that the student is unlikely to have experienced before. Two points follow from this. First, it is extremely important for both parties to put time and energy into this relationship, particularly during the stages when the student tends to feel most vulnerable and isolated. In my experience, this means in the first six months or so after registration, and then when a first draft is completed and there is a desperate need for feedback about whether the draft is close to — or has even achieved — the required 'standard'.

Second, it is important that the student does not rely totally on the main supervisor for advice and guidance. A number of additional sources of support are normally at hand. Most universities and polytechnics have now introduced some kind of 'supervisory committee', which provides the student with direct and legitimate access to other members of academic staff. The committee may also review the student's progress at regular intervals and make recommendations on matters such as changes in registration — e.g. upgrading to PhD candidature — and the name(s) of external examiners.

Apart from the supervisory committee, other research students can also be a vital source of information and support. Informal meetings and discussions with members of one's own peer group — whether via participation in research training schemes or on a one-to-one basis — can be very useful when, as will almost inevitably happen, the student goes through the phase of thinking it is just they who are confused or worried. They will soon recognize that (a) they are not the only ones who are confused; and (b) that a degree of confusion is a necessary stage in doing postgraduate (or, for that matter, any) research.

Organization for Meetings with Supervisors

The golden rule is always to have an appointment booked with your supervisor. At the end of each session, make another appointment and agree the objective(s) for the next meeting so that you have something clear to work towards. If possible, submit something in writing at least three days in advance of each meeting, even if it is only a page of headings or questions. This means that supervisor and student can both give some preparatory thought to the meeting and then check at the end if the objectives have been achieved.

Preparation of Dissertation Outlines at Regular Intervals

As soon as possible — say around four or five months into the research — it is a good idea to begin drawing up outlines or structures of the eventual dissertation. This may sound very early, but it is crucial that you begin this sooner rather than later to concentrate your mind on the end product.

I would suggest aiming for a maximum of one sheet of paper on which you should draw up a list of, say, between five and nine chapter headings plus dissertation title. The latter is often the most difficult of all as it requires you to identify the 'key variables' or issues which hold your research together. When you complete such outlines, date them and keep them for future reference.

First time round, I suggest you clear your desk/computer screen, put all your notes to one side, start with a blank sheet of paper/screen and simply concentrate on the main features of the research. This procedure is about architecture and design, not bricks and mortar. Submit the outline to your supervisor and take out some time in a supervision session to discuss it. I suggest you do this at three to six monthly intervals throughout the research process.

Over time, you can begin to extend the process, filling out the sub-sections in each chapter and writing in the margin what percentage of the eventual dissertation each chapter will constitute. The latter is a useful exercise as it concentrates the mind on the relative importance and weight of each section in relation to the whole.

What is an MPhil/PhD?

This is very difficult to define in the abstract, particularly since the criteria have been changing over the past decade in many of the social sciences. This has entailed a move away from what might be termed the arts-based model, with its focus on an original individual scholarly contribution to knowledge, towards the apprenticeship model of natural science, engineering and the 'harder' social sciences. Ultimately you need to look at the specific regulations in force in your own institution and discuss this question with your supervisor in the context of your own research project and discipline. The dissertation outline — mentioned in the previous section — is a good basis for such a discussion.

However I think it is important that students have at the very least a broad definition of general requirements and expectations. The following is based on the formal regulations governing higher degrees by research at Southampton University (published annually in the *University Calendar*). I have amplified the criteria slightly on the basis of my own experience as a supervisor and examiner of higher degrees.

An MPhil normally requires you to:

— show satisfactory knowledge of the background of the subject
— write clearly and in a logical and ordered fashion
— use appropriate research methods and techniques competently
— display ability to analyze critically and evaluate independently the relevant 'literature' and other sources of data
— make some advance in knowledge of the subject.

A PhD normally requires you to:

— show mastery of the background and 'context' of the subject
— write clearly and in a logical and ordered fashion
— use appropriate research methods and techniques with a high level of competence
— display ability to analyze critically and evaluate independently the relevant literature and other sources of data
— make a significant original contribution to knowledge.

In my view a PhD should also normally contain material worthy of publication — in whole or in part — in a learned journal.

If you find this all too abstract, the best advice is to ask your supervisor — and maybe also fellow research students in your department or faculty — which past MPhils and PhDs they would recommend you to read. All higher education libraries contain copies of dissertations, and this can be a good starting point.

The 'World at One' Question

This question has been the bane of my research students' lives, but I do strongly recommend it. Imagine you are invited to appear on a national news programme such as 'The World at One'. The interviewer puts a microphone under your nose and asks you to summarize the aims of your research and its main findings — *in three minutes*. The aim of the question is to try and get you to identify:

(a) the 'context' of your research, i.e. which debates, issues, problems, it is addressing
(b) the 'red thread' of your research — the idea that binds it together and
(c) its main findings, i.e. your (major) contribution(s) to knowledge.

Trying to answer these three questions is also a good way of preparing for the oral — or viva voce — examination for a higher degree (where there is one). It is one of the classic opening gambits of external examiners, after an initial question to set the candidate at ease, to ask a question along these lines!

Research as Vocation: The Marriage of Inspiration and Hard Work

I would like to conclude this contribution with two pieces of wisdom from the German sociologist Max Weber. First, he suggested that it is one of the primary tasks of the teacher (here the supervisor) to teach the student to 'recognize inconvenient facts', i.e. evidence relevant to the subject under discussion which does not necessarily fit with the student's own argument or views. I see this as an important function of higher degree supervisors, although it is not one which always endears them to their students!

Second, Weber argued that the pursuit and generation of knowledge do not simply come from hard work alone, but also from 'passionate devotion', intuition and inspiration:

Intuition cannot be forced. Ideas occur to us when they please, not when it pleases us. The best ideas do indeed occur to one's mind ... when smoking a cigar on the sofa [having a drink with friends in the pub?] or ... when taking a walk on a slowly ascending street [when going for a walk in the country?] ... In any case, ideas come when we do not expect them, and not when we are brooding and searching at our desks. Yet ideas would certainly not come to mind had we not brooded at our desk and searched for answers with passionate devotion.... Both enthusiasm and work, and above all both of them jointly, can entice the idea. (Weber, 1948:136)

In my own case I find that new perspectives, insights and ideas tend to come when I am mowing the lawn! In contrast, my first ever PhD student swore that ideas came to her when she was taking the dog for a walk. As you can imagine, I was always delighted when I rung her up to discuss something to be told that she was out walking the dog. Only later did I find out that this was a standard joke in her family and was regularly used by her as an excuse to avoid talking to me!

But the basic point stands. If you are not getting anywhere sitting at a desk, go and do something completely different. This may well clear the mind. Try, too, to have some kind of outside pursuit which takes you completely away from your research on a regular basis. Finally: don't enter on research unless it comes from within, unless you really passionately want to do it and to delve deep into the subject in the interests of the pursuit of knowledge. There are going to be some tough times ahead, and this will be absolutely vital to help keep you going.

Jon Clark

Supervisors: 2

I am writing from the perspective of someone who has supervised mainly part-time students registered for a higher degree while working in the human services. There is a need to pay particular attention to the requirements of these students, but in doing so I would hope to identify aspects of supervision significant for all higher degree students.

Reflecting on the experience and practice of higher degree supervision leads me to the conclusion that over the years there have been significant changes in the tasks and expectations of supervisors. Examining these changes helps us clarify what students can demand from the supervision process. The days when a senior academic in a department took over the supervision of the bright young graduates and, in prima donna fashion, influenced and controlled the methodology and thinking of the research in order to replicate and develop ideas which were of particular interest, are long since gone. However, the positives of this situation, referred to as the apprentice model (Howard and Sharp, 1983), hopefully have not disappeared. Supervisors are chosen, or should be chosen, because they have special expertise and knowledge in the field in which the student wishes to research. For this reason they are *educators*, and students should expect that knowledge will be passed on, reading directed and learning facilitated. This does not demand a didactic style, a supervision session which is the reiteration of the supervisor's personal view or an expounding of her or his latest hypothesis. It has to be a process which incorporates listening and responding. The supervisor should be a sounding board for ideas and an inquisitor or trouble-shooter. Primarily this process is one in which the student should be given feedback.

In practical terms there is a need to create the climate in which this educative process can occur. This involves the need to map out a plan or programme of meetings but this programme must have a purpose which is supported by appropriate tasks — for both student and supervisor. Aimless supervision sessions are unproductive and time-consuming. The tasks, of course, can be many and varied and will often be related to the specific discipline in which the research is taking place, or indeed to the methodology chosen. What is important is that they are identified and agreed in advance of meetings and designated as being the responsibility of student or supervisor. To present a draft of a questionnaire or chapter outline at the beginning of a supervision session, or even the night before, is not helpful and will not create opportunities for appropriate and informed feedback. The strategy therefore is to identify a realistic hand-in date and, having done this, to ensure that all work prepared is given appropriate attention and that feedback is clearly presented. The student who sits and writes down every word may be flattering to the supervisor's ego but if the process is happening because they have not done their own thinking (and don't intend to) then it is not helpful. The student who nods dutifully at every suggestion made then leaves the room and changes nothing can be equally frustrating for the supervisor! Alternatively, the supervisor who perpetuates the image of the eccentric academic or even the overworked academic, losing drafts, forgetting to read them or going off at a seemingly unrelated tangent, is not only frustrating for the student but also unprofessional.

Part of the process of feedback has to acknowledge that at some stage supervisors themselves have to become students and the student becomes the expert. It is a function of all research that it is expanding the boundaries of knowledge and that while a student will commence the research dependent on the knowledge and expertise of the supervisor, there will come a time when, in the specific area of the student's research, they will, indeed they should, know more than the supervisor. This is not to say that supervision becomes redundant but that the relationship needs to change. Students need to communicate their knowledge and the supervisor's task is to question, and to assist in the framing of the research in an appropriate form, whether this relates to writing and presentation styles, limiting the scope of the research or requiring further clarification.

There is also a need for the supervision process to be a *management process*. Management functions occur in every stage of higher degree research. At the outset what is required is the crystallization of the ideas, the inevitable process of working to ensure that the student's 'grand idea' is translated into a workable research topic and that this is related to a realistic timescale, with landmarks identified to encourage and give incentive. For students where a taught research scheme is available or where there are opportunities for joining other courses related, for example, to methodology, the management of time and access or availability is critical. Similarly where the knowledge and skills of members of the academic staff are sought, for instance with micro-computing, it is the responsibility of the supervisor to set up the contact rather than expect the student to introduce themselves and tentatively request help. The institution as a whole needs to have a commitment to ensuring that students, both full- and part-time, complete their higher de-grees; the institution, after all, reaps some of the benefits. However it is for the supervisor to act as intermediary, to be the point of contact for the student within the institution and to ensure ease of access of the student to the facilities of the institution.

The reference to completion raises for me another essential management task in supervision and that is to enable the student to understand the effect of and to use appropriately the regulations relating to registration and time boundaries. There is a research topic to be completed on the motivation of all students who undertake research degrees and their subsequent personal his-tories. Part-time students may be extreme examples of an observable pattern. They tend to be mature students who may have reached a critical point in their career or personal life which precipitates them into academia. My experience is that once registered these students are at risk of all sorts of life events — illness, divorce, birth of a child, death of a close elderly relative, a house move or career change to name but a few. It is possible to negotiate these 'hazards' and still complete, but it takes skill, determination and good management. The sadness is the student who said on withdrawing from her MPhil, 'I started it because I thought I couldn't get pregnant. I now have two children and I can't see myself completing in the time left.' It is lack of time, the looming of the final deadline, which often leads students to with-draw precipitately or to produce a thesis which does not adequately reflect their work and their abilities.

One of the problems is the pressure felt by students to carry on regardless. This is in part related to a lack of knowledge that you can suspend, take time out. At any point during registration if there are circumstances which mean the student is unable to undertake his/her research a student can, with the support of the supervisor, request a period of suspension. This means that there will be no fees for the period and no supervision and the time will not be counted towards the final deadline for the submission of the thesis. Therefore, you don't have to watch the research clock tick by while you are sorting out a personal crisis and spending no time on data collection, analysis, reading or writing and kid yourself that you can cope! A realistic fear is that, once having suspended registration, it will be impossible to come back. The reality is that it *is* difficult to return but not impossible and, even though not in supervision, a student can, and should, keep in touch with the supervisor. This can provide the incentive and the encouragement to return.

Much of this leads into a further function of supervision and that is to provide the student with a *counsellor*. The process of research is an intense and potentially isolating one causing stress at all levels. The supervisor is sometimes the only person with whom you can share your deepest anxieties and greatest frustrations. Partners and colleagues don't always understand the significance of the lost file on the computer, the low response rate to a questionnaire or the frustration of chasing the essential reference, or the joy and relief at finding it!

As well as sharing these earth-shattering events with the supervisor, students can also expect help with some of the difficult decisions. Such decisions can include limitations on the research task or changing the focus, but can also involve more painful ones such as suspending, not going for an upgrading and, most difficult of all, withdrawing. It is the supervisor's responsibility not just to ensure that a student completes but that a student completes successfully. The pain and the demoralization of a rewrite are sometimes too great for students and they cannot summon up the energy or will. It is in many cases less painful to acknowledge the limitations and to call a halt at a much earlier stage. This should not mean that work is lost. A more appropriate medium such as a research report or a journal article might be found. It is important that this is an agenda which must be part of every review, if not every supervision session. From the beginning there is a need to be realistic about the potential of both the student and the project they are undertaking and students need to be prepared to accept this realism.

At the very beginning of this chapter I referred to the process of selecting supervisors and I would like to return to this because from my experience as a supervisor and as someone with responsibility for allocating students on a higher degree programme I see this as a highly sensitive area for both students and supervisors. Supervision of higher degree students carries with it a certain status for supervisors. I have indicated in the preceding paragraphs that it ought to be a major commitment of anyone undertaking supervision and can be time-consuming and onerous. The other reality is that it is stimulating and enjoyable for anyone to have the opportunity to discuss at length ideas which contribute to the development of one's own discipline. It can widen horizons and spark off further areas of study either for the supervisor or other research students. There is also a sense of satisfaction and pride to be had from seeing the completed thesis and participating in the graduation celebrations. All this brings a number of pressures to the allocation of supervisors. Essentially there has to be choice and that means choice on both sides. For students to make an informed choice a number of strategies are necessary. The first is that members of staff should identify and share their areas of specialism, their favoured methodological approach and their own research areas. Prospective students should be given information about what is on offer and a provisional allocation of supervisor made at the point of a candidature being offered. Such arrangements are not immutable. It is possible that at an early stage, for a variety of reasons, supervisor and/or student may acknowledge that the allocation is an inappropriate one. While the transfer of supervision should not be undertaken lightly, because it is time-consuming and causes delays in the progress of the research, it is important to acknowledge the possibility without suggesting that this is a 'failure' on anyone's part. Also, the joint involvement of two people who have shared responsibility for supervision can widen the scope for the student but also has implications for the management of the project. The role of second supervisor, frequency of contact and whose word is final are some of the issues which need to be acknowledged and decided at the commencement of the supervisory relationship, or the student may end up feeling like a tennis ball, rather than an equal partner in an exciting and productive relationship.

I conclude by reiterating that my experiences of the supervision process have convinced me that it is demanding and at times frustrating for all involved, student and supervisor alike. This is outweighed for the supervisor by the satisfaction and rewards of contributing to the completed research task and for the student by the acquisition of a higher degree.

Joan Orme

References

BUCHANAN, A. (1989) 'Soiling and sexual abuse: The danger of misdiagnosis', *Newsletter of the Association of Child Psychology and Psychiatry*, **11**, pp. 3–8.

EICHLER, M. (1988) *Nonsexist Research Methods: A Practical Guide*, Boston, Allen and Unwin.

HARDING, S. (Ed.) (1987) *Feminism and Methodology*, Bloomington, Indiana University Press.

HOWARD, K. and SHARP, J. (1983) *The Management of a Student Research Project*, Aldershot, Gower.

PHILLIPS, E.M. and PUGH, D.S. (1987) *How To Get a PhD*, Milton Keynes, Open University Press.

SHAVER, P. and HENDRICK, C. (Eds) (1987) *Sex and Gender*, London, Sage.

WEBER, M. (1948) 'Science as Vocation', in GERTH, H. and WRIGHT MILLS, C. (Eds) *From Max Weber*, London, Routledge and Kegan Paul.

WILKINSON, S. (Ed.) (1986) *Feminist Social Psychology*, Milton Keynes, Open University Press.

WILSON, A. (1980) 'Group sessions for postgraduate students', *British Journal Of Guidance and Counselling*, **8**, pp. 237–41.

Chapter 4

What are Examiners Looking For?

John H. Smith

The examination and award of a higher degree by thesis is properly seen as the climax of a lengthy, sustained and disciplined effort by the candidate. In British higher education the principal role and final decision in that examination is assigned to an expert assessor who is external to the institution. This independent endorsement by a scholar who has no prior knowledge of the candidate's work provides public recognition that it meets the standard required for admission to full membership of the research community.

Recent concern about completion rates and the efficacy of supervision and indeed, about the value of the research degree itself, have prompted a great deal of discussion about the expectations and limitations of present arrangements. Other contributors to this volume have emphasized the importance of proper preparation for each of the various stages of the research student's career. Concerted attempts are being made to remove the doubts and ambiguities encountered along what can be a long and difficult journey and reduce the isolation and possible loss of purpose of research students. While new approaches to research training programmes rightly give priority to the nature and organization of the research itself and the skills required as a framework for success, so far little or no emphasis has been placed on the expectations that the examiners themselves bring to their task. The fact that the external examiner is drawn from another institution is assumed to provide sufficient explanation of his or her role. But this is questionable. The regulations of institutions provide little help to anyone looking for guidance about these expectations, other than in general terms. The 1987 Winfield Report to the ESRC on Submission Rates covered the question as follows:

> Requirements for a doctoral thesis are stringent ones. It must be such that the author can show originality, that it will be different from other work already published, that it will make a contribution to knowledge and still be bounded in such a way as to be manageable in terms of the material to be assembled and the time available.

This passage conveys ideas about the overall standard of the PhD but it can hardly be said to identify specific objectives. It simply echoes the way in which an institution's instructions to examiners for higher degrees will require them to certify in recommending an award that the thesis meets such requirements as contributing to knowledge of the topic, discovering facts not already known, advancing learning and so on.

It is the job of the examiners to relate these general and admittedly idealistic standards to what is actually in front of them. Examiners, like research students, have a problem of bridging the gap between expectation and reality. The observations given here on how this is approached arise from the writer's own experience over the years as an examiner in a fairly wide range of institutions and in particular as an external examiner. What is said applies to research theses presented both for the MPhil and the PhD degree. The standard practice nowadays is for the student to begin with registration for the MPhil and to demonstrate that up-grading to the PhD has been earned. Examiners faced with judging a thesis must apply the standards appropriate to the level of the registration, i.e. is the award of the MPhil or the PhD justified? What happens when there is a fundamental discrepancy between expectation (level of registration) and reality (performance of the candidate)? In the case of the PhD, the examiners may decide that while that particular standard has not been reached, the thesis merits the award of the MPhil. Among the possible reasons for such a decision would be lack of depth in the investigation or analysis of the topic, methodological shortcomings, insufficient development of the material in the form of conclusions and its relation to existing work.

Knowledge that such a provision exists for a lesser award is, of course, yet another of the uncertainties confronting candidates but it is not much of a comfort to have it referred to as a fail-safe procedure. Nonetheless, it is worth noting how this emphasizes the qualities of judgment and absolute discretion which examiners are called upon to exercise. It is also possible that a thesis first submitted for the MPhil ends up with the award of a PhD. In the writer's experience, this is a very rare (and welcome) occurrence; but the fact that it may happen provides a further safeguard of independence, in that the final external judgment on a thesis may exceptionally override the opinion of the supervisor or the normal procedures of the institution.

Having said that, the majority of theses submitted will be successful. The decision to submit and the final form in which the thesis appears should represent above all a declaration of confidence both by the supervisor and by the candidate that the work will be judged satisfactory. For the external examiner then, the formal invitation to act suggests that the research has been satisfactorily completed and that it is ready to be assessed. At this stage candidates would do well to put aside all their doubts and to forget the disappointments and compromises which will have been an inevitable part of the experience. All of which is by way of saying that an external examiner's primary expectation is one of success and that it is the job of the candidate to fulfil that expectation through the finished form of the thesis and, where appropriate, an oral examination.

We can now consider how the external examiner approaches the thesis itself and the preliminary appraisal of the work of the candidate. The first question for an external when approached is whether he or she is willing to act. The choice of an external will be governed by field of research expertise, availability and willingness. All three factors are important, but the last is crucial. Reading and adjudging a thesis is not a lightweight task. It is something which is usually tackled at home, at evenings and weekends, so the decision to act invariably increases the examiner's workload. Agreeing to examine a thesis constitutes a substantial commitment which is in no way matched by the fee which the external examiner receives (currently in the region of £65 for a PhD, £55 for an MPhil). A far more telling consideration will be the examiner's view of the department and its supervisors and the nature of the research topic.

It seems self-evident that the most appropriate external for a thesis is someone whose particular expertise lies in the area of the research topic itself. This is normally the case, but a few caveats are in order. The obvious examiner Professor X may be away in the States for a year and neither the candidate nor the research council's submission deadlines can wait that long. Or Dr Y, another well-known specialist, is simply too busy or may feel stale on that particular topic. The eventual decision is invariably one which is given careful consideration and it is reasonable for the candidate to be given some idea of who is likely to be approached. Whoever is appointed will have been given a preliminary view of the topic, an informal view of the virtues (at least) of the candidate and an indication of when the thesis is likely to be submitted. A long interval between the appointment of an external and submission of the thesis is not recommended.

We can now consider the expectations of the examiner on receipt of the thesis. In most cases, after the informal soundings about availability and the official letter of appointment, the examiner's initial encounter with the candidate will be when the thesis lands on his or her desk. It is salutary for the candidate to consider the first impressions likely to be given. The examiner already knows the topic and the title and will probably start by reading the abstract and glancing through the table of contents and quite possibly the bibliography. References, footnotes and appendices are important indicators of the kind of work it is likely to be. These constitute a form of provenance, which gives the examiner a sense of the overall quality and plausibility of the work. Prefaces may be important, but excessive acknowledgments can be off-putting. It is good to know that families and friends make the burdens of research and literary composition more bearable, but it is worth asking whether many of these thanks are not best left until after the degree ceremony.

The surest way to secure and maintain the examiner's interest is to focus on the quality of the thesis as a finished product. In the writer's opinion, there are three essential requirements, each of which applies generally to theses in the social sciences and humanities, irrespective of the specific topics or methodologies chosen. They are (1) narrative skill; (2) intellectual argument; and (3) methodological (including bibliographical) support.

The importance of narrative in conveying the strengths, or weaknesses, of a thesis should be properly appreciated. Every research has its own story to tell and the student should consider how to present it in an interesting and challenging fashion. The external examiner will expect to find a clear account of the sequence in which the work was done and when decisions — including decisions to change direction — were made. Mistakes or blind alleys should not be ignored, or glossed over, but treated as data or insights. An examiner may well want to know from the candidate whether things might have been tackled differently, or would be now approached with the benefit of hindsight. These should not be taken as trick or carping questions, but as legitimate enquiries about the candidate's awareness of research as a learning process. It should always be remembered that an external examiner cannot have the close familiarity of the candidate or the supervisor with what happened over a long period; hence the need to provide some sort of narrative framework to explain the conduct of the work itself.

The emphasis on intellectual argument may seem self-evident, but it is quite simply too important to be taken for granted. One of the greatest risks for the candidate bringing material together in thesis form is that he or she will lose sight altogether of the central argument. Important though the individual trees may be, the wood should always be in view and the reader should not feel trapped inside it. Opening and concluding chapters have a vital part to play in defining (and possibly re-defining) the boundaries of the thesis itself. What lies between needs to be carefully reviewed at the final stages, even though it may lead to the exclusion of hard-won and cherished material which turns out to be not strictly relevant to the final argument. The alternative is that the examiner may get bogged down in an excess of theoretical or contextual analysis. Sometimes this may be usefully consigned to an appendix with a brief explanation of why it has been retained and presented in that form. Supervisors will of course be aware of such risks, but it is always sensible for the candidate to try to put himself or herself in the position of the examiner reading the material for the first time.

Similar points can be made about the emphasis on methodological and bibliographical matters. Each of these is directly related to the two considerations of narrative skill and intellectual argument just discussed. The way in which they are approached must inevitably be shaped by the research topic and the specific objectives, but from the examiner's point of view there will always be certain basic questions to which the thesis should provide the answers. Why was a particular method (or methods) chosen and why, where appropriate, were others not chosen or discarded? If they were judged satisfactory (or unsatisfactory), for what reasons? On the bibliographical side, what were the key sources? Some overall assessment of the strengths and weaknesses of the literature may also be in order, but this is probably better confined to particular studies or areas. Finally, footnotes do provide an opportunity to discuss methodological or bibliographical issues, but there is no golden rule about them (other perhaps than length).

Close attention to all these points — narrative, intellectual argument and methodological and bibliographical support — should not only make for a more effective thesis, but also for an easier passage through the viva. A candidate's supervisor will be able to give some advice on preparing for this. Despite all that has been said earlier, a candidate, however well-prepared, will naturally feel anxious about what he or she will be asked, or expected to cover in an hour or so. There is no such thing as a standard viva, but a few general points should be borne in mind. A candidate will not be expected to answer questions from memory and examiners will specify pages or passages in the thesis and allow time to look at them. Usually an examiner will give a general indication of how he or she feels about the thesis, including areas of approval or of possible concern. Questions about what worries an examiner should not be taken as a sign that the candidate will be failed, but it is important that they should be answered directly and backed by references to the text of the thesis itself. Finally, a candidate should always be prepared to discuss how the work represented by the thesis might be developed further, especially for publication. He or she should also be prepared for the sense of anticlimax as well as relief which marks the successful completion of a long, arduous but ultimately rewarding experience.

Part 2

Study Skills and the Management of Research

Chapter 5

Organization and Management of Research

Chris Colbourn

Introduction

In discussing the organization and management of research work while studying for a postgraduate research degree, it is worth bearing in mind the ultimate goal — the production and defence of a thesis, i.e. the coherent written account of the research carried out by the student during their course.

Having specified in a relatively general way where we want to go, I shall now describe some of the techniques that students may find useful in reaching this point. I have divided these up into three groups which reflect the structure of the activities necessary as I see it. First, I shall discuss *research organization* itself in terms of the global organization of the three, four or more years over which your research degree is to be studied for. Second I shall discuss *planning* matters, which are techniques more local to particular stages in one's work and are used over and over again. Finally I shall review what I have labelled a *management toolbox* of craft-like skills (e.g. acquiring and handling information, communication, and using information techno-logy) which are also used constantly throughtout one's studies.

Research Organization

Most of the standard pitfalls that postgraduate students can encounter have been well and amusingly recounted by both Bundy, Du Boulay, Howe and Plotkin (1984) and Hodgson and Rollnick (1989). Although the frames of reference for discussing research work were widely different for these two sets of authors, the problems outlined and the advice given were remarkably similar. Probably the most important point to reiterate here from these accounts is the fact that research work rarely runs smoothly and rarely follows the strictly logical progression that one encounters in other theses, monographs and journal papers. It must be realized that the final thesis is a construction where many of the thoughts, constructs, empirical and/or theoretical studies, etc. were generated and carried out at different times and quite likely in a different order from that in which they are presented. The thesis is geared to presenting a coherent exposition of the research topic, though the research itself commonly occurs in a very different way.

Identifying the Problem and Formulating Hypotheses

An important and early stage of organization must be to define the area or topic upon which you intend to work and to identify key issues, questions, etc. that might make a good thesis. To some extent this will already have taken place in the manner whereby you were taken on to do the research degree in the first place. However, institutions and supervisors vary considerably in the amount of detail they expect potential students to have outlined their ideas.

The first stage should therefore be to refine your initial proposal by talking extensively to your supervisor and other experts in the department and faculty, and of course searching the literature for relevant material. This may seem obvious but it is all too easy for the new student and the supervisor to let things settle down and to become involved in general 'housekeeping' activities almost to the exclusion of the real purpose of one's endeavour. The point is that the 'housekeeping' (e.g. learning about facilities available and developing new relevant skills) needs to be done anyway as we shall discuss later, but it can be done in parallel with the more substantive task of working towards your thesis.

At this stage, discussion and feedback from others regarding your proposed project are essential to avoid you falling into the 'solving the world' trap. You only have a finite time and your project is only a means to an end — a research degree — not necessarily the earth-shattering magnum opus that we would all like to produce. Keep it all in proportion and allow others to help you in this task, especially your supervisor whose duty this is. This is not meant to suggest that creativity and radical new ideas are out, but that the chances of success in their application need to be evaluated against pragmatic criteria. Also, do write it all down! It helps to keep track of your ideas and to allow you to look back over your ideas, developments and meanderings. I shall discuss techniques related to note-taking and writing in the later section on the 'management toolbox'.

Implementing Your Project

It is not unknown for the first stage of producing a project proposal to absorb the whole of the first year, especially when the student is attending a research training course and various other 'skill' courses. But to take so long over this stage is really a mistake, and far too leisurely a pace for the constraints of time that exist. I feel that the proposal should be worked up to an implementable stage after the first three months of full-time study at the latest (six to nine months of part-time study) since even then there are likely to be other small and/or large problems to solve.

Your project may involve empirical work, whereupon you will need to produce the detailed operational design of the investigations. Decide upon the techniques to be used and the measures to employ (and possibly consider the development of new measures if necessary — although this could be a major undertaking and should not be entered into lightly; see Powell, 1989, for a consideration of some of these issues in a broad social science context). It is likely that if you are going to be involved in data collection you will already have taken courses in the necessary basic skills during your undergraduate training and probably also have carried out some small-scale empirical projects of this kind. However it is at this, the design stage, where you need to consider how you are going to analyze and interpret the data to be collected. You should have some plan of what statistical, graphical, qualitative, etc. methods will be appropriate, and this should be discussed with the 'experts' before you carry out the study. No 'analysis expert' will welcome you warmly if you meet them for the first time with a sheaf of your latest data under your arm! Whatever plans you formulate should include simply looking at the data. Serendipity often plays a substantial role in revealing things about your data and there are now many exploratory techniques that assist in this task which can be applied either manually or using various computer software packages.

Equally, your research may involve the use of documentary evidence, as discussed in Chapter 10, where access to archives may be important. These days, much archival material is either held or at least indexed via computer databases. This will possibly require you to learn how to access and search such facilities, and commonly will need an outline plan of how to tackle such tasks (see Chapter 6).

When your work gets well under way and you are conducting a series of investigations (either experiments, surveys or archival searches), it is easy to fall into a 'production line' trap. The work can become monotonous in appearance and while all tasks, occupations, etc. do indeed have their routine, somewhat boring side, it is best to try and minimize this because it can quickly sap motivation and thereby the rate of productive work. Bundy *et al.*

(1989) pointed out that doing research shares many of the same psychological difficulties as other creative endeavours and identified a number of problems and their possible antidotes. In general these can be summarized respectively as being related to mental attitude and having faith in what you are doing.

Communicating the Findings

We started this chapter by noting that a written thesis and its oral defence were the ultimate goals of your postgraduate work, and of course, these are concerned with *communicating* what you have been doing and what you have found. It used to be the case that many postgraduate students would complete the work for their thesis without having written very much that they would consider appropriate to put into the final submitted thesis. Starting to 'write up' was thus a dreaded prospect for many. Writing from the very start, and writing with a view to inclusion in the final thesis, not just rough notes, is the main way to circumvent this problem. The ready availability of quite sophisticated writing tools, like wordprocessors, has made this easier to do. The ease with which text can be manipulated and altered also convinces the user that their efforts will not be wasted and changes can easily be made. It also provides a more presentable product for others to read and comment on. (See Chapter 8 on 'Writing Skills'.)

Another activity worth considering is doing some teaching in your subject area. While you do not want to overburden yourself with too much additional work (and also provide yourself with excuses for avoiding thesis-related activities), a certain amount of lecturing and tutorial work can help develop your communication skills and understanding of your own subject. I personally found that having to explain to others quickly established what I really understood and what I needed to comprehend more fully. In this way I learned a lot more about my subject in a small space of time and this fed back into my own postgraduate work in a beneficial way.

Planning

The overall organization of your research work that was discussed in the previous section requires a certain amount of *planning* if everything is to run smoothly. There can be enough upsets with regard to the content of the research without letting general organizational matters create difficulties as well. As I have emphasized, time is of the essence, and good temporal planning in particular can help you stay on course to finish your thesis more predictably.

Coordinating Activities

Like building a house, carrying out an experiment or survey, or even producing a complete thesis, is a complex and multi-faceted activity requiring the coordination and efficient scheduling of the various different phases. For instance in planning an empirical study, you might break down the separate stages and estimate both time and the resources required for each stage and plot these out to see how they fit together using something like the network diagram shown in Figure 1. Such techniques can also be valuable in simply getting you to consider the resources you will require, e.g. technical help, equipment, or access to special facilities, and any special skills you might need.

While such planning can be done manually, more complex activities could benefit from the use of computer software aimed at 'project management'. Commonly such software is based on 'critical path analysis', about which the user needs no knowledge. From simple specifications by the user, the program will derive the optimally efficient scheduling of the different phases of a complicated task and can present this in a variety of graphical forms, one of which being that shown in Figure 1. The advantage of the program is that any inaccuracies can soon be corrected in the light of experience and a new diagram produced to give you a revised esimate of how the study (or whatever task you are planning) will proceed.

Regular Routines

Regular routines are also essential because they help to circumvent times of low motivation and keep you going. It is often useful to establish a set of daily, weekly, and perhaps monthly routines, though what is included will depend on whether you are a part-time or full-time student. The daily ones will probably be the most flexible depending on exactly what aspect of the research you are focusing on at the moment but even here it is important to try and maintain a regular working schedule involving a definite time of day when you start to work. The alternative will inevitably be getting involved with the seemingly endless pile of domestic 'stuff to do' (see Elton, 1989, pp. 173–4), and never actually starting work that day (or perhaps the next).

One valuable antidote to the problem of the morning 'cold start' is to leave yourself some non-threatening, attractive task to do first of all. This can be especially important when you are writing. Leave something easy to write first of all, don't stop the day before at the start of a difficult new section. Some routine paragraph or a diagram can often get you going and provide the momentum to steam into that problem section without hesitation (Bundy *et al.*, 1989).

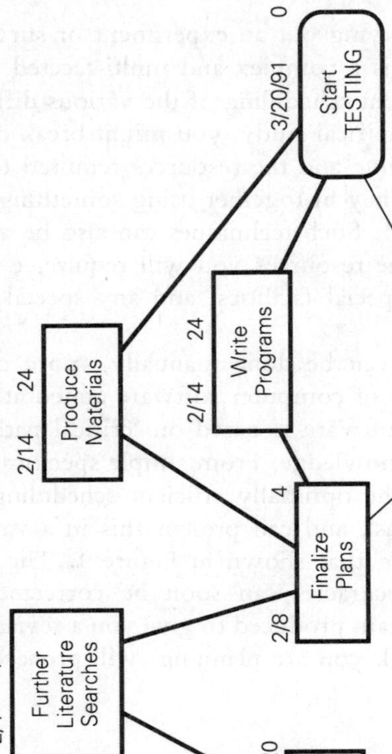

Start
TESTING
3/20/91   0

Produce
Materials
2/14   24

Write
Programs
2/14   24

Recruit
Plans
2/14   11.20

Finalize
Plans
2/8   4

Further
Literature
Searches
2/4   4

Planning
Meetings
1/30   3.20

Research
Visits
1/24   4

Initial
Planning
1/14   8

Literature
Search
1/14   11.20

Start
Project
1/14/91   0

Figure 1: Project planning using such network diagrams can help assess realistic time scales and practical approaches.
(Lines join dependent tasks and bold outlines indicate 'milestone' tasks)

Weekly routines will probably be of a more established nature, such as a visit to the library to check the latest journals received for material relevant to your topic, or whatever other strategy you adopt for this 'updating' function (see next section). Monthly routines could be similar, and are likely to include an assessment of your progress (using your 'project plan' as above) in conjunction with your supervisor.

Do not underestimate the value of these types of regular routines. While you may not adhere to them rigidly, nor would anyone necessarily expect you to, given the valuable flexibility in the way you can organize your life, they are important to give a structure to your work as a research student, particularly when you are feeling less than optimistic about progress at any given time.

Having discussed general organization and planning aspects of research work for a higher degree, let us now turn to what I have labelled the *management toolbox*, a collection of what might be called 'craft skills' and techniques that will be valuable in putting the previous advice into practice.

Management Toolbox

Using Computers

Many if not all of the techniques that I intend to discuss in this section can be perhaps most efficiently implemented using information technology based around a personal computer. I have written in more detail elsewhere about most of these techniques (Colbourn, 1989, 1991) and so I shall only provide a summary here. However, when I have presented this material to students, the question inevitably arises as to whether they should purchase their own personal computer and if so, which one. Such questions are not at all straightforward (Colbourn, 1991) and any specific recommendations can be quickly out of date. Therefore I have aimed to tackle this issue at a generic level and indicate techniques and facilities that are available on just about all 'business-type' personal computers (as opposed to what are often called 'home computers').

For some students owning one's own computer is not a viable option for economic reasons. Also it is now common for institutions of higher education to provide a substantial number of readily accessible personal and other computers available for use by all their students. These machines and their software are often considerably more powerful and sophisticated than the student is likely to be able afford themselves. Part-time students especially though may not always find it convenient to come to the university or polytechnic to use them. If students decide to purchase their own equipment then it would be most economical to satisfy the major function of word-processing in the first instance, which can be accommodated on just about all types of 'business' personal computer (and on which there are usually substantial educational discounts from major suppliers of computing hardware and software), and use the institution's facilities for other functions. Clearly compatibility between your own and your institution's or department's equipment will be important here. Another important issue will be access to institution-based workstations simply because demand may still exceed supply especially at certain times of year. These are all 'local' issues and it would be necessary for you to establish what access you are likely to have against what you use such a computer for. However let us first review the techniques and facilities that I am referring to and return to such matters at the end of the section.

Acquiring Information

Whatever type of research you are doing the need to acquire relevant information will be paramount. The main means by which this will be done will no doubt be through library services. This is the subject of the two following chapters and hence here I will restrict my comments to the importance of doing this systematically.

There has probably nearly always been the difficulty that there is too much seemingly relevant information, and it is essential to maintain a balance between reading about the work of others and carrying out one's own work. As Bundy *et al.* (1989) suggest, it can be helpful 'to think of the work of others as arranged in concentric circles around your own, where the relevance of the work decreases as you get further from the centre'. Thus the inner circles would consist of work that is directly relevant to your own and concerned with the same topic, while the outer circles would consist of related topics of your discipline as a whole. Clearly you will have to spend less time staying in touch with these 'outer circles' than with the inner ones. Therefore different study techniques will be appropriate.

First of all you need to identify where the relevant information is likely to appear, say by drawing up a list of journals that you will need to scan regularly, perhaps prioritized in terms of their likely relevance to your research. Obviously the frequency of appearance of these periodicals will be known to you and you should keep records of when you have seen the latest issue and thus know when to expect the next. You may find that your institution's library doesn't subscribe to all the journals you need to consult and therefore alternative means of access may be necessary. Obviously your local library staff will be able to assist you here but it is quite likely that there will be a local subscription to one or more of the abstracting or contents-listing journals which cover your needs; this can provide a partial solution to staying in touch.

Apart from keeping up to date there will also be the need for a retrospective literature search. While these can be carried out manually using abstracting journals and citation indices, this can be incredibly time consuming and you would be well advised to investigate the computer-based methods of conducting such searches described in Chapter 6. Libraries are rapidly introducing information technology techniques, such as an on-line public access catalogue (OPAC), which are starting to supplement if not largely replace the card and microfiche-based catalogues. These allow a much more rapid search of whether particular books and periodicals are held by your library and can often be conducted remotely from a terminal or suitably equipped personal computer almost anywhere on campus. Other facilities such as determining whether the book you require is out on loan, and reserving it, are gradually being added which again can save you considerable time in your library work. Therefore it is worth spending a while familiarizing yourself with this technology if it is available at your institution and perhaps attending the brief courses often provided by libraries.

Another method of keeping up to date in one's field is to attend conferences and seminars. However increasingly such events if held on a national or international basis are beginning to be very expensive and funds for supporting such activities from institutional sources are often limited. It is important to explore what support is available and your supervisor should be able to help here in selecting the most appropriate events to attend. Choice is likely to be made on such criteria as the number of relevant presentations and the attendance of other key researchers in your area. The function of such events for bringing like-minded people together for informal discussions is as important as the more formal paper-giving aspects.

In addition there is an increasing number of electronically mediated conferences going on in a whole variety of research areas. Access to these simply requires you to be the user of an appropriate computer system, usually a campus-based service that provides electronic mail (E-Mail), and/or access to remote computer systems at other institutions (see Colbourn, 1989, pp. 88–90). The use of E-Mail as a rapid means of communication between researchers throughout the world is well worth investigating. Details of such services, including short training courses, are usually available via your local computing services organization. However more specific information regarding your discipline may better be established by talking to the staff and other postgraduate students in your department. In the UK, the Computers in Teaching Initiative (CTI) has established subject-based centres and electronic bulletin boards which often provide basic information on these kinds of facilities. Again local enquiries will establish how best to contact these.

Handling Information

I mentioned earlier the notion of concentric circles of relevant information in the literature, and the fact that different study techniques would be necessary to handle them. The outer, more general, circles will best be dealt with at the level of reading abstracts and perhaps keeping very brief notes on those items of interest. The inner circles though will require much more detailed handling with more thorough reading of complete papers and more comprehensive notes. Given the amount of study required, it is obviously necessary for you to obtain your own copies of the most central papers you encounter. Copies can be obtained by writing to the author for an offprint, or of course via a photocopier. If you write to the author, a personal letter may often pay more dividends than the standard offprint request postcard usually available in departments for this purpose. Such a letter might explain briefly what you are researching and how you see the relevance of your work to that of the author.

Keeping Records

It is essential to keep records of your reading in the form of a personal bibliography with attached comments about the paper or book and its relevance to your work. This has traditionally been done using a card index system readily available at most stationers. Commonly one card per item is used to provide the exact reference and your comments. There are many ways of classifying the cards but it is important that you note down your own particular method and use it consistently. Such records can, of course, be kept using a computer system. Many database packages are now available for personal computers which can be used for bibliographic purposes although often such a package may be overkill for just this purpose. There are also a number of dedicated bibliographic packages available (e.g. 'Auto-Biblio', 'EndNote' and 'Pro-Cite') which would be more suitable, and some personal computers come already equipped with 'personal information handling' software that can be readily and easily tailored to one's own personal use (e.g. 'HyperCard' on the Apple Macintosh computer and 'ToolBook' on IBM PC compatible computers).

Of course, the sophistication of current wordprocessing software, in terms of search and organizational facilities, makes this approach quite a viable proposition for maintaining files of bibliographic information as well as all your other writing. However, these packages are somewhat less amenable if you suddenly wish to reorganize a very large amount of material and they are often relatively slow in handling large files compared to more specific purpose-designed database-type software.

The pros and cons of using a computer for this purpose depend heavily on whether you have ready access to a personal computer. Given that maintaining a bibliography can be a time-consuming task, and assembling the final version for your thesis even more time-consuming, I feel the balance falls towards the computer-based method. If you wish to reclassify an electronic bibliography partially or completely, and perhaps create some new sub-bibliographies, then the advantage truly shows through in the speed and ease with which such manipulations can be carried out. However cards are readily portable and easily used in libraries and elsewhere. The use of a personal electronic organizer (a small genuinely pocketable hand-held data input unit complete with keyboard and screen — thus not a portable personal computer as such) in conjunction with a personal computer can provide a ready solution. I have found that one of these, the Microwriter AgendA which uses a five-finger chord keyboard, can be used to take notes at about the same speed as handwriting. Having keyed material into this device while in the library, I can connect it to my personal computer on returning to the office and upload all my notes into a wordprocessor or bibliography handling package. The main limitation that such devices currently have are that they cannot handle graphics, though no doubt that will be overcome in the not too distant future. I feel that for the purposes I am considering here, these devices are much more useful than current types of portable computers, and are certainly a fraction of the cost.

Taking Notes

When taking notes on papers and books that you read, it is essential to do so with a particular purpose in mind, otherwise you will find yourself writing down virtually everything in the paper. If the reference is so crucial that you need so much detail then it should be clear that you need a copy of the original. Abstracting the essence of a paper must be done for your purposes, which may or may not coincide with those of the author. Read the item with some questions in mind, like 'Does this paper offer a solution to problem X?', 'Is the experimental technique used appropriate for testing the theory I am working with?', 'Can the author really use this data to test theory Y?'. For key papers it is useful if you can discuss these with others. The obvious possibility would be to draw your supervisor's attention to such a paper (if the supervisor is not already aware of it) and suggest that you discuss it together.

You should also regularly go over your notes and try to summarize all your reading into a survey of the state of the field relevant to your thesis topic. This will gradually build into the introduction chapters of your thesis. It will also provide a good basis for meetings with your supervisor and provide a good record of your progress and present position. As I mentioned earlier, I feel it is essential that you start writing very early on in your research work and keep writing throughout. This will give you excellent practice at this often difficult task and minimize the effort needed to produce the final thesis.

Information Technology Skills?

As I stated at the beginning of this section, I shall conclude with a brief assessment of the value of information technology or IT skills and the use of a personal and perhaps other computers in postgraduate research work. I trust that I have made it sufficiently clear already how valuable the use of a computer can be in the organization and management of research. There is now a plethora of easy to use software packages that can make the production of your thesis much easier and more directly under your control. This is also likely to have some beneficial economic consequences in terms of savings on the production costs. The use of wordprocessors (e.g. 'Microsoft Word', 'WordPerfect', etc.) to enter your text is the most well-known type of application, but similar facilities are available for the production of graphics — diagrams, data tables and charts, etc. (e.g. 'Cricket Graph', 'Corel Draw', 'MacDraw', 'Adobe Illustrator', 'Harvard Graphics', etc.). Often the data for such charts can be taken directly from spreadsheets or statistics packages used in the actual analysis. Such analysis packages may themselves have facilities for producing charts, graphs, and tables and allow you to export these directly into your wordprocessing files (e.g. Stat-Graphics, SPSS Mac, SPSS/PC+, Systat, Microsoft Excel, Lotus 1–2–3, Borland Quattro, etc.). Nearly all such software also supports output on high quality printers, like laser printers, which are likely to be available at your institution and can be used for the final output of your thesis (usually charges at least equivalent to photocopying charges are made for the use of such facilities). Thus overall I feel that it is essential for all postgraduates to spend some time acquiring the necessary skills to use personal computers in their work. The relatively small amounts of time required initially to get you going will be more than repaid in terms of the time and effort saved in the longer term. Many educational institutions 'standardize' on particular software packages both to take advantage of economies of scale when purchasing or economical licensing arrangements and to provide a pool of expertise in the user community. It is worth assessing the local arrangements which exist since they can certainly be valuable for users. This is especially true given that many software packages designed for specific functions, like wordprocessing, graphics, etc. usually only differ in presentation and in their very advanced features. Colbourn (1989) provides a fuller treatment of the kinds of software that you may find useful, but do seek out what facilities you have available locally and try them out. I think you'll find it will be worth your while.

References

BUNDY, A., DU BOULAY, B., HOWE, J. and PLOTKIN, G. (1989) 'How to get a PhD in AI', in O'SHEA, T. and EISENSTADT, M. (Eds) *Artificial Intelligence: Tools, Techniques, and Applications*, New York, Harper and Row.

COLBOURN, C.J. (1989) 'Using computers', in PARRY, G. and WATTS, F.N. (Eds) *Behavioural and Mental Health Research: A Handbook of Skills and Methods*, London, Lawrence Erlbaum.

COLBOURN, C.J. (1991) 'Issues in the selection and support of a microcomputer system', in AGER, A. (Ed.) *Microcomputers in Clinical Psychology*, Chichester, Wiley.

ELTON, B. (1989) *Stark*, London, Sphere Books.

HODGSON, R. and ROLLNICK, S. (1989) 'More fun, less stress: How to survive in research', in PARRY, G. and WATTS, F.N. (Eds) *Behavioural and Mental Health Research: A Handbook of Skills and Methods*, London, Lawrence Erlbaum.

POWELL, G. (1989) 'Selecting and developing measures', in PARRY, G. and WATTS, F.N. (Eds) *Behavioural and Mental Health Research: A Handbook of Skills and Methods*, London, Lawrence Erlbaum.

Chapter 6

Using Libraries: Computer-based Methods

Chris Parker

There are several special services which libraries may offer via computer terminals or microcomputers, apart from ordinary data-processing, word-processing, spreadsheets or database managers. These services provide a faster and more sophisticated way of searching for information than previous traditional methods. They include:

1   access to library catalogues/services
2   access to external online vendors/databases
3   access to CD-ROM's (databases on compact disks)

Since all searching for information is done for a reason, we shall assume here that we have a project: 'Assessing the means of recovering hostages in prison riots' — inspired by the 1990 riots in Strangeways Prison, Manchester. This means that we are interested in violence in prisons, especially rioting and the taking of hostages.

In the examples which follow, the searcher's input is in bold type and can be in upper or lower case; both input and computer responses are shown in boxes.

Library Catalogues/Services

This facility may simply tell you if a particular book is part of your own library's collection, or it might be part of a very sophisticated 'integrated system' which would enable you to see whether the book was out on loan or on order, to reserve it, to borrow it from a different library, to search the catalogues of other libraries, etc. Libraries with this kind of service usually provide terminals at various locations which you may use on your own via simple screen menus or options.

Preparation

For specific author/title searches, make sure that you use the exact spellings (although some systems permit 'fuzzy' searching). Be prepared to try alternative spellings (color/colour), acronyms, abbreviations, and synonyms.

The example below covers two searches on a simple OPAC (online public access catalogue) for books on hostage taking and books on how to control a riot. Usually library terminals are set up with a menu already on the screen, so that all you have to do is to make an appropriate selection.

In the menu below, entering '1' followed by a 'return' gives the main library catalogue menu:

```
                University of Southampton Information Group
                ═══════════════════════════════════════════
Services available

1   Library Catalogue
2   Library News
3   Computing Services News
4   Teaching Media News

Type number of option and press <return>

Users connecting through JANET should type QUIT<return> to break connection
.1
*** Selecting CATALOGUE file ***

Southampton OPAC: Menu of Catalogue Search Options

** Not ALL LIBRARY STOCK IS INCLUDED **
** see HELP for details                **

1   TITLE and AUTHOR/EDITOR/ISSUING BODY
2   AUTHOR/EDITOR (Persons)   only
3   ISSUING BODY only
4   TITLE or SUBJECT keywords
5   SUBJECT INDEX keywords
6   CLASSMARK
7   EXPERT MODE (fast command searching)
8   HELP on all searches
9   EXIT from search program

Type number of option, and press RETURN
.4
```

As we are looking for information on a particular subject, option 4 may be selected by entering '4'. This results in a request to enter search words. Hostage is not a common word, so it is worth trying it on its own. On this particular system, there is no facility for word truncation or 'wild cards', so it would be wise to search for 'hostages' separately. Options 5 and 6 could also have been used to find books via their subject classmarks.

Title or subject search
Enter significant words from TITLE or SUBJECT
or H (help) or M (menu) and press RETURN
.HOSTAGE

1   A review of the literature on hostage incidents/ Shirley McLean. 1986.
    Main Library p HV 6431 MACL / 86-121981

2   The emotional hostage: rescuing your emotional life; Leslie Cameron-Bandler,
    Michael Lebeau. 1986.
    Main Library BF 531 CAM / 89-092381

3   The hostage/ Brendan Behan. 1962. 3rd ed.
    Main Library PR 6003.E42 / 62-049847

4   An giall/ Brendan Behan; translated and edited by Richard Wall; The hostage; edited
    by Richard Wall. 1987.
    Main Library PR 6003.E42 / 90-023952

N = Next or P = Previous records, F = change display Format, T = Try
again, H = Help & M = Menu. Type a command letter and press RETURN.
    T

The display above shows the first four items that contain the word 'hostage'. Only item 1 looks promising and the location of the document is given on the second line as a pamphlet at subject classmark HV 6431. The number '86–121981' is the unique number by which the computer recognizes that particular pamphlet. There can be any number of books at class HV 6431. Additional information may be obtained by changing the format by entering 'F', or further items viewed by entering 'N'. In the example above, 'T' was entered in order to restart with a different search strategy, such as how to control a riot.

Title or Subject search
Enter significant words from TITLE or SUBJECT
or H (help) or M (menu) and press RETURN
CONTROL RIOT

1   Riot control: material and techniques/ Rex Applegate. 1981. 2nd ed.
    Main Library HV 8055 APP / 82-042873

2   Riot control agents & herbicides in war 78/ Verwey, W.D.
    Main Library JX 5133 / 78-058699

End of list.

In this system entering two or more words, separated by spaces, will retrieve all those items containing the words in any order. Separate searches using combinations of words such as rioting, riots, and controlling would be needed for an exhaustive scan. Both items appear relevant. The system can now be left by entering 'M' to return to the main catalogue menu shown earlier, and then '9' to return to the main Information Group menu, if appropriate.

Online Vendors/Databases

These services effectively provide you with instant literature searches (lists of references on a specific topic, possibly with abstracts), directory information (such as who makes what product and their address), factual information (such as properties of silicon), or the full text of certain journals, reference material, encyclopedias etc. There are four main components to the service:

(a) databases, which may be compared to abstracting journals, directories, data compilations or other reference works;
(b) vendors, who may be compared to libraries with copies of databases which they mount on their main-frame computers and make available for searching;
(c) terminals or microcomputers which you can use to communicate with the vendors;
(d) telecommunications networks to connect your terminal to the vendor (such as a normal telephone line or local network).

In most cases, because the services work on a pay-as-you-use basis, and can be quite expensive (usually £5 to £50), they have to be operated by library staff acting on your behalf. The common procedure is to agree a mutually convenient time and work at the search together. Where special bulk subscriptions are possible, self-service terminals may be available. The academic community in the UK is currently working on a system for 1991. There are four main stages in using these services as far as you are concerned:

(a) choosing databases (such as SOCIAL SCISEARCH);
(b) choosing vendors or hosts (such as DIALOG);
(c) searching (which means you must know what you want and which words or phrases describe it);
(d) obtaining results (which can be displayed, printed online or offline, downloaded onto disks, or sent via electronic mail).

Preparation

The same process is used as for Library Catalogues/Services above, but also try to predict which words, combinations of words, phrases, or subject headings may have been used in titles, abstracts or indexes. Also be prepared to say how quickly you need the results, how exhaustive you wish the search to be, if abstracts are required, and if the search should be limited in any way (such as language or year of publication).

All four stages interact with each other. The same database may be mounted on several different vendors, but only one vendor may provide the best way of searching and obtaining results for your particular topic for the minimum cost. Making the right choices depends on experience and skill, so assistance from trained library staff is usually necessary for this reason as well. There are various general directories published, and each vendor provides their own database guide, giving such details as subject and time period covered, and file name or number. Some vendors also have a 'cross-file facility' which effectively surveys a selection of databases to see what hit rate they would give if they were searched directly. The main point of the cross file search is that it is cheap and saves wasting time and money searching barren databases.

Some of the more general databases which are used by social scientists are listed below so that you can get a feel for what is available. For real searches, comprehensive listings should be used to pick out the more narrow, specialist databases which may be relevant (such as CHILD ABUSE AND NEGLECT).

SOCIAL SCISEARCH (Social Science Citation Index) with international coverage of social science journals back to 1972, and available via DIALOG, BRS, and DIMDI.

SOCIOLOGICAL ABSTRACTS with international coverage of sociological and social science literature back to 1963, and available via DIALOG, BRS, DIMDI and DATA-STAR.

SOCIAL WORK ABSTRACTS with international coverage of journals and dissertations back to 1977, and available via BRS.

SOCIAL SCIENCES INDEX with international coverage of English language journals back to 1983, and available on WILSONLINE.

PSYCINFO (Psychological Abstracts) with international coverage of the literature of psychology back to 1967, and available via DIALOG, BRS, DIMDI, and DATA-STAR.

DHSS-DATA (Department of Health and Social Security Library, London) with coverage of social services literature back to 1983, and available via DATA-STAR and SCICON.

Other databases cover accounting, management, law, economics, education, politics, religion, and the European Community. Some cover specific types of sources such as books, broadcasts, newspapers, theses or reports; and some are multidisciplinary or cover application areas such as the NASA database which includes some social and psychological work.

The example below covers two searches on one of the largest vendors —
DIALOG in the USA. The search topics are hostages in prison riots, modelling prison riots, and any news on hostages in the Strangeways prison riots
of 1990.

```
DIALOG INFORMATION SERVICES
PLEASE LOGON:
  *************
ENTER PASSWORD:
  *************
```

After connection to DIALOG via telephone or network, DIALOG requests you to enter your identity number and then your password. Whenever
Dialog types a question mark on a new line, it means that you are being
prompted for an entry or command of some kind. A typical library–run
service would use a communications software package such as PROCOMM
PLUS or CROSSTALK XVI to automate some or all of the logging on
procedures. Strict security is required for passwords as these control access to
the systems and also the resulting charges and subsequent invoices.

In this example, HOMEBASE is automatically entered. This file is
effectively a cheap, 'empty' database that permits requests for information
and various housekeeping tasks.

```
Welcome to DIALOG
Dialog level 23.02.3A

Last    logoff   13jun90   04:21:02
Logon   file405  13jun90   08:59:33

File  405:DIALOG HOMEBASE

     Set    Items    Description
     ----   ------   ----------
              *** DIALOG HOMEBASE Main Menu ***
Enter an option number and press ENTER to view information on any item listed below;
enter /NOMENU to move into Command Mode; or enter a BEGIN command to search in
a different database.

  1   Announcements (new databases, price changes, etc.)
  2   DIALOG HOMEBASE Features
  3   DIALOG Free File of the Month
  4   DIALOG Database Information and Rates
  5   Database Selection (DIALINDEX/OneSearch Categories)
  6   DIALOG Command Descriptions
  7   DIALOG Training Schedules and Seminar Descriptions
  8   DIALOG Services

Enter an option number, /NOMENU, or a BEGIN command and press ENTER.
     /H = Help      /L = Logoff      /NOMENU = Command Mode
?B411
```

The cross file database on DIALOG is called DIALINDEX or file No. 411. It is entered via the BEGIN command 'B411'

```
Menu system v. 5.38 ends.
      13jun90   09:00:02   User006649   Session A484.1
            $0.12    0.008 Hrs FileHomeBase
   $0.12    Estimated cost FileHomeBase
   $0.08    DialnetE
   $0.20    Estimated cost this search
   $0.20    Estimated total session cost   0.008 Hrs.

File 411:DIALINDEX (tm)
       (Copr. DIALOG Inf.Ser.Inc.)
?SF 7,11,21,35,171
```

The databases chosen for scanning are selected via their file numbers or Group names such as SOCSCI or TOXICOL using the SELECT FILES (SF) command as above or e.g. 'SF SOCSCI'. The selected files may then be listed showing their periods of coverage. There are various guides available to help you choose appropriate databases including the DIALOG annual 'Database Catalogue', which gives information about each database including its file number.

```
File    7:  SOCIAL SCISEARCH 72–90/WK21
File   11:  PSYCINFO — 67–90/MAY
File   21:  NCJRS — 1972–90/APR
File   35:  DISSERTATION ABSTRACTS ONLINE 1861–JUN 90
File  171:  CRIMINAL JUSTICE PERIODICAL INDEX — 75–90/MAR

File    Items    Description
----    -----    -----------
?S (PRISON? OR JAIL?) (S) (RIOT? OR DISTURBANCE?) (S) (HOSTAGE? OR MODEL?)
```

A single line search statement may now be entered using the SELECT or 'S' command. The question marks at the ends of words are truncation or wild card symbols, so that 'PRISON?' will search for 'prison' or 'prisons' or 'prisoner' etc. Note that the '?' is also used as a prompt by the DIALOG computer. The '(S)' means in the same subfield (e.g. in the same sentence in some databases), whereas the 'S' at the beginning of a search statement is the SELECT command.

The strategy shown will retrieve any item which contains either the word-stem prison or jail, and also the word-stem riot or disturbance, and also the word-stem hostage or model, all in the same sentence. So an item with a title 'Modelling prison riots' would be retrieved. Other terms like gaol, revolt, strike, disorder, rebellion, may be included if appropriate.

The 'hit' rates are then displayed separately for each database or file, clearly indicating which databases are worth searching directly. DIAL-INDEX is a cheap way of finding relevant databases, but it only tells you what the hit rate is. It cannot provide any other information such as references.

```
  7:  SOCIAL SCISEARCH — 72–90/WK21
       3562   PRISON?
        301   JAIL?
        471   RIOT?
       1707   DISTURBANCE?
        220   HOSTAGE?
      40850   MODEL?
          2   (PRISON? OR JAIL?) (S) (RIOT? OR DISTURBANCE?) (S) (HOSTAGE?
              OR MODEL?)

 11:  PSYCINFO — 67–90/MAY
       4091   PRISON?
        331   JAIL?
        183   RIOT?
      14394   DISTURBANCE?
         66   HOSTAGE?
      58760   MODEL?
          8   (PRISON? OR JAIL?) (S) (RIOT? OR DISTURBANCE?) (S) (HOSTAGE?
              OR MODEL?)

 21:  NCJRS — 1972 –90/APR
      13494   PRISON?
       3876   JAIL?
        957   RIOT?
       1090   DISTURBANCE?
        787   HOSTAGE?
      10859   MODEL?
         76   (PRISON? OR JAIL?) (S) (RIOT? OR DISTURBANCE?) (S) (HOSTAGE?
              OR MODEL?)

 35:  DISSERTATION ABSTRACTS ONLINE 1861–JUN 90
       1408   PRISON?
        171   JAIL?
        209   RIOT?
       3491   DISTURBANCE?
         74   HOSTAGE?
     108812   MODEL?
          2   (PRISON? OR JAIL?) (S) (RIOT? OR DISTURBANCE?) (S) (HOSTAGE?
              OR MODEL?)

171:  CRIMINAL JUSTICE PERIODICAL INDEX — 75 –90/MAR
      10033   PRISON?
       1984   JAIL?
        491   RIOT?
        204   DISTURBANCE?
        303   HOSTAGE?
        899   MODEL?
         10   (PRISON? OR JAIL?) (S) (RIOT? OR DISTURBANCE?) (S) (HOSTAGE?
              OR MODEL?)
```

At this stage, the search strategy may be saved temporarily to prevent having to retype the search strategy again later. The DIALOG computer automatically allocates a saved search identity 'TA107'.

```
?SAVE TEMP
Temp SearchSave 'TA107' stored
```

There were two hits for the first database — 'Social SciSearch' which corresponds to the 'Social Science Citation Index', file No. 7. This database can be entered using the command 'B7' and the saved search re-executed using the command 'EXS TA107'.

```
?B7
      13jun90   09:04:02   User006649   Session A484.2
            $3.74      0.083 Hrs File411
   $3.74   Estimated cost File411
   $0.83   DialnetE
   $4.57   Estimated cost this search
   $4.77   Estimated total session cost     0.083 Hrs.
File   7: SOCIAL SCISEARCH — 72–90/WK21
         (COPR. ISI INC.1990)

      Set    Items    Description
      ----   -----    ----------
?EXS TA107

            3562    PRISON?
             301    JAIL?
             471    RIOT?
            1707    DISTURBANCE?
             220    HOSTAGE?
           40850    MODEL?
     S1        2    (PRISON? OR JAIL?) (S) (RIOT? OR DISTURBANCE?) (S)
           (HOSTAGE? OR MODEL?)
```

When the search has been completed and hits have been obtained, it is possible to type out or display the references or records using the type or 'T' command. 'T1/3/1–2' means type out from search statement 1, in format 3 (which is references only), items 1 to 2.

```
?T1/3/1–2

1/3/1
01034848   Genuine Article#:  MR413   Number of References: 14
   THE TREATMENT OF HOSTAGES IN PRISON RIOTS — SOME HYPOTHESES
   DESROCHES FJ
```

UNIV WATERLOO,UNIV ST JEROMES COLL,DEPT SOCIOL/WATERLOO N2L
3G1/ONTARIO/CANADA/
CANADIAN JOURNAL OF CRIMINOLOGY-REVUE CANADIENNE DE
CRIMINOLOGIE, 1981, V 23, N4, P439–450
Language: ENGLISH   Document Type: ARTICLE

1/3/2
00508930   Genuine Article#: DR317   Number of References: 9
MODEL FOR PRISON DISTURBANCES
ZEEMAN EC; HALL CS; HARRISON PJ; MARRIAGE GH; SHAPLAND PH

WARWICK UNIV,INST MATH/COVENTRY/ /ENGLAND/; PRISON DEPT,HOME
OFF,MIDLAND REG/BIRMINGHAM/ /ENGLAND/; WARWICK UNIV,DEPT
STATIST/WARWICK/ /ENGLAND/; PRISON DEPT,HOME OFF,SE REG/SURBITON/
/ENGLAND/
BRITISH JOURNAL OF CRIMINOLOGY, 1977, V17, N3, P251–263
Language: ENGLISH   Document Type: ARTICLE

At this stage it would be normal to search other databases and type out additional hits. For example, the NCJRS database (National Criminal Justice Reference Service, USA) produced 76 hits.

In this example, we shall proceed straight to the other aspect of our search by exploring the Strangeways topic in the 'Newswire' group of databases back in the cross file DIALINDEX (file No. 411).

?B411
    13jun90 09:05:32 User006649 Session A484.3
            $3.96   0.033 Hrs File7
              $1.12   2 Type(s) in Format 2
              $1.12   2 Types
  $5.08   Estimated cost File7
  $0.33   DialnetE
  $5.41   Estimated cost this search
  $10.18 Estimated total session cost   0.116 Hrs.

File 411: DIALINDEX(tm)
      (Copr. DIALOG Inf.Ser.Inc.)
?SF NEWSWIRE
>>>   611 is unauthorized
>>>   649 is unauthorized
File 258:   AP NEWS — 1984–12 Jun 1990
File 261:   UPI NEWS — 01/90–06/12/90
File 260:   UPI NEWS — APR 83–DEC 1989
File 609:   KNIGHT-RIDDER FINANCIAL NEWS — 89–90/Jun 13
File 610:   BusinessWire — 86–90/Jun 13
File 612:   Japan Economic Newswire Plus — 84–90/Jun. 12
File 613:   PRNewswire — 87/May–90/Jun 13

File   Items   Description
- - - - - - - - - - - - - - - - - - - -
?S STRANGEWAYS (S) HOSTAGE?

In this case our search strategy is looking for any news items containing 'Strangeways' in the same sentence as the word-stem 'hostage'.

```
258:  AP NEWS — 1984–12 Jun 1990
                 58   STRANGEWAYS
              16172   HOSTAGE?
                  0   STRANGEWAYS (S) HOSTAGE?

261:  UPI NEWS — 01/90–06/12/90
                 57   STRANGEWAYS
                896   HOSTAGE?
                  5   STRANGEWAYS (S) HOSTAGE?

260:  UPI NEWS — APR 83–DEC 1989
                  2   STRANGEWAYS
              11937   HOSTAGE?
                  0   STRANGEWAYS (S) HOSTAGE?

609:  KNIGHT-RIDDER FINANCIAL NEWS — 89–90/JUN 13
                  4   STRANGEWAYS
                364   HOSTAGE?
                  0   STRANGEWAYS (S) HOSTAGE?

610:  BusinessWire — 86–90/Jun 13
                  0   STRANGEWAYS
                 67   HOSTAGE?
                  0   STRANGEWAYS (S) HOSTAGE?

612:  Japan Economic Newswire Plus — 84–90/Jun. 12
                  0   STRANGEWAYS
                248   HOSTAGE?
                  0   STRANGEWAYS (S) HOSTAGE?

613:  PRNewswire — 87/May–90/Jun 13
                  0   STRANGEWAYS
                229   HOSTAGE?
                  0   STRANGEWAYS (S) HOSTAGE?
```

The search indicates that the only Newswire service that satisfied our search was UPI News (United Press International, file 261) with 5 hits. This database is then entered using the Begin command (B261), and the search strategy re-entered or re-executed if previously saved.

```
?B261
      13jun90   09:07:08   User006649   Session A484.4
   $1.49   0.033 hrs File411
   $1.49   Estimated cost File411
   $0.33   DialnetE
   $1.82   Estimated cost this search
  $12.00   Estimated total session cost   0.150 Hrs.

File 261:UPI NEWS — 02/90 — 08/06/90
                  (COPR, 1990 UNITED PRESS INTERNATIONAL)
```

```
Set    Items   Description
----   ------  -----------
?S STRANGEWAYS (S) HOSTAGE?
        58     STRANGEWAYS
      1034     HOSTAGE?
S1       5     STRANGEWAYS (S) HOSTAGE?
```

UPI NEWS is a full text database, but a short version of each record may be examined before printing out the entire text. Failure to obtain authorization has meant that we are unable to reproduce sample records.

The session is terminated using the 'LOGOFF' command. The vendor's computer provides a summary of connection times and, possibly, of costs. The network computer may then provide details of the call duration and the amount of information received and transmitted.

```
?LOGOFF
     13jun90   09:09:55   User006649   Session A484.5
          $2.86      0.033 Hrs File261

    $2.86   Estimated cost File261
    $0.33   DialnetE
    $3.19   Estimated cost this search
   $16.21   Estimated total session cost   0.219 Hrs.
Logoff:   level 23.02.3 A   09:09:55

Call duration:   00  :07:50       Segments out:  15       Segments in:  197
Resets:  0                        Breaks:  0              Errors:  0
*** Cleared
```

CD-ROMS (Compact Disks)

These systems are the equivalent of running databases on a microcomputer without having to connect to an online database vendor. Each workstation consists of a microcomputer and a CD-ROM player, CD-ROM disks, and possibly a printer. Each disk contains a database or part of a database such as PSYCLIT (Psychological Abstracts), and may be searched via a menu system in a similar way to the OPAC services.

The technology is changing rapidly and multi–disk players and networking are already possible to increase searching power, amount of information available and efficiency. Some vendors provide a combined online CD-ROM hybrid service.

Preparation

This is the same as for Online Vendors/Databases above. Libraries usually have workstations set up for self use, and will provide initial training and advice. The following search is a simulation of searching the Social Science Citation Index on CD–ROM for information on prison violence.

The first thing you see is a menu display which allows you to choose the 'search' mode by pressing the F3 key. This brings down a second menu which allows you to select 'Enter search' by entering E.

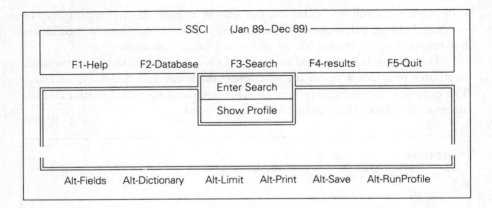

If we assume that you wish to search for titles containing the word stems Prison and Violen, a third menu may be brought down by pressing the Alt and F keys together. This enables 'Title' to be selected from the new menu by entering T.

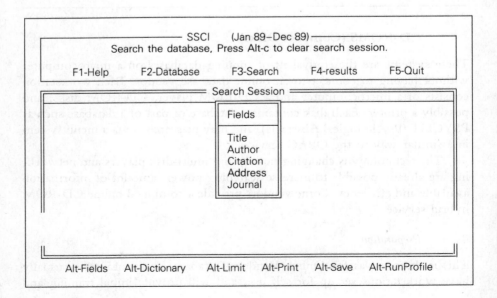

The search strategy 'PRISON* AND VIOLEN*' is then entered, and the hit rate display tells you that four references have been retrieved.

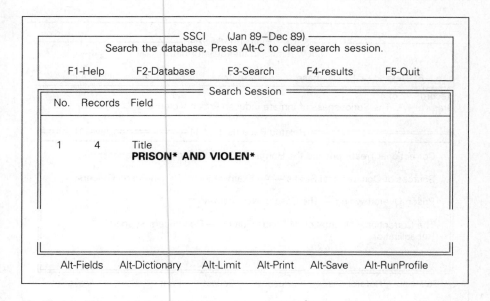

```
┌─────────────────── SSCI    (Jan 89–Dec 89) ───────────────────┐
│        Search the database, Press Alt-C to clear search session.│
│                                                                 │
│    F1-Help      F2-Database      F3-Search    F4-results    F5-Quit│
│  ┌═══════════════════ Search Session ═══════════════════┐      │
│  │ No.   Records   Field                                 │      │
│  │                                                       │      │
│  │                                                       │      │
│  │  1      4       Title                                 │      │
│  │                 PRISON* AND VIOLEN*                    │      │
│  │                                                       │      │
│  │                                                       │      │
│  │                                                       │      │
│  │                                                       │      │
│  └═══════════════════════════════════════════════════════┘      │
│  Alt-Fields   Alt-Dictionary    Alt-Limit   Alt-Print   Alt-Save   Alt-RunProfile│
└─────────────────────────────────────────────────────────────────┘
```

The F4 key is pressed to bring down a 'results' menu which gives the option of displaying titles only or full records as below.

```
┌─────────────────── SSCI    (Jan 89–Dec 89) ───────────────────┐
│                 Show results as full records.                   │
│                                                                 │
│    F1-Help      F2-Database      F3-Search    F4-results    F5-Quit│
│  ┌═══════════════ Records: 2 of 4 ═══════════════ (Set 1) ═══┐  │
│  │ Braswell-MC   Miller-LS                                   │  │
│  │                                                           │  │
│  │ The Seriousness of Inmate Induced Prision Violence – An   │  │
│  │ Analysis of Correctional Personnel Perceptions (English)  │  │
│  │                                                           │  │
│  │ JOURNAL OF CRIMINAL JUSTICE                               │  │
│  │ Vol 17  Iss 1  pp. 47–53  1989  (T8082)                   │  │
│  │                                                           │  │
│  │ Related Records: 11    References: 18                     │  │
│  └═══════════════════════════════════════════════════════════┘  │
│    Related    References    Addresses    Collect   Print   Save │
└─────────────────────────────────────────────────────────────────┘
```

Chris Parker

At this stage you may enter P to print, F to display the eighteen references cited by Braswell, or R to display related references (as below) which also cite one of more of the same eighteen references cited by Braswell.

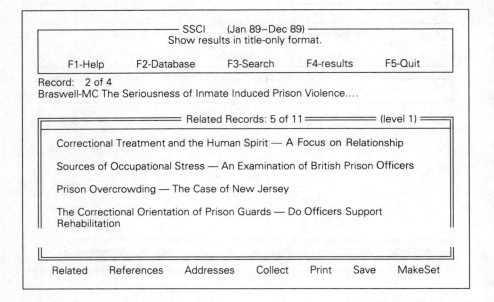

Acknowledgments

The author is pleased to acknowledge the kind assistance of iSi, and DIALOG in providing advice and permission to use copyright material.

Chapter 7

Using Libraries:
British Official Publications

Diana Marshallsay

An enormous and varied amount of information useful to social scientists is published by different branches of government. As well as Parliamentary debates, Green Papers, White Papers, Bills and Acts, government departments regularly issue reports and publish research. Mention of a few of the topics covered in official publications in recent years, chosen more or less at random, will suffice to indicate the wide range of matters encompassed: abortion, accidents, acid rain, AIDS, birds, chat lines, community care, company investigations, computers, cowboys, discrimination, drugs, education, environment, health, Hong Kong, legal services, local government, modern languages, nature conservation, official secrets, planning policy, remote sensing, sentencing, summer time, vandalism and wildlife. The purpose of this chapter is to provide a guide to the bibliographic sources that will help you find material relevant to your research. Of course, different libraries have different resources and are organized in different ways. Nonetheless what follows should provide you with sufficient information to begin your search.

Parliamentary Papers and Their Indexes

There are currently three main categories of official publication — parliamentary, non–parliamentary and non–HMSO. The first two categories, parliamentary and non–parliamentary, are both published by Her Majesty's Stationery Office. Parliamentary papers comprise Public Bills, House of Commons Papers and Command Papers which together form the sessional papers of the House of Commons. The sessional papers of the House of Lords consist of just two categories of papers — House of Lords Bills and House of Lords Papers.

The sessional papers of the House of Commons can be traced by using the Sessional Index which forms the last volume in each set of sessional papers. There is also a Sessional Index on microfiche, produced by Chadwyck-Healey Ltd. as part of their microfiche edition of the current parliamentary papers. The microfiche version is more up to date than the printed version, which is prepared only after the House of Commons library has prepared a set of sessional papers for binding.

There are now no such indexes to the sessional papers of the House of Lords, merely detailed contents lists for the volumes; a complete set of these is bound in at the front of the first volume of each sessional set. All House of Lords Papers and Bills can, however, be traced by using the *Daily Lists*, *Monthly Catalogues* and *Annual Catalogues* of HMSO, as can the recent House of Commons sessional papers, thus giving access to all recent parliamentary papers.

In the past, Sessional Indexes have frequently been cumulated to form Decennial Indexes and subsequently General (Alphabetical) Indexes which may cover any period up to fifty years. The whole of the nineteenth century is also now covered by the *Subject Catalogue of the House of Commons Parliamentary Papers 1801–1900* (Cockton, 1988), a definitive work which also includes references to the microfiche edition of the parliamentary papers, which may be held by more libraries than the hard-copy sets.

Subject Approach to Parliamentary Papers

The *Subject Catalogue* (Cockton, 1988) provides a broad subject approach to all the parliamentary papers of the nineteenth century, a period selectively covered by Hansard's *Catalogue and Breviate of Parliamentary Papers 1696–1834* (Hansard, 1953) and *A Select List of British Parliamentary Papers 1833–1899* (Ford and Ford, 1953). These last two works provide a good starting point for research as they list just the reports and other papers produced by Select Committees, Royal Commissions and other kinds of enquiring body, omitting the many thousands of Bills and Accounts and Papers. The reports are grouped under broad subject headings, further sub-divided by topic. The selective coverage of parliamentary papers has been extended to the year 1983 by a series of works, all aiming to lead those researching into public policy changes to the most important reports and policy statements, (Ford and Ford, 1951, 1957, 1961; Ford, Ford and Marshallsay, 1970; Marshallsay and Smith, 1979; Marshallsay and Richards, 1989). The three *Breviates* (Ford and Ford, 1951, 1957, 1961) provide summaries of the reports and other papers included, so that it is possible to discover in advance whether or not a particular report is likely to be relevant to the subject being studied.

All the works listed above which cover the twentieth century also include materials from the other category of HMSO publication — the non-parliamentary. Few of these existed prior to 1921 but in the year, in an economy drive, the Treasury issued Circular 38/21 which instructed departments that in future only papers dealing with subjects likely to be legislated on fairly soon or which were otherwise essential to Members of Parliament, were to be issued as Command Papers. The rest, including virtually all the statistical series, were to be published in the non-parliamentary category. This edict had the effect of making the early non-parliamentary material quite difficult to trace as the HMSO annual catalogues were then very basic sales lists, not intended for bibliographic searching. The Treasury instruction also resulted in the evidence taken by Royal Commissions and Departmental Committees being published as non-parliamentary publications, whereas the reports of these same bodies would have been Command Papers. This dual system means that those libraries which bind the sessional papers have to make different provision for storing evidence. The *Breviates*, *Select Lists* and *Ford Lists* referred to above, all indicate whether or not reports were accompanied by published evidence. The original reasons for a report's publication in the non-parliamentary category appears to have been lost sight of over the years; such a report can have significance just as far-reaching as one published as a parliamentary paper.

Chairman Approach (to HMSO Publications)

Many reports, parliamentary and non-parliamentary, have become known by the name of the chairman or author and there are a number of indexes which can be used to trace reports from this information. A series of volumes published by the Library Association cover the period 1800–1982. The three Ford *Breviates*, the *Select List* and the *Ford Lists* cover the period 1900–1983 on a selective basis and all contain indexes to chairmen and authors. *Committee Reports Published by HMSO Indexed by Chairman* has been issued quarterly by HMSO since 1983. The *Monthly* and *Annual Catalogues* of HMSO also include chairmen, authors and editors in their indexes.

Online Services

There are two online services which cover HMSO publications. *British Official Publications* (HMSO) is available on DIALOG. The database holds records from 1976 to the present, is updated monthly and, in February 1990, held approximately 130,000 records. In addition to HMSO's own publications, this database also includes the publications of many European and international organizations for which HMSO acts as sales agent.

The other online service is the Parliamentary Online Information System (POLIS) developed for use in the House of Commons library but available to other libraries on subscription. This database includes references to parliamentary questions, parliamentary debates (Lords and Commons), early day motions and petitions, parliamentary papers (Lords and Commons), unprinted papers listed in Votes and Proceedings, Bills, Acts, Statutory Instruments, selected non-parliamentary and departmental publications, European Community publications, publications of other international organizations, some foreign official publications and books and pamphlets added to the House of Commons library stock (including papers deposited by Ministers). As there is some variation in the dates from which various categories of material are available on the database, the publicity information about POLIS should be checked before planning a search. Also at the search planning stage, the *House of Commons Library Thesaurus* should be consulted. This provides the controlled subject-indexing language for POLIS. The most up-to-date version of the thesaurus is available only online but subscribing libraries should have the printed version available for consultation. The information provided by POLIS is very up to date, unlike *British Official Publications* (HMSO) on DIALOG, which is updated monthly, and IT's third contribution to the official publications scene — *Catalogue of United Kingdom Official Publications* (UKOP) — which covers HMSO and non-HMSO official publications and is updated quarterly (see below.)

Non-HMSO Official Publications

The emergence of the third and last category of official publications — the non-HMSO or departmentally published material — can be said to date from the Government's nationalization programme which started after the Second World War. A few official bodies had already been publishing independently for many years, but mainly in the realm of specialist publications, e.g. Admiralty, Ordnance Survey. But the appearance of policy statements from public corporations such as the National Coal Board, the British Electricity Authority and the Gas Council heralded a new era, that of the decentralization of official publishing in this country. From modest beginnings the non-HMSO official publications category has burgeoned to the point where it has, for the last ten years or so, comprised some 80 per cent of British official publishing. The nationalized industries were followed by government departments, most of which also publish through HMSO, and now the category comprises many other types of public body, including executive, advisory and research organizations. A word of warning here — references found in the literature to some items in this category may, wrongly, include the name of HMSO as publisher, simply because HMSO handled the printing contract and their name appears near the end of the publication concerned — but they will be looked for in vain in the HMSO *Catalogues*.

The main printed catalogue for the non-HMSO material is the *Catalogue of British Official Publications not Published by HMSO*, (COBOP) which was first published by Chadwyck-Healey Ltd. for the year 1980. It is published six times a year with an annual cumulation. There is a printed index in each issue as well as a cumulating keyword index on microfiche which, in spite of its name, indexes every word other than definite and indefinite articles. The keyword index also indexes by subject even though the subject may not be referred to specifically in the title. The *Catalogue* provides details of addresses from which almost all the publications can be obtained but many of them are included in the microfiche collection which accompanies the *Catalogue*. The existence of the text on microfiche is indicated alongside the relevant catalogue entries.

HMSO and Non-HMSO Combined on CD-ROM

Non-HMSO official publications also feature in the *Catalogue of United Kingdom Official Publications* (UKOP), which is available only on CD-ROM, updated quarterly. UKOP also includes all HMSO publications from 1980, together with all the publications of international organizations for which HMSO acts as sales agent. This combined database, of considerable and increasing size, offers a very flexible approach. Searchable fields include HMSO publications only, non-HMSO only, both combined, departments or agencies, personal authors, titles, series, chairmen, subjects, keywords and dates. For HMSO publications there is also information as to whether or not a particular title is in print. Provided the hardware and services are available, data can be printed out or downloaded on to floppy disks and, using appropriate software, be manipulated in a number of ways.

The third means of tracing some non-HMSO official publications is by using the catalogues and lists produced by the various government departments and other public bodies themselves. However, lists have different starting dates and not all government departments publish such lists. Coverage of other public bodies is very incomplete and new bodies are being created as existing ones merge or are wound up. This method is, therefore, hardly satisfactory unless the research interest lies with just one department which produces a good catalogue. The individual catalogues and lists do still have their uses, however, as the *Catalogue of British Official Publications not Published by HMSO* (COBOP) relies for its comprehensiveness on the co-operation of its contributors and these contributors may change their policy over the years. Government departments with multi-site operations have great difficulty in keeping track of their own department's publications, often leading to the incompleteness of their own catalogues and items which cannot be traced in COBOP.

> In the larger, more complex organizations with multiple objectives absolute control becomes far more difficult, and indeed sometimes almost impossible; only in a very few departments of state is there total coordination of all forms of publishing, allied to full bibliographical recording of the whole output (Howard, n.d.).

Problems of Definition

There is a further problem when dealing with official publications and this relates to the definition of the words 'published' and 'publication':

> Many officials engaged in disseminating information do not appreciate that they are generating what libraries would nominate as 'publications'. They are writing research reports, feasibility studies, explanatory papers; they are not officially secret and are often made available to interested parties. The originators however genuinely do not consider the document to be of any real outside interest, copies are not lodged in the departmental library; it may even be claimed that the papers cannot be publications because they are not priced (Howard, n.d.).

Current Information

The preceding two paragraphs contain warnings. In spite of an increasing bibliographical network providing information on official publications, important items can still slip through this net. Therefore, constant vigilance must be maintained while research is in progress if current topics are involved. Press Notices issued by the relevant department can often provide the only source of some official information.

> A Press Notice is sometimes used as the sole vehicle for the communication of 'hard' official information. This practice is not always helpful ... particularly if the journalist does not differentiate between the original message and his comment on it (Howard, 1985).

Press Notices often advise of new official publications, both HMSO and non-HMSO, and also highlight information otherwise buried in answers to

Parliamentary Questions. The News Distribution Service, run by the Central Office of Information on a subscription basis, provides libraries with Press Notices on request from a daily listing. This service is also available online.

While Parliament is sitting the *Weekly Information Bulletin*, produced by the Public Information Office of the House of Commons library, provides details of the previous week's parliamentary business and looks forward to forthcoming business in the House of Commons. It lists recent parliamentary publications, has the most comprehensive listing of Consultation Papers and also has a table showing the progress of Public Bills. The *Sessional Information Digest* is in part a cumulation of material from the *Bulletin* but does not completely supersede it. The *Digest* forms an index and companion to the *Bulletin* and also provides information not available elsewhere. The 1987–88 *Digest* provides an analysis of time spent on various types of business, use of the guillotine, the total number of Parliamentary Questions, a subject index to White Papers and policy documents and an index to Green Papers and consultation papers.

Official Statistics

For some researchers the only contact with official publications will be in their need for official statistics. HMSO issues a number of statistical publications, some fairly general in coverage, others more specific. Of the more general ones attention is drawn to the *Annual Abstract of Statistics, Economic Trends, Financial Statistics* and the *Monthly Digest of Statistics*. Reference will be found in these publications to the fact that much of the data they contain is available from the CSO Databank in computer readable form and in longer runs than appear in the published tables. The *Annual Abstract* contains a useful Index to Sources, referring to other official publications in which more detailed figures can be found. A fuller subject guide is provided by the *Guide to Official Statistics* (CSO, 1976). Note should also be taken of the series entitled Reviews of United Kingdom Statistical Sources (Maunder, 1974); this series provides critical reviews of many official statistical publications, dealing with them on a subject basis.

Many of HMSO's statistical publications are kept up to date by departmentally-published Statistical Bulletins. These can be traced either by using the *Catalogue of British Official Publications Not Published by HMSO* (COBOP) or by using UKOP on CD-ROM, where the HMSO and non-HMSO series on the same subject will appear together on the screen if the appropriate search strategy is used. COBOP or UKOP will also provide references to many other non-HMSO statistical publications. It should also be remembered that the· most recent statistical information and statistical information not regularly published can sometimes be given in the answer to a Parliamentary Question — and here the indexes to *Hansard* or POLIS should be used.

For keeping up to date with new developments in official statistics, and for articles on many aspects of the subject, together with information on unpublished material which can be made available, *Statistical News* (1968) should be a constant companion.

Libraries and Librarians

This chapter has detailed the bibliographical sources that are available for students interested in official publications. Not all university, polytechnic or large public libraries will be able to offer all the publications and services which have been described, albeit briefly. But most of them should be able to offer some. A list of libraries which currently receive virtually all HMSO publications can be found in the HMSO *Annual Catalogue*.

Libraries also treat official publications differently. Some may hold them in special collections. Others may integrate them with the rest of their stock. Yet others may use a combination of these methods. For nineteenth-century material some libraries may have only the Irish University Press 1000 volume reprint series, to which the *Checklist* (IUP, 1972) provides the key.

Many libraries which hold large collections of official publications will also provide guides to them, but the printed word cannot replace personal contact between the researcher and the librarian. Work with official publications is a specialist area of librarianship and advice should be sought from the staff as to which of the many bibliographical aids and services are most likely to be relevant for a particular research topic. Research time is precious so none of it should be wasted for want of professional help.

References

Butcher, D. (1983) *Official Publications in Britain*, London, Clive Bingley.

Central Statistical Office (CSO) (1976) *Guide to Official Statistics*, 1st ed. London, HMSO. (2nd ed., 1978; 3rd ed., 1980; 4th ed. 1982; 5th ed., 1986; 6th ed., 1990).

Cockton, P. (Ed.) (1988) *Subject Catalogue of the House of Commons Parliamentary Papers 1801–1900*, 5 vols. Cambridge, Chadwyck-Healey.

Ford, P. and Ford, G. (1951) *A Breviate of Parliamentary Papers, 1917–1939*, Oxford, Blackwell. Reprinted by Irish University Press, 1970.

Ford, P. and Ford, G. (1953) *A Select List of British Parliamentary Papers, 1833–1899*, Oxford, Blackwell. Reprinted by Irish University Press, 1970.

Ford, P. and Ford, G. (1955) *A Guide to Parliamentary Papers*, Oxford, Blackwell; 2nd ed. Oxford, Blackwell, 1956; 3rd ed. Shannon, Irish University Press, 1972.

FORD, P. and FORD, G. (1957) *A Breviate of Parliamentary Paper, 1900–1916*, Oxford, Blackwell. Reprinted by Irish University Press, 1970.

FORD, P. and FORD, G. (1961) *A Breviate of Parliamentary Papers, 1940–1954*, Oxford, Blackwell. Nendeln, reprinted by KTO Press, 1979.

FORD, P., FORD, G. and MARSHALLSAY, D. (1970) *A Select List of British Parliamentary Papers, 1955–1964*, Shannon, Irish University Press.

HANSARD, L.G. (1953) *Catalogue and Breviate of Parliamentary Papers, 1696–1834*, with an introduction by P. and G. Ford., Oxford, Blackwell. Reprinted by Irish University Press, 1969.

HOWARD, B. (n.d.) 'Non-HMSO: Why?', in *Proceedings of the Conference on British Government Publishing*, held at Blackpool 16–17 September 1982, edited by V.J. Bradfield.

HOWARD, B. (1985) 'Government publications "SCOOP'd"', *Library Association Record*, **187**, pp. 183–5.

IRISH UNIVERSITY PRESS (IUP) (1972) *Checklist of British Parliamentary Papers in the Irish University Press 1000 volume series, 1801–1899*, Shannon, Irish University Press.

MARSHALLSAY, D. and RICHARDS, P.G. (Eds) (1989) *Ford List of British Parliamentary Papers 1974–1983*, Cambridge, Chadwyck-Healey.

MARSHALLSAY, D. and SMITH, J.H. (Eds) (1979) *Ford List of British Parliamentary Papers 1965–1974*, Nendeln, KTO Press.

MAUNDER, W.F. (Ed.) (1974) *Reviews of United Kingdom Statistical Sources*, Vols. I–V, 1974–1976, originally published by Heinemann Educational Books. Vols. VI–XXII, 1978–1987 by Pergamon. Vols. XXIII–, 1988– by Chapman and Hall Ltd.

RICHARD, S. (1984) (comp.) *Directory of British Official Publications. A Guide to Sources*, 2nd ed. London, Mansell Publishing Ltd. (Lists some 1,200 official publishing bodies; provides a summary of the types of material published; and, when up to date, provides addresses and contact points, with telephone numbers.)

STATISTICAL NEWS (1968) *Developments in British Official Statistics*, London, HMSO (quarterly since May 1968).

Chapter 8

Writing Skills

Peter Calvert

Writing is a craft, and like any other craft it takes time to learn its skills and it helps to 'keep your hand in'. That is why it is important to start work on the thesis early in the research plan. Trying to express your ideas so that others can understand them is an integral part of the development of your research.

Some people like to write in long, intensive stretches; others in regular blocks of a few hundred words each day. But the latter is undoubtedly the easier and safer pattern for a research student. You should also try to plan your writing sessions so that you make best use of the time of day that you find the words flow most easily. The rest of the day need not be wasted, but you can leave less demanding tasks for that time.

Remember that although a thesis is a book–length piece of writing, each chapter should have a shape and structure of its own. If you find yourself beginning to feel intimidated at any stage, remind yourself that the chapter you are actually working on is the task in hand. If some other problem is bothering you, do not simply forget it, but make notes on it and set them aside to be dealt with at the proper time. Set yourself reasonable goals that you can reasonably achieve, and break up your work sessions with rest and relaxation.

Not all universities and polytechnics impose a maximum word length for a thesis. If yours does not, as a guide, an MPhil thesis in sociology or politics might be approximately 50,000 words; a PhD thesis about 80,000. A doctoral thesis in economics or social statistics may be much shorter: approximately the length of three learned articles, or between 30,000 and 40,000 words. Broadly the more mathematical and tabular material in a thesis, the shorter it is going to be.

Notes and bibliography are extra. Occasionally an appendix may be appropriate, as for example where you have been studying a short text, but this is not usually the case other than in law or political or social theory. Your supervisor will advise you and you should not include an appendix unless your supervisor agrees in advance.

Whatever you may feel, the word length suggested is not particularly restrictive. The average academic article in the social sciences seldom exceeds the 5–7,000 word range preferred by editors, and chapters in books are usually of the order of 10–12,000. Much of the advice that follows will therefore continue to be useful to you when you come to write books and articles.

Writing Clearly

Before you start to write make a plan of what you are going to say, going through your source material to see if you have left anything out.

The wordprocessor is ideal for compiling and rearranging the material in an outline and there are special programs which make it even easier. But given the limitations of the screen, some still like to begin work on each chapter by taking a large sheet of paper and writing all over it, using lines and balloons to connect ideas. Add a brief cue to the source of each idea while you are at it.

While you are working keep a separate sheet of paper or notebook for ideas which you will need later, for example in the conclusion.

Avoid Verbiage

Get your thoughts clear before you start to write. If you cannot understand what you are trying to say the odds are that no one else can do so. Write in ordered paragraphs, each dealing only with a single idea or related set of ideas. Keep your objective in mind throughout. Keep to the point.

Unhappily, many students think it is profound to be obscure. Like other fields of study, the social sciences have their own technical vocabulary, which you have to use. Its purpose, however, is not to impress, but to make sure we all understand what you mean. Otherwise you should aim to put things as clearly and simply as you can.

The following was written by a (successful!) PhD candidate. Do you know what it means? What is the point the writer is trying to make? Could it have been put more clearly?

The investigation demonstrates the fallacy of equating the nationalization of the workers ideology which consolidated an economico-
corporative consciousness, with the strangulation of woman's
potential as a historical subject at this time. (Doyon, 1978)

97

In academic work you should write impersonally, avoiding the use of personal pronouns such as 'I' or 'we'. But this does not mean that you have to be boring. You will, inevitably, have to use the passive voice more than is really desirable: 'On investigation, it was found that ...', but plain statements of fact are clear and quite acceptable. The use of impersonal forms has one advantage: it makes it much easier to avoid forms that imply sex (or other) stereotyping, which you should always avoid.

Liven up your writing by:

— varying the length of your sentences
— turning sentence constructions round where you can
— avoiding repetition
— thinking of the *sound* of your sentences

But avoid slang, and resist the temptation to put in 'throwaway' comments or witticisms. The examiners may not share the same sense of humour.

Many words can be saved by deleting all verbiage which adds nothing, e.g. 'It is the case that ...', 'It should be noted that...'. But, sparingly used, a *few* bridge phrases ease the reader's task. 'Finally', 'In conclusion' should be used at most *once* in each chapter — *at the end.*

Use the Right Word

The English language is constantly evolving, so there will always be arguments about proper usage. Some common usages, however, are definitely undesirable, as they are either incorrect, tired or misleading.

Please take care to use correct *geographical terms*. Do not use 'America' where you mean 'the United States', 'England' when you are referring to 'the United Kingdom (UK)', 'Russia' instead of 'the Soviet Union (USSR)', and 'the Common Market' for 'the European Community (EC)'.

Some words are correct in the right context but are very often used wrongly in everyday speech — you should use them correctly. If in doubt you should check in a good dictionary like the Concise Oxford Dictionary.

Watch Grammatical Points

Our awareness of the rules of grammar is largely unconscious; we do not always know why they exist. The reason is almost always that they help avoid ambiguity and uncertainty.

Do not use pronouns until you have put in the noun they are to represent. 'When we went to see George, he was sitting in his study' is not necessarily the same as 'When we went to see him, George was sitting in his study'.

Avoid double negatives, which produce a positive statement. 'The response was not lacking' means the same as 'there was a response' but it has less impact and is much easier to misunderstand. If you find yourself writing the sort of sentence that begins 'It is not uncommon to find that ...', remember the sentence 'The not unblack dog chases the not unbrown rabbit across the not ungreen field'.

Be careful to select the correct adjectives, and avoid qualifiers which weaken the thing qualified, e.g. 'rather novel', or which contradict it, e.g. 'a strong weakening influence'. It is quite common, but always wrong, to write 'rather unique' — if something is unique there is only one of it, and 'unique' cannot be qualified.

A dependent clause, which is there to explain a word, should always go as near to the word that it qualifies as possible.

Do not split infinitives. Instead of 'to boldly go where no man has gone before' write 'to go boldly' or even 'boldly to go'. And purists say that you should not begin a sentence with a word like 'but' or 'and'. But you can, occasionally.

Check Your Spelling

Social scientists usually have great sympathy with people with genuine spelling problems. Significantly, however, few people have difficulties with learning new words; it is the old ones that they have 'known' (i.e. not known) since childhood that they get wrong. If you spell technical words incorrectly, therefore, it soon looks as if you have not been paying much attention. Be particularly careful about *names*. If in doubt check a good reference work, or, for authors, the Library of Congress or British Library catalogues.

With wordprocessors spelling problems should mostly be a thing of the past. Use of a spell-check program is recommended, followed by a final read through to check names and figures. But remember that wordprocessors do not pick up use of the wrong word (e.g. 'their' for 'there') and do make possible new faults: words only partially erased, or the wrong word(s) deleted or changed.

Spell-checking also presents the problem of confusion between English usage (programme) and American usage (program). Where American usage is required, either in quotations, or where the word concerned has a technical meaning, as e.g. program means computer program, the important thing is to be consistent.

Use Punctuation Carefully

Punctuation marks come where you have a pause or breath in speech. If in doubt, say the sentence over to yourself before writing it down. The standard marks are the *comma*, for a brief hesitation in the middle of a sentence, or to mark off a subordinate clause, and a *full stop* (period) at the end. Use a *semicolon* sparingly; it joins related ideas only. Use a *colon* to demonstrate a point or when followed by a list of items. Make sure lists of items are all of the same kind. There is no comma before 'and' in English usage in the following case: 'apples, pears and onions' (but there is in American usage). If in doubt, always put a full stop and start a new sentence.

Should we not always avoid rhetorical questions? Yes, and the exclamation mark is usually inappropriate in academic writing! Avoid it! Avoid also the dash — which — whether you like it or not — always looks untidy — and (especially when used in combination with brackets) can make it almost impossible to tell — if you use it too much (however much that may be) — where you are in the sentence.

A similar rule applies to hyphens — avoid them wherever possible: 'middle class, Latin America, Vice Chancellor'. But you should have them where two adjectival words are joined together: 'working-class respondents' but 'the British working class'. Use them sparingly and strive for consistency.

Be consistent, too, with capital letters. The general rule is to use them as little as possible. Give capitals to proper names (Peter the Great, the Church of England, the Liberal Party) and to terms formed from proper names (Marxism) — though not to other 'isms': anarchosyndicalism, capitalism, communism. Capitals are not now used for 'left' and 'right' in the political sense.

Watch the position of the apostrophe in all plurals and never use it in the plurals of abbreviations (MPs not MP's) and dates (1990s not 1990's).

Otherwise you should have a consistent 'house style'.

Avoid Abbreviations

Abbreviations look slipshod and should be avoided. Colloquial abbreviations, such as 'can't', 'don't', 'hasn't', are inappropriate in the text of a thesis and should never be used. In direct quotations they should ideally always be reproduced *exactly* as in the original. Irrelevant matter may be left out of a quotation, though you must be careful to retain the sense of the original and not to give a false impression of its meaning. And, you must mark omissions by three dots, so ...; there should, of course, be four dots where the omission comes at the end of a sentence.

Use Foreign Words Properly

Foreign words should never be used simply to impress. If you think they look impressive, they should probably go. Consider very carefully whether there is any real reason why you cannot use an English equivalent. Great confusion exists over accents in words of French origin. With common words which have become normal English usage a useful rule is to accent them only if they could not otherwise be pronounced correctly according to English rules. Hence 'elite' and 'role' are not usually accented, but 'café', 'resumé' and 'coup d'état' are (or should be). Such words are not italicized. All other foreign words should be italicized and spelt exactly as in their own language: *cause célèbre, première, protégé, vis-à-vis.* Note that in German in addition capital letters have to be given to all nouns, whether or not they occur at the beginning of a sentence: *Lebensraum, Weltanschauung.* You can either use the Umlaut or add an 'e', but not leave it out — *Länder, Laender,* but not *'Lander',* (which is a form of space vehicle).

Presentation

You and you alone are responsible for seeing your work is properly presented. None of us ever achieves it, but what is expected of us is always perfection. A thesis should look clean, smart and professional. Three rules will help ensure a good standard:

Give yourself time. It cannot be too strongly stressed that it is up to you to *plan* your work and, if working to a deadline for grant or other reasons, to allow adequate time not only to get the length and balance right, but also for typing, checking and binding.

Do not leave everything to the last moment. Arrange your timetable so that you have adequate time to work on your thesis; you may in this way be able to take best advantage of a weekend or a vacation. Remember that you will have to make more than one draft and probably several revisions, and that if your draft is being typed by someone else it is still up to you to get it properly corrected.

Read it through. When correcting do not try to get everything right in one reading. Read it through several times: once for content, another time for style, a third time to check spelling, a fourth to check punctuation etc.

If you have to rely on someone else to type your thesis, make it clear from the beginning that corrections have to be done and have to be done properly. If you have given them a clear clean manuscript there should be very few mistakes, but you should always insist that they be corrected.

Avoid last minute hasty and/or messy alterations in pen or pencil — they give the worst possible impression to the examiners. Even correcting fluids can be a problem if over-used, as they tend to flake off.

Be consistent. The basic rule of good presentation is *consistency*.

Sources and Citations

What do You Cite?

You *must* cite a source for all direct quotations ('quotes' is slang). Quotations must always appear within quotation marks. Many publishers now prefer single quotation marks but many wordprocessors do not offer them, so double will be clearer. Use one or the other consistently. You *should* give a citation for major pieces of evidence.

How do I Cite It?

There are two principal reference systems. You can use either, unless you are specifically told otherwise by your supervisor. You will find that the first, the Harvard system, is the easier both to use and to understand. Do not make up your own system!

Method one — the 'Harvard' system
a) In the text: you include references in the text by putting the author's surname, the date of publication and, where applicable, the page number, in brackets, e.g.:

> The fact was 'that Britain lagged behind almost all her main industrial competitors and that she failed to solve the problem of sterling' (Pinto-Duschinsky, 1970, p. 58; see also Glyn and Sutcliffe, 1972).

Since all citations refer directly to the bibliography, there is no distinction between first and subsequent citations.

b) In the bibliography: you must list *all* your sources in the bibliography so that the references can be tracked down, thus:

> BERNSTEIN, Basil (1973) *Class, Codes and Control*, St. Albans, Herts: Penguin.

Avoid the common practice of giving just a single initial when more information is available. You will find that 'J. Smith', for example, is not easy to trace in the library catalogue. Then comes the date of publication. If there are two or more publications of the same author they are listed in date order; titles of the same date are identified in *both* text and bibliography as 1972a, 1972b etc. It is good practice, even if often unnecessary, to give the place of publication before the publisher's name.

To distinguish between books and articles, the rule is that a published volume (book or journal title) is underlined and the title of a chapter, an article in a journal or an unpublished source (if it has a title) is not underlined but is placed in quotation marks. Titles of unpublished sources (theses, conference papers etc.) are also put in quotation marks.

Method two: footnotes or endnotes
a) In the text: the alternative is the more traditional system of putting a superscript number in the text corresponding to a footnote or (better) endnote. Endnotes may be grouped at the end of each chapter, but it is much easier for all concerned if they are grouped at the end of the thesis.

Again, to distinguish between books and articles, the rule is that a published volume (book or journal title) is underlined and the title of a chapter, an article in a journal or an unpublished source (if it has a title) is not underlined but is placed in quotation marks.

Thus, for example, for a book:

Caroline Thomas, *In Search of Security; The Third World in International Relations* (Brighton, Sussex: Wheatsheaf, 1987), p. 29.

For an article:

Peter J. Beck, 'Britain's Antarctic dimension', *International Affairs*, LIX, No. 3, Summer 1983, pp. 429–444.

For unpublished sources:

L.G. Espejo, 'Neutral but not indifferent: Colombian foreign policy since 1900', unpublished PhD thesis, University of Southampton, 1981.

b) In the bibliography: if Method Two is being used the bibliography entry for each source should be identical with the full citation only with surnames first. Unlike Method One the date stays at the end. For example:

HINDESS, Barry. *The Decline of Working Class Politics*. London, Paladin, 1971.

c) Short citations: To save space, it is only necessary to cite a work in full on the first appearance. On second and subsequent appearances use the author's surname and page number only; if more than one work is cited by the same author give a short version of the title the first time and use it the next time each reappears. Avoid 'ibid.', 'op. cit.' etc.

Maps, Tables and Graphs

Before including any of these think carefully why you want them. Properly used, they present information in a most economical form, saving many precious lines of text. Wrongly used they can be a disaster.

Maps. Try to get these on to a normal-size piece of paper if you can — it causes great difficulty for the binder to bind in oversize folded maps and they easily get torn.

Tables. A thesis will often be based on tabular material which will be needed for *reference* purposes (it will have to be consulted several times). Such tables will most conveniently be grouped together at the end. Discussion of the material presented, however, will also require tables for *demonstration* purposes, to illustrate a specific argument. These should be inserted in the body of the text itself, as close as possible to and accompanying the explanation of their meaning. Generally speaking, demonstration tables should be as simple and clear as is consistent with the needs of accuracy.

Number all tables consecutively and clearly within each chapter, e.g. 1.1, 1.2 ..., 2.1, 2.2 ... etc. Each individual table should contain a clear and complete explanation of the figures it presents. Both axes should be clearly labelled and the units stated in each case. Number the columns from left to right and give them clear headings. Avoid long-winded headings and above all avoid abbreviations, which may be misunderstood. *Check* all figures with particular care. Sub-totals and totals should be clearly distinguished. At the bottom, give the *source(s)* of your data. Footnotes may be used to explain any changes which would invalidate direct comparison. For a full discussion of the problems and pitfalls see Chapman (1986).

Graphs. Graphs, bar charts, pie charts etc. are less accurate than tables and only really suitable for demonstration rather than reference purposes. Remember to label both axes and make clear what units are being used. If there are several lines, distinguish them clearly. Again, give the source(s) of your data.

Writing for Publication

The techniques you have developed or improved while writing your thesis are the same that you will need when writing books or articles for publication.

Your first problem comes with your thesis itself. You have invested years of work in it, and you may well want to get it published. Given the very different needs of the commercial market, it is, however, likely to need a great deal of rewriting, much of the purpose of which will be to remove or reduce the 'academic' features. In the meantime you may wish to publish part of it as an article or articles for a learned journal.

Be clear what you want to say. An academic article is usually between 5,000 and 7,000 words long, unless the journal in question specifies otherwise. It must have a definite point to make, and for most journals this means one that is of interest to its readers generally and not just to specialists.

Study the requirements of the journal. Once you have the first draft ready study the requirements of the journal you propose to approach. The lay-out and contents lists will tell you broadly what sort of thing they like to publish. Often quite detailed instructions are given on technical aspects of the production and submission of typescripts, and you should follow these to the letter. (Editors of journals seem to delight in inventing quirky requirements specific to themselves, but you must remember that you have to please them, not the other way round.)

You can submit an article to only one journal at a time. Submission generally implies a warranty on your part that the article is original and is not being considered for publication elsewhere, and more often than not this is a formal requirement.

Pay careful attention to criticism. Editors and academic readers will be looking for an article that is clearly written, has a well defined theme, is based on a sound methodological approach, sets out evidence in a way that is concise and meaningful, and states its conclusions at the end. It goes without saying that they will expect it to recognize all appropriate sources and to be set in the context of a debate in which both argument and counter-argument should appear.

Even if an article is not accepted 'first time out', therefore, all is not lost.

Most academic journals will give you extracts from or a paraphrase of the reader's reasons for their decision, and may even go so far as to offer very specific advice on how to revise it so that it is acceptable. In either case, pay careful attention to their reasons even if you do not agree with them. If you decide to try another journal instead, their views and/or approach may well be different. So, too, however will be their technical requirements, so remember to conform to them while preparing your revised version.

Helpful Aids

You should always keep a dictionary and thesaurus on hand (or on disk), and a copy of H.W. Fowler's *Dictionary of Modern English Usage* is useful, as is Sir Ernest Gower's *The Complete Plain Words*. Those who use US materials will find H.W. Horwill's *A Dictionary of Modern American Usage* helpful. Myra Chapman's *Plain Figures* is worth consulting before you plan your tables. Finally, Howard Becker's *Writing for Social Scientists: How to Start and Finish your Thesis, Book or Article* covers much of the ground of this chapter in more detail.

References

BECKER, H.S. (1986) *Writing for Social Scientists: How to Start and Finish your Thesis, Book or Article*, Chicago, University of Chicago Press.
CHAPMAN, M. with MAHON, B. (1986) *Plain Figures*, London, HMSO.
DOYON, L.M. (1978) 'Organized Labour and Perón [1943–1955]', unpublished PhD thesis, University of Toronto.

Chapter 9

Presentation and Communication Skills

Haydn Mathias

Introduction

Presentations are a fundamental means of communication between professionals and between professionals and lay people. We live in a world where communication, whether by print, vision or speech, has powerful influences on attitudes and behaviour. As a research student, you will be called upon increasingly to explain and justify your work to colleagues and others. This means that you will need to develop the skills necessary to deliver effective presentations.

Standing up in front of a group of people is not everyone's idea of a good time. Fear, terror and anxiety strike at the heart! One consolation is that, as a presenter, you are not alone in feeling nervous in such a situation. Actors and actresses experience the same feelings. It is a normal reaction and one which can be productively used to enhance a performance. Your confidence will increase with practice so you need to take every opportunity, e.g. at departmental seminars, meetings and conferences, to give presentations and receive feedback on them. Practice and feedback, as well as observing good and poor presentations, should contribute to the development of your own presentation skills.

There are no guaranteed procedures for delivering excellent presentations. Judgment and the unique interaction between presenter and audience are factors which cannot wholly be prescribed in advance. To a large extent these are acquired through experience. Moreover, the development of an individual style is to be valued, much the same as it is in other forms of communication. What we can do, however, is to identify a set of guidelines and suggestions which will contribute to the development of an effective presentation. The aim of this chapter is to consider three aspects of presentations: preparation and planning, the use of audio–visual aids, and delivery. It should offer you some initial thoughts and insights as to how to develop presentations which are effective and to help you to evaluate the feedback you receive from your own presentations.

Characteristics of Presentations

We have all been to lectures and presentations and are probably as expert as anyone in identifying what makes for a good and a poor presentation. Although we may differ on some points, and expect to do so, in general we could probably arrive at a fair consensus. We like presentations to be interesting, relevant, clear and well-organized. We do not like presentations which are rambling, poorly organized, dull and difficult to follow.

In trying to define the characteristics of an effective presentation we should begin by recognizing that, as a means of communication, an oral presentation is not the same as a written communication. Each has to be prepared and delivered differently. Written communications usually contain a lot more detail but are largely under the control of the reader who can scan, browse, re-read sections of text and generally process information in ways which suit his or her needs. Verbal presentations are largely under the control of the presenter. Unlike a conversation where one person can ask the other for clarification or to repeat a point, the presentation moves on like a film with the onus on the audience to keep up with the action. The skill of the presenter is to organize and pace the content in such a way that it is followed and understood by the audience, and engages their interest.

The presentation is essentially a process of one-way communication. In this situation the presenter and the audience are faced with a number of constraints which have to be taken into account in preparation. The audience is relatively passive and may lose attention. A mixed audience makes it difficult for the presenter to judge at what level the message should be pitched. Demands are made on the memory and information-processing capabilities of the audience so the presenter has to be careful about the amount, organization and pacing of the content. Finally, in order to control the delivery the presenter needs to get audience feedback but this can be difficult unless the audience is obviously wildly enthusiastic or visibly asleep!

A considerable amount of research has been undertaken on presentations and lectures. From this we can extract a number of key messages which both reinforce our own experience and provide pointers to preparation and delivery. Studies of audience attention in lectures indicate that attention is initially high and declines after some twenty minutes or so, climbing again in anticipation of the end of the talk. This suggests that variety needs to be incorporated into a presentation, whether it be a change of pace, a break or the use of an audio-visual aid, if attention is to be maintained.

Presentations can make considerable demands on memory and cognitive processing. Information which is organized and structured in meaningful chunks is much easier to absorb and retain. Retention and understanding are also helped by using simple language, emphasizing important points, providing an orientating framework, including frequent summaries and generally 'signposting' the structure much like the headings and sub-headings used in books. Providing examples also helps understanding particularly with unfamiliar material where a new idea can be introduced through an example which links the familiar to the unfamiliar.

One of the most common problems in presentations is including far too much material for the time available. Getting through the material might be the concern of the presenter but if the audience fails to grasp the key ideas from the mass of detail then the presentation has failed. A presentation is not a spoken version of the written word. It cannot deal with the density of material which print can. Part of the planning of presentations involves selecting out the key ideas and excluding much of the detail which can always be followed up by the audience in a handout or through a written paper or report.

The purpose of a presentation is to give understanding to the audience. If the audience departs none the wiser then the presentation has failed to achieve its objectives. This is a vital point to remember. The whole purpose of giving a presentation is to communicate or to persuade. So think about the audience, what you want them to take away from your presentation and build your preparation around that.

Preparation and Planning

The quality of your presentation will ultimately depend on the amount of preparation you put into it. If you have thought through your presentation and are clear about what you want your audience to take away with them, you should find that the delivery largely takes care of itself. Of course, the more familiar and confident you are about your material, the easier you will feel about organizing it to meet your purposes.

There is no one right way to prepare a presentation but there are certain key elements which need to be considered. Below is a simple procedure which you can follow and adapt to meet your own circumstances and preferred way of working. While it may look sequential, in reality you will be moving back and forth between the steps as you refine your ideas. One way to approach planning is to keep your audience firmly in mind. Put yourself in their shoes and ask yourself what you would want them to do as a result of your presentation. In terms of your overall strategy, the familiar advice of tell them what you are going to say, say it and tell them again is not a bad rule of thumb.

The first stage of your preparation should involve considering your objectives in terms of your audience. If you are not sure where to start then write down in outline form on one sheet of paper as much as you know about the topic you will be presenting. Then begin to consider what is going to be important for you to put across and why. Now you need to draw out your purposes and objectives. Are you trying mainly to persuade or to inform? What are the specific objectives of your presentation? What will be the key messages you will want your audience to take away with them?

Defining your objectives at an early stage will help with your subsequent preparation and keep the presentation coherent and focused. It is likely that an audience will be able to remember from three to five key ideas from a presentation, so limit your objectives to not more than these. These will be your 'take home' messages. It might also help to focus your presentation and arouse interest by turning your topic into a question for which the talk will provide the answer. For example, a presentation called 'student learning' says very little about what it might contain but a title such as 'How do students learn?' or 'Why do some students fail to learn?' gives the presentation more direction, increases interest and anticipates answers.

Defining objectives for the presentation and deciding its slant and emphasis will also depend on the audience. It is unlikely that you will be giving the same presentation to a group of lay people and to a professional conference. You need to identify your audience's level of knowledge, interests and the reasons that they have for attending your presentation. You can then determine what needs to be explained, what you can take for granted and what examples you need to choose to illustrate your ideas.

With your objectives defined and your audience identified you can then proceed to develop the organization of your presentation. From your initial outline or map of ideas you should begin to see what elements of your topic are important and less important, and to identify the gaps for which you need to do further reading. Your objectives should be governing this process of organizing and sifting of ideas by this stage. You need to develop a coherent structure to your presentation which will reflect your objectives and reinforce them.

One major problem facing you will be in selecting content. The temptation is to cover everything which you feel is important rather than to look at the presentation in terms of your objectives and your audience. It is not going to be possible, nor productive, to try to cover all the ground. You have to be selective otherwise you will end up with a jumble of ideas presented far too quickly to be comprehended meaningfully by your audience. One way of approaching content selection is to categorize content into what is essential, important and desirable. By doing this you will be forced to keep to the most essential content in relation to your objectives. Some important elements may have to go and even all of the desirable elements, but by so doing the presentation will be kept focused, coherent and meaningful.

Following this process of refining ideas, you will be aiming to identify a set of key ideas or points which will be related in some logical structure and will form the skeleton of the presentation. This, in essence, is what your audience will take away with them and provides a summary of the key messages of your talk.

However, you will need to highlight your key messages and the structure of your presentation so that the main points are not lost among the rest of the supporting detail. There are various ways of doing this. You can emphasize and repeat your key ideas in different ways and point to their importance by using simple verbal cues such as: 'Now, this is an essential idea'. You will also need to 'signpost' the structure so your audience know where they are in the presentation. This means indicating where the main sections begin and end. Signposting statements can also be used, such as: 'Having dealt with how the research was undertaken let us move on to consider the main findings...'. Finally, rhetorical questions can be used to indicate the beginning of a new section and raise interest in what is to follow, e.g. 'So, what are the implications of these findings?'

Summaries are important in reminding an audience of the key ideas and main arguments. In some presentations, where a sequence of steps or a central line of argument is important, more frequent summaries may be needed. A final summary is certainly important to draw the various strands of the presentation together, to remind the audience of the key ideas and, in many cases, to point to the implications of the presentation for the audience.

The final element in your design will be developing an introduction. This is left until last because in order to orientate your audience to what is to come, you will have had to work out the objectives and structure of your presentation. Your introduction should indicate your objectives and how they relate to your audience as well as the structure of your presentation. In effect you are selling your presentation before it begins and, hopefully, arousing interest and expectation in what is to follow. Your introduction also serves as a social device to establish rapport with your audience and to introduce yourself as a person.

At the end of this process of preparation you should have a presentation outline which can be summarized as a structure of key points and sub-points on one sheet of paper and which could be used as part of your introduction and final summary. You will also have to add timings for each part to ensure that the presentation will fit into the time available. In this respect, it is always best to plan to undershoot rather than aim to finish on time since the actual presentation will take longer to deliver than you think. It is easier to expand to fill the time available than to cut material during the delivery.

Audio-Visual Aids

When used appropriately audio-visual aids can enhance the effectiveness and impact of a presentation. However, it is important to be clear about why you are using them rather than to use them for their own sake. They need to contribute directly to the achievement of your objectives and complement your verbal presentation. In general, audio-visual aids can be used to add interest and variety, to provide relevant examples and illustrations, to add emphasis and impact, and to communicate ideas which are best conveyed other than by the spoken word alone.

Before you embark on a splendid multi-media display you really need to think about the practicalities of managing even the simplest piece of equipment. The more equipment you use and the more complex it is, the more likely it is that problems will occur. It is best to keep it simple and preferably to stick to one or two audio-visual devices. The most common audio-visual aids used in presentations, apart from chalkboards, are the overhead projector and 35mm slide projector, so we will focus on these, although many of the considerations applying to them should also apply to other media.

The overhead projector is widely available, simple to use and generally reliable. It has the advantage of requiring little or no blackout. Materials can be prepared in advance and added to during the presentation. It is a flexible and dynamic visual aid with a wide variety of creative uses. As well as images, shapes can be projected and even moving models. The basic materials are acetate sheets and special overhead projection pens. Spirit-based or permanent pens should always be used for prepared material since the water-soluble type can easily smudge.

Slide projectors contain more moving parts so are slightly less reliable, particularly when poor quality slide mounts are used which can jam in the machine. Room blackout is required and either an operator needs to be employed for slide changing or you will need to have a remote control at the end of a long lead. Slides and their sequence have to be prepared in advance and it is vital to run all slides through the machine to ensure they are all the correct way round. A mixture of the usual horizontal and less usual vertical slide (long side up) should be avoided since the latter may project off the screen. The main compensation for the greater preparation required for slides is that very high quality images, whether graphics or pictures, can be produced.

Unless you are on familiar territory with familiar equipment, you really need to check everything with your material at the venue. Have they got the right equipment for you? Is there space for your overhead projection transparencies? Is the slide remote control working? Are the lamps working? Have you a spare available? What would happen if a piece of equipment failed? Does the room have blackout facilities? Is the mains lead long enough? Can the audience see the screen clearly? Where will you stand? In other words, always anticipate the worst that can happen and run through any material with the actual equipment you will use in the room you will use well in advance of your presentation.

When designing either slide or overhead projection material the basic message is to keep it simple, readable and relevant. Simplicity is really the key. Your audience will need time to absorb a visual image so give them time before launching into your explanation and keep the visual simple. Break down a complex visual into a series of simpler ones. Do not cram on too much information. While you are speaking your audience will be reading what is on the screen. Include only what is absolutely essential and keep words to a minimum. If you need to use word visuals then try to limit these to not more than seven double-spaced lines and do not include too many words on each line. A simple test of readability is to look at the slide or overhead projection transparency at a distance of eight times its vertical height. If you cannot read it nor will your audience, especially from the back of a room.

Visuals come into their own when you display visual material rather than words. But again you need to keep it simple. Taking materials directly from books and papers is rarely suitable since they are designed for detailed reading, and usually contain far too much information which is printed too finely for projection. It is easier to redraw and simplify such material. Avoid the temptation to include large tables. These will only confuse. Extract the essential data for display or convert the data into a graph, histogram or pie chart which is easier to absorb. Just think of the presentations you have attended where visuals were used and you should appreciate the importance of simplicity in visual design for impact and communication.

When using either slides or overhead projection transparencies you need to relate your verbal message to your visual message, and to control the attention of your audience to the points you are making. This means not leaving images displayed which are no longer relevant. These will only distract attention. Using a pointer to link what you say to what your audience sees will also help to focus attention on your argument. As your audience is in front of you be sure to talk to them and not to the screen. Again this can distract attention and make you difficult to hear.

Delivery

Having put in the preparation, the delivery of your presentation should practically take care of itself. Many of the problems related to presentations tend to be associated with poor organization of the material rather than the act of standing and speaking. However, there are a number of guidelines which can be offered to ensure your investment in preparation pays dividends in the delivery.

From the viewpoint of the presenter, facing a sea of faces can be quite intimidating. However, looked at from the viewpoint of the audience, you will be seen as an individual. One way to look upon the presentation, therefore, is as an enlarged conversation between yourself and a member of the audience. This means being yourself and assuming that you are talking to another person. However, the situation is artificial in that you will be engaged in a one-way conversation some distance away from the other person. There is also more than one person you will be addressing so you have to make your normal conversational style exaggerated and larger than life to hold your audience's attention.

You may be nervous at first. This is quite normal. However, you can diminish your initial nervousness by fixing your mind firmly on the purpose of your presentation and the key ideas you want your audience to take away with them. Controlled deep breathing should also help to relax you while keeping your necessary level of arousal sufficiently high to deliver a good performance. Some presenters find it useful to rehearse their introductory words thoroughly so as to get them off to a positive start. However remember the analogy of the enlarged conversation; smile, introduce yourself and welcome your audience. First impressions are extremely important and if you get a positive, warm response from the faces of your audience, it should give you the boost you need to overcome your initial nervousness.

If we continue the analogy of the enlarged conversation, then we need to look at the person we are talking to. In the presentation this implies maintaining eye contact with the audience. This does not mean fixing your gaze on one or two individuals but constantly scanning round the faces and, where possible, picking up reactions to what you are saying. If you appear actively interested in them, they should respond by maintaining attention on what you are saying. This is another reason why you should not read a script but rather use notes. You will be able to maintain eye contact and come across more naturally.

Other aspects of delivery you should bear in mind are voice and mannerisms. Because you are in a large room, probably at some distance from your audience, and because you will need to hold their attention in a form of one-way communication, you will need to project your voice. This is not quite the same as simply raising your voice for this may well make it sound harsh and thin. Voice projection comes from the stomach in as much as it will be your stomach muscles pressing on your diaphragm which will produce the volume and intensity you need.

Attention and emphasis will also be enhanced if you vary the speed and pitch of your voice to match the points you are making. For example, a slower and more deliberate pace, coupled with a pause just before, will highlight a key message. For less important points and asides a faster speed will do. However, you will also need to be aware of your articulation, particularly at the end of sentences where there is a tendency for the voice to drop. Clear pronunciation of consonants and word endings should help to avoid indistinctness of speech.

Do not be afraid to be natural in your gestures. In fact, you can afford to exaggerate them to add variety and maintain attention as long as they complement your verbal message. Gestures are only distracting when they do distract. If you do not know what to do with your hands, then hold on to something. Holding your notes will keep at least one hand occupied. In order to project yourself and hold attention you should stand more erect, but not stiff, and convey a business-like style. The larger the audience, the larger the performance. Being too casual and too visually 'quiet' may well detract from what you are saying. You need to control attention and maintain interest, and the impact of your physical presence is therefore important.

You can afford to take risks in your delivery. Novelty will help maintain attention and impact. That is not to say that you should be loud and distracting but rather to have something different to offer, and making your delivery larger than life to help to make it and you more memorable and appreciated. The alternative is to withdraw into your shell and come across as a diminutive figure, lacking presence and soon losing your audience's attention. Making what appears to you as something of a fool of yourself is likely to be more respected and better remembered than having little or no impact at all.

Summary

You do not have to be a gifted orator to produce a good presentation. There are many elements of preparation and delivery you can control and develop to ensure you communicate effectively. These boil down to:

— Keep it simple (not simplistic)
— Be clear about your objectives
— Organize your material
— Signpost the key messages and organization
— Consider the presentation as an enlarged conversation
— Keep your audience firmly in mind

Giving presentations is very much of a practical activity. In order to develop your presentation skills it is vital to gain feedback. Take every opportunity to do so.

Haydn Mathias

Further Reading

Brown, G. and Atkins, M. (1988) *Effective Teaching in Higher Education*, London, Methuen. (Chapters 2 and 3 provide a useful account, coupled with practical suggestions, on preparing and delivering lectures.)

Mandel, S. (1987) *Effective Presentation Skills*, London, Kogan Page. (A cheap, short guide to practical presentation skills. Although orientated to the commercial presentation, many of the ideas are applicable to other kinds of presentation.)

Goodlad, S. (1990) *Speaking Technically*, Richmond, Sinclair Goodlad. (An inexpensive, concise and very helpful practical guide to preparing and delivering technical presentations developed from the author's communication skills programmes at Imperial College. Covers a variety of situations, including presentation to funding bodies, conferences, lectures, schools talks, project reports, etc.)

Chapter 10

Using Documentary Sources

Peter Calvert

All times before the instant in which you read this are already past. For the present, we can actively seek information by a variety of means. For the past, we are the passive recipients of only two sorts of evidence: remains and records. Documentary research is concerned with the latter, the use of written records as a source of information. In the past, this limited our access to those cultures that possessed a system of writing and to those matters about which they chose to write. We know how the Roman Empire was governed; we can only guess at the politics of the peoples who built Stonehenge. Today we have access to far more written records than we can conveniently handle, and records may also take the form of photographs, film, audio disks, videotapes or computer diskettes, each of which requires slight modifications of our traditional techniques of study. Collections of records are termed *archives*.

Documentary research is associated principally with the discipline of history. However wherever a research project in the other social sciences involves any study of, or comparison with, a period before the present, documentary sources immediately become the main source of information for that period. If they are not properly used, comparison with the present will be misleading or at worst completely wrong.

In addition, a search of the relevant literature forms the essential preliminary to every research project, and the history of a problem is the vital background to applied policy research. Fuller understanding of the nature, advantages and limitations of different forms of documentary sources will make this task much easier and more interesting.

Archives

An archive is any collection of original documentary material, such as letters, lists, diaries, drawings etc. However the fact that an archive exists does not mean that it is available for inspection by researchers. Archives may themselves be public or private; and in either case any or all of the documents in them may be open or closed.

Public Archives

All organized governments maintain collections of public records, though their state of preservation and the degree of accessibility varies widely.

State papers in the United Kingdom, including all correspondence of government departments or of public figures in their official capacity, are not open to inspection for at least thirty years (the 'Thirty Year Rule'). In the case of some categories of material, that relating to members of the Royal Family, to the work of security agencies or the Census, the closed period is much longer (up to one hundred years). In the United States, on the other hand, most categories of public records are available in the National Archives after some twenty-five years, and an American citizen who can demonstrate knowledge that a specific document exists can obtain sight of it at any time under the Freedom of Information Act.

Public figures naturally wish to retain their personal papers for their own use during their lifetime and certainly do not wish to open them to opponents or critics. Fortunately in Britain many leading politicians, administrators, artists and literary figures have deposited their personal papers in a public collection where they can be inspected by scholars, but there is no obligation for them to do so. Papers remaining in private hands may well be inaccessible or, even where their owner is willing to give access to them, may be badly stored, and they will almost certainly be unsorted and uncatalogued.

When public figures die their papers are in particular danger. Some have given instructions for all their papers to be destroyed at their death and these instructions have been carried out with thoroughness and zeal. Others have died unexpectedly and their papers hare been wholly or partly destroyed by their next of kin before (or perhaps because) their importance was realized. However where relatives have been more farsighted, or the particular importance of the collections has been appreciated, the papers may then be deposited in a public collection. Examples are the Churchill Papers at Churchill College, Cambridge, and the Wellington and Mountbatten collections at the University of Southampton.

It is obviously difficult to produce, and even more difficult to keep up to date, a union catalogue of personal papers, that is a catalogue of items in all libraries. Hence the serious researcher has to rely on a combination of methods to locate relevant material:

1 union catalogues of documentary sources, where these exist;
2 biographies of key figures, where available, and where based on documentary sources;
3 the separate guides and/or handbooks of major archives, such as the Bodleian Library, Oxford, the University Library, Cambridge, or the British Library of Political and Economic Science, at the London School of Economics;
4 word of mouth.

Getting to Use Archives

Permission to use a private collection must be sought by personal letter to whoever owns it. A personal introduction from a sympathetic figure known to the owner can do much to smooth the way. If this is not available, would-be researchers should explain concisely but clearly who they are, what their project is about, why the material they seek is important to it, and what use they propose to make of it. Permission to consult material does not constitute permission to publish it, and if you go on to publish your thesis you will have to secure specific permission for that purpose.

A general letter of introduction from your supervisor will normally give access to public collections. You will be informed on what conditions (if any) you may publish the material you are allowed to consult.

Sources

Social scientists (other than historians) are usually interested in sources only for the data that they can get out of them. Unfortunately not all sources are equally valuable or reliable, and if the sources of data are bad, research based on them will have little value. We must, therefore, distinguish between different sorts of source.

The main distinction to make is that between primary and secondary sources. *Primary sources* are books, papers and other documents that were produced by the people being studied during the time when the action you are studying was actually in progress. Typical primary sources are: the originals of official correspondence, parliamentary papers (as far as they relate to the purpose for which they were issued), minutes of meetings, wills and other legal documents, personal letters and diaries, eye-witness accounts of events, transcripts of speeches, pamphlets, and (where they report current events) newspapers.

Secondary sources are books, papers and documents written after the event, or by someone who was not personally a witness of the events described. They represent only indirect evidence about the events you are studying. Typical secondary sources are: academic books and articles, annual reports, official statistics.

Two other categories of documentary sources come in a special position: memoirs and oral history. The published or unpublished *memoirs* of participants are not primary sources, as they were not written at the time of the events they describe, but they are evidence of a very special kind about how the individuals concerned wanted their actions to be seen by others.

Official history has often been criticized, sometimes unfairly, for dealing with kings and queens, and battles and other public events to the exclusion of the lives of ordinary people. *Oral history* is therefore of particular interest to the sociologist or economic historian. In the technique usually used, the subject is interviewed and the entire interview recorded. A skilled interviewer, directing questions towards specific areas, can elicit information that the subject might not consider important or simply have forgotten in the course of time (see Chapter 17 on interviewing; Hoopes 1979). However there is a strong tendency for respondents to put the best possible light on their previous actions, as in the case of the writers of memoirs. So the researcher reading an oral history transcript should be careful to consider whether it is confirmed by the written evidence available.

Finally, we have to be able to find the references we need. *Tertiary sources* are indexes, abstracts and other bibliographies which help us to do this. There are even bibliographies to help us find bibliographies.

The value of sources depends on their accuracy, completeness, degree of detail and proximity to the event(s) recorded. Generally speaking, the *earlier* a primary source (the nearer it is to the moment of the action) the stronger its value as evidence. However if it is neither accurate nor complete its value will be much diminished.

As a general rule, also, the evidence of primary sources should be preferred to that of memoirs, and that of memoirs to that provided by other secondary sources. Yet the author of a secondary source is likely to have had access to information that was not available at the time to the participants. This in turn will have come from other primary sources. Hence if a secondary source is to be preferred to a primary source, it must be because it provides evidence from some other primary source that the researcher has not been able to use personally. For this reason, generally the *later* the secondary source is, the more likely value it has to the researcher.

Weighing Evidence

No documentary source should ever be accepted uncritically. Every source read should be assessed with six questions in mind:

1. *Is the document what it purports to be?* The credibility of a document depends first and foremost on its authenticity. The question of whether a document is what it seems to be is a highly technical one, and the episode of *The Hitler Diaries* (so-called) is an excellent example of how not to judge authenticity. The first step is to check if paper, ink etc. are of sufficient age and whether the pedigree of the document is a realistic one. Judgment of authenticity from the internal evidence of the text comes only when one is satisfied that it is technically possible that the document can be genuine. (Of course, most documents that postgraduate social scientists need to use will not require scientific authentication.)

2. *What is the relation of the author to the event?* Having first established whether we are dealing with a primary or a secondary source, we must next try to assess how good a witness the author was. For this purpose we can use, if we have time, supplementary information about the life, education, religious and political affiliations, etc. of the author of the record to ascertain how far that individual had a specific point of view and how far that point of view may have coloured the evidence presented by the record.

If we judge that it has, then the next step is to try to assess how much evidence we can recover from the record. The fact that a record is defective does not necessarily mean that it is useless. Even an eye-witness such as Samuel Pepys could not see all of the Great Fire of London but Pepys had more opportunity to do so than most and his record is therefore of great value to us. Nevertheless his account of how the fire first started is hearsay. In cases of obvious bias, the very fact that an effort has been made to weight the record may in itself be evidence of a kind.

3. *What is the record trying to show?* Some classes of records, memoirs in particular, are written to present their authors in a positive light. Rare indeed is the political memoir whose author admits to having made a mistake. This is not altogether a reflection on the author's sincerity. From the moment the event occurred, the phenomenon of cognitive dissonance has been acting to smooth away inconvenient details which conflict with the evolving self-image of competence and honour. It comes as no surprise, therefore, to find that no one admits to having started the First World War.

Some inaccuracies can be easily checked because of the volume of evidence that is available. Newspapers are frequently inaccurate, but many of the errors are caused by haste and carelessness, and in democratic countries with freedom of the press we can check them against the reports in other newspapers. But few of us do.

On the other hand, personal letters do not have to contain very careful judgments. Even in Britian, where libel laws are strict, they do not cover personal correspondence. Hence although personal letters give us much information that we could not get in any other way, we must remember that just because a letter was written at the same time as or soon after the event does not mean that the author was as well informed as others who wrote later.

Authors of secondary sources, too, have their own points of view, which at times can be very obtrusive. There is, for example, a strong tendency among biographers to present their subjects in the most favourable light possible. The obvious remedy in such cases is to try to get information where possible from more than one source. The more sources from which information comes, the higher the degree of confidence, if the sources agree, that the deductions drawn from it are likely to be valid.

This applies not only to literary material but also to economic and social statistics, many of which are produced by official bodies and presented in a form which reflects the best possible light on their performance. The researcher should not fall into the trap of believing that because a document is official, or because the information it presents is numerical, it can therefore be uncritically accepted. The belief in accuracy is a relatively modern phenomenon, and many governments do not have the capacity to produce accurate statistics, even if they want to, which is not always the case (see Chapter 20).

4. *How representative is the document of the written record*? For social scientists the problem of representativeness is therefore of particular importance, since they will often have to use the documentary record as a basis for making quantitative judgments. The question of how well the document as seen represents a whole possible category of documents is fundamental. Throughout history many documents have been deliberately destroyed to avoid them being read, and recent protests in the United States about systematic bias in the latest volumes in the series *Foreign Relations of the United States* are a reminder that in today's conditions the huge bulk of archives make such selectivity easy.

On the other hand many documents of social interest, e.g. accounts, receipts, inventories, are simply destroyed when they seem to be no longer of interest. For sociologists and economic historians this presents an interesting problem in sampling theory.

5. *What does the document mean*? Even when all these questions have been dealt with, the question of meaning is not automatically transparent. Words change meaning and new usages are generated; documents contain allusions familiar to the writer and reader, but not to the researcher. Meaning derives from context and if the context is imperfectly understood, the meaning of the source may be distorted.

6. *What is the researcher's relation to the subject*? Finally, researchers should take care to consider their own prejudices. Are they more willing to accept one piece of evidence rather than another because it supports their own argument and not because it is inherently more reliable? If so, they should think again.

Literature Search

For most researchers their first contact with their topic will be through a literature search using in the main secondary sources. The purpose of the literature search is obvious, it is to acquaint you with the full range of material available that is relevant to your field, and to avoid the risk of 'reinventing the wheel'. Two basic points cover the requirements of all disciplines and types of thesis:

1. *Start with your bibliography*. The bibliography, which comes at the end of your thesis, should be a complete record of all sources used in the course of the research. Works consulted but not used should not be listed in the final bibliography, but you will need to keep check of them while the work is in progress.

Therefore the first thing you should do, before beginning the research proper, should be to start your bibliography. As well as the electronic version which you will edit, there is much to be said for keeping a duplicate bibliography on 5″ × 3″ cards. You can take a few to the library each time you go, check them off when found, and move them from the back of the box to the front when you get home to give yourself encouragement. You can also scribble occasional notes on the front or back, where a book or article (as quite often happens) turns out to have practically no relevance to your chosen subject.

2. *Use bibliographical sources properly*. There are four types of source which you will use to build up your bibliography.

(i) *Indexes*. There are many standard bibliographical indexes available. In addition, a University library will have available a selection of specialist bibliographies in your own particular field. Printed bibliographies, however, are inevitably rather out of date by the time they reach the shelves, and a number of online services are now available (see Chapter 6).

(ii) *Abstracts*. Most of the social sciences have their own abstracting journals. These are journals which give brief (100 words or so) summaries of the contents of recently published articles, usually prepared by their author(s). If you are not sure from the title whether or not an article is likely to be relevant, the abstract ought to give you a reasonably good idea.

(iii) *References*. Bibliographical references from key books or recently printed articles are not only a good way to begin your search, they are also an invaluable way to cross-check on other references. It is becoming common to substitute an essay on sources or annotated bibliography for the traditional 'block' bibliography in many printed books, and this can have advantages (because comments are available to guide your choice) and disadvantages (because they are less complete in their coverage).

(iv) *Reviews*. The principal journals in your field will carry reviews (of individual books) or review articles (essays on a number of books on a particular subject area). Reviews can, however, be a disappointment, particularly where an opinionated reviewer has forgotten that the first task of the reviewer is to explain what is in the book, not what he or she thinks ought to have been in it.

Using Documentary Sources in the Project

Because of the practical, policy-oriented nature of much social science research, most if not all theses will have to contain a *history statement*, setting out the past history of the problem to be studied, setting out alternative policies that have been tried, evaluating their effectiveness and explaining the background to the research design of the thesis (see Mayer and Greenwood, 1980). This will utilize documentary sources exclusively, but in addition many theses will use documentary sources throughout. Whatever use is being made of such sources the obvious hope is to find a source or set of sources that will provide the sort of data that are most likely to be of use in answering the questions posed by the research topic. Such information, however, is not always directly available. The researcher may instead have to find out just what information is available and then see if it can be adapted to the purposes of the investigation.

In all cases, it is an absolute requirement of reputable academic work that future researchers must as far as possible be able to follow the same trail and if necessary to replicate the research. Given the intense and often acrimonious debates that have raged within the social sciences about the validity of certain approaches, other workers in the field expect to be able to 'decipher' the research, to uncover the assumptions on which it was based, to see how the data was obtained and analyzed, and to determine how far the results presented are based on the research and how far on other sources.

The following four points apply equally to research for the history statement or to research for the project itself:

1. *Assemble data systematically*. Remember you are reading for information and not for amusement. If you cast your net widely, as you should, you must

also discipline yourself and skip all but essential material. Avoid being side-tracked into interesting but profitless digressions.

The ideal is to be able to assemble and read sources in the logical order demanded by your project. Unfortunately this is rarely possible. By sensible planning, however, you can avoid being left, when you wish to use documentary material in the course of your research, in the position of wasting time for lack of some essential work or piece of information. By taking full and accurate notes you can also avoid the embarrassment of finding you have failed to recognize some vital piece of information when it finally falls into place.

You will almost certainly want to consult other theses on related topics. These are usually available on microfilm, but they take some time to arrive, so order them as early as possible. The inter-library loan system is very efficient, but it may still be worth your while to plan a short visit to certain other libraries instead. The best guide is *Dissertation Abstracts*, published annually by University of Michigan Press, Ann Arbor.

2. *Take notes selectively*. If you rely too much on memory, you remember your best quotation the day after you have handed in your thesis. But to do good research you have to master your material and be in full command of it, and this means exercising your memory to the full. Accurate note-taking serves as an essential record if memory fails. But the exercise also develops the memory in the way that you want it to, if you remember at all times that notes should be *selective*. Simply copying out paragraph after paragraph serves no useful purpose — you have to get the essential gist of the argument, together with the most telling points. If the record is of little or no value, a simple note to that effect will serve as a reminder not to bother with it again.

Keep notes on *standard sized* sheets of paper and record details of the source used (author name, title, publisher, place and date of publication, and, for an article, the name, volume, part, date and page numbers of the journal in which it occurs) *on the notes as well as in the card index/electronic bibliography*. A clear abbreviation or code on succeeding pages helps when you come to reassemble the material in outline form for writing up. A running note of the page number on which quotations or data occur can be conveniently kept in the left-hand margin. Notes on talks, lectures, conferences and all oral material should be properly identified by time, place and speaker.

3. *Never throw anything away*. Your records are the essential base on which your thesis depends, so make sure you keep them safe. Do not entrust irreplaceable material to the post if you can possibly help it; if you must,

divide it into a number of packets and keep a duplicate where possible. If you are doing fieldwork abroad, take extra care, and carry the most essential notes in your personal baggage.

If you are using a computer/wordprocessor, set the automatic backup facility for (say) ten minute intervals and back up *everything* on to floppy disks *every time* you leave the machine. You soon get used to this. Best of all, make and keep a duplicate of key data (and of your first draft chapters) on disk somewhere else, i.e. in a different building. For the cost (60p a disk) you get a lot of extra peace of mind.

However many times you have reworked your material, *never* destroy your records of the original data on which it is based and keep all notes which would enable you to reconstruct your chain of reasoning if any accident happened to it.

4. *Use the photocopier sparingly.* Photocopying something means that its content passes straight from one piece of paper to another without going through your head. If there is not much information on the page concerned, notes are a better and cheaper way of recording it. Excessive use of the photocopier is bad for the memory, and in extreme cases suggests that you do not really possess the faculty of selectivity essential to effective research. Photocopiers come into their own in enabling you to study tables, statistics and graphs in more detail and more quiet than a university library normally permits.

Conclusion

This chapter has tried to give you broad guidelines about the use of documentary data. Research students will need to spend time ensuring they are familiar with the source material for their own topics. Obviously your supervisor will help in this, but remember too that librarians have specialist knowledge about their collections. Do not be afraid to ask for their help.

Further Reading

One of the best generals books on documentary sources is John Scott's *A Matter of Record*. Derek Heater (1970), Elias Tuma (1971) and John R.M. Wilson (1974) are all useful, while James Hoopes (1979) *Oral History: An Introduction For Students* has relevance for social scientists generally. Finally, Robert R. Mayer and Ernest Greenwood (1980) address basic questions in the nature and purpose of social science research.

References

HEATER, D. (1970) 'History and the social sciences', in BALLARD, M. (Ed.) *New Movements in the Study and Teaching of History*, London, Temple-Smith.

HOOPES, J. (1979) *Oral History: An Introduction For Students*, Chapel Hill, University of North Carolina Press.

MAYER, R.R. and GREENWOOD, E. (1980) *The Design of Social Policy Research*, Englewood Cliffs, NJ, Prentice-Hall.

SCOTT, J. (1990) *A Matter of Record: Documentary Sources in Social Research*, Oxford, Polity.

TUMA, E. (1971) *Economic History and the Social Sciences: Problems of Methodology*, Berkeley, University of California Press.

WILSON, J.R.M. (1974) *Research Guide in History*, Morristown, NJ, General Learning Press.

Chapter 11

Negotiating with Agencies

Jackie Powell and Robin Lovelock

Introduction

This chapter is concerned with an important aspect of research practice which is commonly under-emphasized in methodological texts. Empirical research in the social sciences generally requires access to data and to research subjects. Where a public service agency or a commercial undertaking is involved, the ultimate quality of a piece of research, indeed the very possibility of carrying it out, depends upon the researcher successfully negotiating and sustaining such access. If, as is often the case in applied work, the researcher hopes to influence future policy and practice in the agency concerned and/or more widely, negotiating the findings and recommendations is similarly crucial. In this chapter we shall examine in some detail various aspects of negotiating with agencies, using the stages of the research process as a framework.

Agencies vary in their openness to change and more particularly in their willingness to look critically at their own activities. How they perceive 'research' is influenced by previous experience of investigations of various sorts. Further, organizations cannot adequately be understood as unitary wholes. Identified sub-groups within an agency are among the interested parties to a piece of research, and may well hold differing views about its relevance (Smith and Cantley, 1985; 1988). For example, where a particular service is to be investigated, professional practitioners such as social workers, GPs or nurses may be primarily concerned about the impact of the proposed study on service users, clients or patients; service managers may question the appropriateness of devoting staff time to the research and its other resource costs. There will usually be particular areas of shared concern, but with differences in interpretation and perceived importance. In addition, there are usually a number of interested parties outside the organization itself. By no means least important are the users or consumers of the service, who themselves also generally contain several sub-groups (Powell and Lovelock, 1987a).

The authors' view is that research involving agencies, whether for a higher degree or not, is best conceived as a partnership. A balance has to be achieved whereby the researcher is perceived as both an 'outsider', largely free from the influences of any particular group within the agency, essentially independent and open-minded, and as 'one of us', an 'insider', with an understanding of the agency and the issues important to it as perceived at different levels in the organization. Taking some account of each of the different views is an important part of clarifying the researcher's role and interests relative to those of people within the agency and others outside. However, actual negotiations will vary with the nature of the research proposed and the type of access required. For example, the need for access may be limited to one particular group, such as the users of the agency's services or its senior managers.

The research student may have a number of particular issues to handle, depending upon whether they are employed by the agency concerned and wish to carry out a piece of practice-based research or whether they are outsiders wanting to investigate that particular aspect of the 'real world'. In any case it is imperative for the student to negotiate a degree of freedom over the scope of their study and the dissemination of its findings, especially where the preparation of a higher degree thesis is concerned, with the requirement that it be publicly available.

A number of issues concerning negotiations with agencies will now be examined, using the several broad stages in a research study as a framework. Adopting this approach reflects the authors' view that the process of negotiation mirrors the process of the research, beginning with early informal discussion of ideas as a first step towards gaining approval in principle, to a formal research proposal, proceeding ultimately to discussion around the dissemination of findings. Readers should try to keep in mind that the stages are not entirely discrete and that the negotiating tasks themselves interrelate, both conceptually and in practice. This being so, there are inevitably areas of overlap and some repetition in our discussion of them.

Underlying what is seen as a continuous process of negotiation lies the view that access to any agency cannot be presumed or taken for granted, but is rather given as a privilege not to be abused. It requires careful and well-considered negotiation from the outset, while its maintenance is an ongoing task for the researcher, resting to a large extent on the way they present and conduct the study throughout the period. While we make much of the number of different individuals and groups with whom access may have to be negotiated, our primary concern might be said to be with the quality rather than the quantity of access.

Formulating the Aims and Purposes of the Research

This aspect, perhaps more than those which follow, is affected by whether the researcher is an 'insider' or an 'outsider' in relation to the agency concerned, and whether the study is primarily the idea of the researcher or is essentially initiated and commissioned by the agency. Often, and particularly for the research student, the reality may be rather less clear-cut than this, with the agency prepared to lend its support to an idea initiated by the researcher but seen as relevant to the organization.

The would-be researcher needs to be or to become familiar with the agency, including any formal procedures for considering research proposals. They also need to identify likely sources of data and useful personal contacts at an early stage. Early discussion of initial ideas is necessary, to establish the level of interest and possible support within the identified agency for research in the general area proposed. The immediate responses of people in various parts of the agency may indicate the feasibility or otherwise of alternative ways of investigating the topic. Notwithstanding our stress on the fact that an organization consists of a variety of groups, 'the official line' — in practice usually that of senior management — is most important here. For the member of staff contemplating a study of part of their own agency, their line manager and training/personnel section are crucial actors and may well be the route to 'the agency's view'.

As part of formulating a proposal and planning a research strategy — particularly if several groups or agencies are involved — it is sometimes worthwhile for researchers explicitly to set down for themselves the various 'stakeholders' and to try to identify their current involvement in the area which the research seeks to examine, the possible benefits of the research to them, its possible costs in their terms, and the power of each group — and of key individuals — to influence the completion of the research positively and/or adversely. In doing this, it is helpful to distinguish which of the stakeholders are internal and which external to the specific research setting: in other words, from which of them will a direct and from which an indirect contribution be required.

Presentation of a Formal Proposal

The next stage is the preparation of a formal research proposal, setting out the aims of the study, research methods and sources of data, and the time-scale and/or phases into which the study will fall. Depending on the nature and degree of agency participation required, there may be a need for detailed discussion of the overall proposal with appropriate agency representatives.

Among the key topics likely to be involved, in addition to probable demands on staff time, intrusiveness with respect to service users, and the relevance of the research to the agency, are arrangements for any possible feedback. It is vital to secure an understanding that whatever form(s) of feedback the agency may welcome or require, the student's primary aim is the production of a thesis. The agency must be left in no doubt about the fact that this document will be publicly available. Ownership of the research data is thus a key issue, with no room for lack of clarity if later difficulties are to be avoided (Punch, 1986). Any proposal should contain appropriate statements about confidentiality in respect of individual respondents and rights to publication, both for the thesis and for other possible publications in academic or professional journals.

The way in which the proposal is documented is an important demonstration to the agency of the researcher's ability to communicate ideas, and a general indication that the research will be conducted in a professional manner. At this stage negotiations will normally be with fairly senior staff, although these may not be the people most directly affected by the actual carrying out of the research. Where appropriate, the research proposal provides the framework for obtaining agreement in principle. It forms the basis for seeking further specific access to various parts of the agency and areas of its work, which in certain contexts will require further written or formal application.

A proposal of a rather general nature also makes it possible to take account of organizational developments and changes. In some contexts this is particularly relevant: for example where the study is concerned with researching either the management of change or the impact of change. In such cases the overall strategy or framework for the research must necessarily state only broad aims, retaining the flexibility which will be necessary to incorporate both anticipated and unexpected changes as they occur (Powell and Lovelock, 1989).

Although it is natural to be defensive about your proposal and to seek a swift and positive response, the old adage 'marry in haste, repent at leisure' is very pertinent. If at all possible, direct contact with those making decisions about the research is highly desirable. It may be helpful if the research supervisor is involved at this stage. Find out what questions in the general area they feel are most relevant. Try to help them identify possible benefits from the research and, equally if not more importantly, encourage them to articulate any uncertainties or negative concerns they may have. These should then be directly discussed. In one sense this amounts to seeking to delay the central decision, 'yes or no?', in the interests of thoroughly exploring what is involved. The benefits of so doing are to be found later, when a sound relationship between researcher and key agency staff will assist the resolution of any difficulties and the acceptance of critical comment.

Identifying Sources of Data

At the proposal stage, likely sources of data to which access will be required must be identified and any conditions imposed by the agency established. For example, access to personal case files will require some guarantees regarding confidentiality and individuals' entitlement to anonymity; this is not simply a likely agency condition, but a central part of professional research ethics (Social Research Association, 1984; Social Services Research Group, 1990). As well as personal files, information covered by the Official Secrets Act or by legislation governing commercial initiatives may be required by the research. Even if only names and addresses are sought it is important that those responsible in the agency see the relevance and appropriateness of this information being passed to an 'outsider'.

It is important to remember that information kept on a computer about living identifiable individuals is governed by a number of principles enshrined in the 1984 Data Protection Act. With certain exemptions, 'data users' — people controlling and using such data (often corporate bodies) — must be registered under the terms of the Act. 'Data subjects' — individuals about whom non-exempted forms of information are stored on computer — have certain rights of access to such information and are entitled to any errors being corrected, to erasure in certain circumstances, and to compensation for damage suffered as a result of inadequately protected or inaccurate data about them. It is necessary to ensure that you are allowed to use the data for research purposes and/or that you are registered through your institution under the Data Protection Act.

The need to attend meetings and otherwise to observe the activities of the agency and its staff should also be clarified and agreed at this stage. Whilst some of the required contact with agency staff will necessarily be informal, it is important to clarify the extent to which formal observation of staff or users of agencies' services is a proposed method of study.

Gaining access to formal documentation other than personal files can also need careful negotiation. For example, a well argued explanation may be necessary as to why access to minutes of meetings or to files of correspondence concerning the development of policies is required, if they are to be made available.

Gaining Access to Agency-Generated Data

Clearing official channels regarding access to existing sources of information, whether manually or electronically stored, forms the first stage of gaining access to particular bodies of data. Once achieved it is generally followed by more specific negotiations, often involving some element of personal contact. There are two important points here.

First, there is always a need for realism regarding the actual availability of recorded data. While access to agency records and other documentation may be given, this is no guarantee of its overall quality nor its uniformity. There may be considerable discrepancies between what is reported as routinely recorded and the reality at the 'coal face', both in terms of procedures and actual records. This applies to the important area of financial systems, which agencies increasingly wish to see incorporated in evaluative research on services.

Second, access to case files or similar records necessitates direct negotiation with administrative and clerical staff, as well as with front-line professionals and their immediate managers. An instruction from 'higher up' to comply is rarely conducive to a good relationship with staff in direct control of access to files. Clerical staff have limited power, but their cooperation is invaluable and irreplaceable. The researcher is well advised to respect them and to earn their cooperation. Clear explanations of what is involved are essential; any workload implications for the staff concerned should be acknowledged openly.

Collecting Research Data — Involving Agency-Based Participants

We now turn to agency staff as possible research subjects, rather than as gatekeepers to agency records of various kinds. Ensuring the collaboration of staff in the agency, which in some practice-based research means one's colleagues, is crucial where the study involves the generation of research data either indirectly, for example through observation, or directly, from questionnaires or interviews with agency staff. Once again, automatic cooperation cannot be assumed on the basis of 'higher' approval. Adequate explanations must be offered regarding the nature of the study, why the specific information needs to be acquired in the ways proposed, and how it might be used. Appropriate guarantees of confidentiality and subsequent anonymity should be fully discussed. In doing this it is important to be realistic about the use of key informants and the extent to which some personnel are readily identifiable by their role or particular activities. For example, although posts rather than names would be used, it is very difficult to conduct an evaluative study of a particular agency service without key individuals in responsible and possibly unique positions being identifiable, at least by those in the agency concerned.

Gaining colleagues' cooperation may require some bargaining, for example by offering additional feedback or an early opportunity to discuss the presentation of findings. It is important to remember that there normally has to be 'some pay-off for them in giving access' (Preedy and Riches, 1985, cited in Bell, 1987:43) as well as, often, their time and commitment to the research task.

While there can be advantages in being an insider researching the agency in which you practice, there are also important potential difficulties. Changing roles is not always straightforward. Receiving the confidences of one's professional colleagues as research data can be problematic, as it can lead to a conflict of commitments to the research and to professional practice (Bell, 1987). If this has not been anticipated and, preferably, discussed in advance, colleagues may feel compromised or seek to withdraw at a later stage. This is another example of the advisability of 'delaying the decision' — to agree to cooperate as much as to withhold participation — until the possible implications have been discussed in some detail.

Particular problems can arise with the observation of staff activities. Attendance at meetings is generally easier to negotiate than observation of 'professional activities.' In both contexts, non-participant observation can be experienced as intrusive, whereas semi-participant observation requires considerable expertise to maintain the right balance. Researchers in meetings where issues central to the questions being addressed by the research are under discussion tend to get asked their views. This is all the more likely to occur where a good rapport has been established. In most situations of this kind neither blank refusal on methodological principle nor giving one's inevitably half-formed thoughts are adequate responses. Some brief but relatively non-committal contribution will often serve to sustain one's credibility. There are obvious ethical difficulties where subjects are unaware of being observed (see Chapter 12). If data collected in this way are likely to be used and presented as findings, *post hoc* consent may be necessary.

Collecting Research Data — Establishing Contact with Users of the Agency's Services

Many research projects in areas where agencies are explicitly or implicitly involved require the collection of the views of users of services. In some cases the researcher may be permitted to make the initial contact on their own behalf; in others the agency concerned may wish to retain a role as intermediary. This is an area where the researcher's credibility is most important; the most careful attention must be paid to how the research is presented and access or consent negotiated (Cassell, 1982). There must be adequate discussion with agency staff, who will need to be confident that their clients will be treated with respect. Having one's own work with clients open to investigation by a third party can be an uncomfortable experience, particularly if much of that work is conducted through an essentially personal relationship.

As with negotiating access to agency staff as research subjects, the issues of confidentiality and anonymity are of central importance; the principles and procedures involved are also similar. In detailing the procedures proposed, account must be taken of the ethical principles and conventions of the relevant disciplines. Staff from a range of professions will require guarantees and assurances regarding the likely benefits of involving users in the study and of any possible harm which could result to their clients or patients: for example a degree of upset to elderly, mentally or physically ill or otherwise vulnerable people. The ways in which informed consent will be sought and the right to refuse indicated are of special concern. In negotiating agency approval for direct access to users of its services, the researcher needs to convey an awareness of the ethical issues involved and to be sensitive to professionals' concerns in this area.

The agency may wish to make the initial contact with its users, in order to introduce the research and to ensure that the right to refuse is made clear. Sometimes there are advantages for the researcher in being thus identified with the agency in the eyes of the respondent. In other contexts, for example when the service is being evaluated, it must be clear to all concerned that the research is independent. In such cases there can be disadvantages for the researcher and the agency in the latter making the contact. In these situations it is appropriate and preferable for the researcher to argue for direct initial access to the users of the agencies' services, giving proper assurances regarding the ways in which individual subjects will be invited to participate or to refuse further contact.

Analyzing the Data and Preparing Reports

This is often the stage in which the researcher is least directly involved with the agency. However, the rewards for careful initial negotiations become evident at this stage, and likewise the penalties for inadequate preparatory discussion are exacted. The quantity and, perhaps more importantly, the quality of the data collected over time will reflect the level of success achieved in gaining access to agency documentation, staff and users. It is also the time when 'bargains' struck have to be acknowledged.

Although secondary to the preparation of the thesis, it may be important to keep the agency context in view when writing up. Where immediate colleagues have been significantly involved, or where some specific feedback has been requested by the agency, it is important to give some attention not only to the professional and technical issues surrounding the analysis and interpretation of the data, but also to how this information can be presented in ways both accessible and relevant to the agency.

In some situations feedback, for example by means of an interim report, can constitute an important part of the research study itself (Powell and Lovelock, 1987b:41–5; 1989). It can be consciously used as a tool for 'respondent validation' (McKeganey and Bloor, 1981), checking the researcher's interpretation of practices and situations with those involved in them day by day.

Presenting and Disseminating Findings

The research student's primary goal is the successful completion of their thesis, which will need to contain discussion of both methodology and findings with due respect for confidentiality. We have emphasized the public status of the thesis and the importance of this being clearly understood from the outset by any agency involved. The question of dissemination in a wider sense then arises and it may well be necessary and appropriate to discuss proposals with representatives of the agency concerned. It is commonly the case with commissioned work from professional researchers that several different forms of report are produced for different audiences.

A short report, identifying key findings and their implications for the agency, may have been requested. This should anyway be supplied in acknowledgment of the agency's consent and in most cases hopefully active support, particularly where the researcher is in its employ. More than one form of feedback, written and/or verbal, may be appropriate to the agency, given the different needs and interests represented within it, although this has consequent time and resource implications for the researcher and a degree of caution is appropriate.

Conclusion: Partnership and Credibility

The manner in which negotiations are conducted can substantially influence the quality and the quantity of data collected and thus the overall success of the project. As a means of emphasizing the importance of the personal and professional credibility of the researcher, both on paper and in person, this chapter concludes with a brief discussion around the need to develop and sustain a shared or common interest on the part of the agency and the researcher throughout the study period. Whether the person undertaking the research is an 'informed outsider' or an 'insider standing back', some form of dialogue has to be established at the outset, whereby certain expectations and obligations for both parties are acknowledged. There is then a continual need to demonstrate and sustain the principles of such a dialogue in specific contexts.

Much of this relies on the manner in which researchers present themselves in the many and varied negotiations with members of the agency, and crucially on their ability to present the work involved as useful and relevant. This has to be done in a variety of ways. The ability to prepare a formal written research proposal for a key agency representative and an accessible letter of introduction to a service user are equally important research tasks in this context, and both can be significant dimensions of the continuing process of negotiation. The ability to communicate clearly and concisely both in formal meetings and in informal settings may each also be part of fulfilling the researcher's role. Personal credibility and the ease with which the researcher can relate both to people working within the agency and to those who use its services are crucial. Given the many potentially interested parties, implicitly or explicitly acknowledged in most of the foregoing discussion, this is a demanding task and one which involves a high level of interpersonal skill.

Differing expectations about the value of research, both in general and regarding the specific project in hand, have to be recognized and areas of common interest continually sought. In some situations research is seen as being a low priority for the agency and a luxury for those able to undertake it. It may be necessary to challenge this view, albeit in a way which enables some agreement to be reached about gaining and sustaining access. Persistence and tenacity, accompanied by a cheerful and gently encouraging manner, are often needed in the face of delaying or obstructive tactics. The value of the research may well be judged by the degree to which the researcher demonstrates her/his own belief in its value and its relevance to the agency and the wider community.

By way of final comment, successful negotiations lie at the heart of successful research studies. They have two essential ingredients: the credibility of the individual researcher working within an acknowledged code of practice, and the ability of the agency to 'enable social enquiry to be undertaken as objectively as possible, with a view to providing information or explanations rather than advocacy' (Social Research Association, 1984). Together the researcher and as many relevant members of the agency as necessary and appropriate to the study concerned can then establish a relationship based on partnership.

Suggestions for Reading

This chapter has deliberately concentrated on the practical matters involved in gaining and sustaining access to service-providing agencies. This is in part a recognition that other methodological texts have a tendency not to give adequate or sufficiently direct attention to this area, addressing it only in passing, usually as an aspect of a discussion of surveys or interviewing, observational work, or some other research method. Judith Bell's Open University text, *Doing Your Research Project: A Guide for First-Time Researchers in Education and Social Science* (1987), is a valuable exception. It contains a short chapter (pp. 42–7) on negotiating access, with a useful example of 'inside(r)' research in the educational field and a checklist of tasks and issues. Also in a similar spirit to our own contribution is Buchanan *et al.*'s paper 'Getting in, getting on, getting out, and getting back' in *Doing Research in Organisations*.

More generally, there is a growing body of 'experiential methodology' — historical, sociological and/or autobiographical accounts of actual studies — along with historical and sociological analyses of the role of research in policy-making. Works in this area include Bell and Newby (1977), Bell and Roberts (1984), Booth (1988), Bulmer (1982), Fletcher (1974), Punch (1986) and Thomas (1985). On similar themes, albeit in a specific area, *Research, Policy and Planning*, one of the two main British journals serving the community of researchers doing academic or 'in-house' work closely related to the activities of social services departments, has since 1983 published a number of interesting short papers. For example, Poland (1988) reveals the difficulties caused by failing to recognize different interests and expectations. *Social Services Research*, published by the Department of Social Policy and Social Work at Birmingham University, is also a valuable source for researchers in the social services field. While its contents mainly report substantive studies, recent editorials have reflected on the role of research in local authority and health service contexts and a number of articles in recent years have had an experiential dimension.

References

BELL, C. and NEWBY, H. (Eds) (1977) *Doing Sociological Research*, London, Allen and Unwin.

BELL, C. and ROBERTS, H. (Eds) (1984) *Social Researching: Politics, Problems, Practice*, London, Routledge and Kegan Paul.

BELL, J. (1987) *Doing Your Research Project: A Guide for First-Time Researchers in Education and Social Science*, Milton Keynes, Open University Press.

BOOTH, T. (1988) *Developing Policy Research*, Aldershot, Gower.

BUCHANAN, D., BODDY, D. and MCCALMAN, J. (1988) 'Getting in, getting on, getting out, and getting back', in BRYMAN, A. (Ed.) *Doing Research in Organisations*, London, Routledge.

BULMER, M. (1982) *The Uses of Social Research*, London, Allen and Unwin.

CASSELL, J. (1982) 'Harms, benefits, wrongs, and rights in fieldwork', in

BEAUCHAMP, T.L. *et al.* (Eds), *Ethical Issues in Social Science Research*, Baltimore, Johns Hopkins University Press.

FLETCHER, C. (1974) *Beneath the Surface: An Account of Three Styles of Sociological Research*, London, Routledge and Kegan Paul.

MCKEGANEY, N.P. and BLOOR, M.J. (1981) 'On the retrieval of sociological descriptions: Respondent validation and the critical case of ethnomethodology', *International Journal of Sociology and Social Policy*, 1, pp. 58–69.

POLAND, F. (1988) 'Some dilemmas of in-house social services research: Problems in evaluating services to childminders', *Research, Policy and Planning*, 6(2), pp. 7–14.

POWELL, J. and LOVELOCK, R. (1987a) 'The role of consumers' views in the evaluation of services: A case study — the travelling day hospital', *Social Services Research*, 16(1), pp. 16–29.

POWELL, J. and LOVELOCK, R. (1987b) *Northern Road: A Study of Developing Services for Drug Misusers*, Portsmouth, SSRIU, Portsmouth Polytechnic.

POWELL, J. and LOVELOCK, R. (1989) 'The development of community based adult mental health services — A research contribution', *Psychiatric Bulletin*, 13, 51, pp. 662–6.

PUNCH, M. (1986) *The Politics and Ethics of Fieldwork*, Sage University Paper series on Qualitative Research Methods, Volume 3, Beverly Hills, Sage.

SMITH, G. and CANTLEY, C. (1985) *Assessing Health Care: A Study in Organisational Evaluation*, Milton Keynes, Open University Press.

SMITH, G. and CANTLEY, C. (1988) 'Pluralistic Evaluation', in LISHMAN, J. (Ed.) *Evaluation: Research Highlights in Social Work 8*, 2nd ed., London, Jessica Kingsley Publishers.

SOCIAL RESEARCH ASSOCIATION (1984) *Ethical Guidelines*.

SOCIAL SERVICES RESEARCH GROUP (1990) *Code of Good Practice for Research, Evaluation, Monitoring and Review Studies in the Personal Social Services*.

THOMAS, P. (1985) *The Aims and Outcomes of Social Policy Research*, London, Croom Helm.

Chapter 12

Ethical Issues

Tony Rees

Over the past two or three decades, disquiet about the standard of ethics in social research has been chiefly occasioned by a few projects which achieved notoriety. Some of these involved allegations of straight fraud: Sir Cyril Burt, for example, doyen of the psychological profession, stood accused of inventing not only experimental material but also research collaborators in his anxiety to bolster his preconceived notions about the nature of human intelligence (Hearnshaw, 1979). Others were community studies in which the identities of localities or individuals turned out to have been insufficiently concealed (Vidich and Bensman, 1958). Another category consists of deceitfully constructed psychological experiments: Milgram (1974), for example, conned volunteers into administering so-called 'electric shocks' to subjects who failed to comply with the instructions of a scientist impresario. In a fourth group of cases, the problems were ones of sponsorship: Project Camelot, concerned with charting the propensity for 'internal conflict' in a number of Latin American countries, had to be called off when the involvement of the United States Army and Defence Department became known.

Most of the highly contentious projects, however, utilized covert participant observation, sometimes involving deception on a spectacular scale. Laud Humphreys observed numerous homosexual acts in Chicago public lavatories ('tearooms') by acting as a 'watch-queen' or look-out. He noted the numbers of the automobiles in which the participants had driven to the scene, obtained the names of the vehicles' owners from the police while concealing why he wanted them, and then interviewed the men over a year later, disguising his appearance, ostensibly as part of a 'health survey' totally unconnected with the activities which had determined their inclusion in the sample.

Although the rights and wrongs of covert research is an important subject in itself, concentration on a few sometimes lurid examples probably does a disservice to those embarking on social research. The implication is that ethical questions mainly arise on the extreme margins of the research endeavour, whereas in fact they are commonplace: most researchers will encounter one or two in the course of their enquiries. They occur in all the social sciences and with research dealing with all types of materials. They may affect, or be raised by, any of the actors involved in a project. They may arise at any stage in the research process (in the initial conception and design of a project, in the obtaining of funds, while negotiating access to field settings, during the course of fieldwork, or on publication of the results).

These matters will need to be treated systematically, but first of all I want to make the point that the more one emphasizes the 'normality' of ethical problems in social research, the more difficult they become to spot and to sort out unambiguously. Barnes's definition seems straightforward:

> By ethical problems I mean those that arise when we try to decide between one course of action and another not in terms of expediency and efficiency but by reference to standards of what is morally right or wrong. (Barnes, 1979:16)

However, later in the same paragraph, he blurs this with a caveat:

> in discussing social research, we must look at practical and pragmatic considerations whenever these bear on ethical issues as they arise in practice. Honesty may sometimes pay but there are other times when a price has to be paid for being honest.

Circumstances, therefore, alter cases: and it is perhaps not surprising that the protagonists in recent debates on research ethics, both from within and without the academic community, have given several and varied answers to such general (and relevant) questions as:

— Should researchers aim to be totally open and above-board with the other parties involved in their project? Should they seek 'informed consent' from all research subjects before administering any research instrument?
— Are there research topics, areas of private behaviour or methods of enquiry which should be 'off bounds' to researchers?
— Should any promises made be kept (as an absolute requirement)?
— Should researchers be able to avail themselves of a 'public interest defence' in which the social scientific or public policy importance of enquiries or findings overrides other considerations?
— Should the aim be the avoidance of any foreseeable harm to research subjects, especially placing them (and junior researchers) in physical, legal or moral danger?
— Should researchers have in the forefront of their minds the interests of

those who may come after them, since their own activities, and the reputation they engender, may close off settings for further research, at least while wounds heal?

Bearing these questions in mind, we can return to the diverse contexts in which ethical problems may arise. They are obviously more often present in psychological experiments or in sociological or social anthropological field-studies than elsewhere. But for an example occurring in another social scientific discipline we can take the occasion in 1985 when a group of academic accountants, who had been afforded cooperation and research facilities by the National Coal Board, published an article in a professional journal which quarrelled with the methods employed by the Board to decide on pit-closures (Berry *et al.*, 1986). The authors are careful to explain that they worked from published data, and did not utilize any additional materials — confidential or otherwise — collected by them in the course of their researches (Berry *et al.*, 1986). However this intervention by a group of apparent 'insiders' understandably generated a good deal of media interest at the height of the miners' strike. I shall consider some of the issues raised by this incident later.

Those political scientists, social policy specialists and others who work essentially with and from documentary materials are also not immune from ethical considerations. Keeping within the libel, copyright, and official secrets laws and the thirty year rule restricting publication of certain official documents may be matters of prudence rather than of ethics, but you cannot be too careful. The writer in the 1920s who wrote about the famous trial of Madeleine Smith who had been found 'not proven' of having poisoned her lover in 1857, must have felt safe enough when he opined that she had, in fact, committed the deed: however, the lady reappeared in the United States, and might have sued him for damages. The British law of libel can strike closer to home. Some extraordinarily inexplicit passages in Colin Bell's retrospective account of the second sociological study of Banbury (Bell, 1977) are owing to a fear — indeed, apparently a threat — that he might be liable to legal action on the part of his own erstwhile colleagues.

Those who write about the recently dead — who cannot be libelled — will often cite other, less self-regarding, reasons for their discretion. It is common to find in the introductions to biographies passages like the following, from Philip Williams's work on Hugh Gaitskell:

It is a political biography. I have avoided amateur psychology, and do not consider it appropriate for an outsider to explore Gaitskell's more intimate relationships while most of his family and close friends are still alive and entitled to their privacy. But I think I have omitted no important influences on his intellectual and political development. (Williams, 1979, p. xiii)

A rather different point raised by the use of documentary materials is that there appears to be a feeling that once a document has been printed it enters the public realm. However those responsible for the production and dissemination of such matter may not see things that way. Homan comments:

> sect literature in the form of weekly magazines, assembly bulletins and missionary newsletters is no more accessible to the stranger or its circulation no less controlled than platform performances in large crusades and convention in which tape-recording is widely practised. Literature searching and content analysis are merely forms of covert non-participant strategy distinguished from observation and interviewing only by the format of observed data. (Homan, 1982:113)

Admittedly, this passage forms part of Homan's defence against accusations that he pursued unacceptably underhand methods in his study of old-time pentecostalists, but his point is surely valid.

Social research has become a complex business, and there are several parties with an interest or stake in its conduct and outcomes. Barnes distinguishes between four sets of actors: 'scientists' (i.e. the researchers), 'citizens' (i.e. the subjects of research), 'sponsors' (who provide the financial or other resources) and 'gatekeepers' (who control access to research subjects and settings) (Barnes, 1979:14). These roles are not necessarily discrete: any of the actors may be instrumental in initiating research, except perhaps for the gatekeepers — and even then sponsors are frequently also gatekeepers, as when an institution commissions research into its own activities, but with restrictions on the access accorded. 'Scientists', of course, are also 'citizens', and the claim made by the accountants who ran into trouble with the National Coal Board was essentially that their responsibilities as citizens outweighed any other obligations they might have.

There are some problems with the nomenclature. The word 'scientist' conjures up the image of someone in a white coat, and many social researchers will not find this an appropriate description of what they are about. 'Citizen' avoids the overtones of subservience contained in the 'subjects' — or, even worse, the 'objects' — of research, but it begs some important questions. Many of those studied are not citizens, or are not yet or not fully citizens — guest workers and illegal immigrants, children, prisoners, the mentally handicapped and others receiving social care. In such instances, permission for access for research purposes may routinely be given by others, supposedly on their behalf. This poses problems, particularly when the population being studied is either literally or metaphorically a captive one, as in custodial institutions or schools. The danger is both that the rights of individuals in such groups may be ignored and that their participation in research is obtained 'under orders', with uncertain results for the reliability of research outcomes. In their prison research, Cohen and Taylor (1972) aimed to get over this through obtaining entrance to their research setting by means of an extra-mural course which they ran — and without clearing with the authorities what they were doing.

Some social scientists — particularly, of course, those of a left-wing persuasion — take the view that the researchers should be particularly sensitive to the interests of those who lack the means of getting their voices heard (Galliher, 1982). The institutionally powerful, it is argued, are well able to look after themselves. In some circumstances, researchers may be fully justified in concealing their true purposes from them. Van der Berghe (1964) makes this case in relation to the South African government. This line of argument is an interesting reversal of the view prevailing in the earliest days of social research, when the anthropologist summoned 'natives' to his verandah to find out about local customs and institutions, or the poverty investigator quizzed the urban proletariat in Britain and North America about the details of their expenditure, at least in part because these groups were not thought as of having rights which could be intruded upon.

However, where the aims of sponsors and researchers diverge the feelings of the former may very well be bruised, especially if it is felt that the researchers have not been completely straight in revealing their intentions. Few social policy specialists took seriously the thesis behind Sir Keith Joseph's initiative for the study of 'transmitted deprivation'. They tended to favour instead a theory of poverty rooted in economic and social structures. Nevertheless some of them understandably felt that the chance of substantial research funding was too good to miss. Berthoud (1983:168) notes:

> If the Transmitted Deprivation Working Party was clear on one
> point, it was that the centre of its programme should consist of the
> study of 'intergenerational continuities'. Astonishingly, this feature
> of 'deprivation' is not a central theme of the final report on the
> programme, and there is no summary of the evidence on this point.

There has been speculation that Sir Keith's sense of betrayal as a result of this experience directly led to the Social Science Research Council losing its name, and only narrowly avoiding losing its life (Cherns, 1986).

Since this episode, too — and more importantly — the balance has tended to shift from the researcher to the sponsor, with the relative shortage of research funds and the acceptance of the Rothschild principle of clearly defined contracts for government-commissioned research. The right of researchers to publish their findings has been dented under such contracts, and there are important reports which have been mouldering on the shelves of government departments — for example Brian McLaughlin's study of rural poverty, completed in 1985.

It is important that researchers should avoid signing away their rights if at all possible. Maurice Punch entered into a legally enforceable agreement with the 'herbivorous progressives' of the Dartington Trust — and found that they could turn to a meat diet when he sought to publish some fairly fundamental criticisms of the progressive education provided by Dartington School (Punch, 1986:79). However the young postgraduate is clearly in a weak position when faced with sponsors (even apparently beneficent ones) who control access to research settings: tough intervention by supervisors may be necessary to lessen this power imbalance in negotiations.

Some sponsorship may be sufficiently tainted to make researchers very wary of accepting money from it, the tobacco industry being a case in point. Some would certainly add the US Army and Defence Department, although a revisit to Project Camelot prompts the reflection that its sponsors were surprisingly open — innocent almost — in the way they proceeded (Horowitz, 1967). Social scientists from all over the world were sent copies of relevant documents and were invited to planning sessions — including Johan Galtung, the distinguished Norwegian sociologist (and pacifist) who was instrumental in making known in Chile what was afoot. It was also made clear that basic research, not applied research, was envisaged. If there was a moral issue — and not just a prudential one — involved in Project Camelot, it was one of 'research colonialism'.

Are there areas of enquiry so sensitive that researchers should be barred from them? This issue was raised by the Wichita jury trials, in which the deliberations of juries were recorded, with the permission of the trial judge, but without the knowledge of the jurors themselves. As Martin Bulmer (1982:220) says, this was 'research which ... flagrantly violated both the privacy of individuals and of a "sacred" social institution.' However there is a danger of obscurantism here: we know all too little about how jurors perform the crucial public role allotted to them in the administration of justice. Nevertheless, there is always the possibility that we can find out what we need by means other than those employed in Wichita. In this area, simulations may be a feasible alternative, with carefully assembled mock cases put to panels of magistrates or the general public (representing jurors). This was the method utilized by Hood in his study of decision-making in cases involving motoring offenders (Hood, 1970).

There may nevertheless be institutions which can only be studied by covert means. Simon Holdaway (1982:63) tells us that he opted for covert research 'without much difficulty' when he returned to the police force after secondment on to a sociology degree course and enrolled for postgraduate work. In his case he was probably right, since the combined role of serving officer and acknowledged researcher into the police would have produced tensions very difficult to sustain. However the possibilities of using covert methods to prise open even such a relatively closed occupational community were amply demonstrated by David Smith and his associates at the Policy Studies Institute in their study of the Metropolitan Police, particularly in their documentation of the racism prevalent in sections of the Force (Smith and Gray, 1983).

No one, therefore, should embark on covert research without very careful consideration of alternatives. The psychological malaise attendant upon deception should also be borne in mind. Homan confesses:

> I must admit that, upon withdrawal from the field, I was troubled by an acute feeling of having betrayed my subjects and that this has endured ... [However] my abiding and retrospective misgivings about covertness tend to relate to the feelings and personal ethics of the researcher rather than to the rights of his subjects. The skills of covert observation and interviewing which I practised in the field carried over to my personal relationships ... with detrimental effect. Even drinking coffee with colleagues, I found I was practising covert observation and storing data in the mind to be recorded at the next private opportunity. Whereas in the field my subjects had become my friends, out of it my friends my subjects. (Homan, 1982:116–7)

However it must also be admitted that research is a peculiar activity, and it is rare for the intentions of researchers to be transparent to the subjects of research. It would clearly not be feasible, for instance, for the interviewer to explain the motives behind each question to the respondent: quite apart from anything else, this would render the results worthless. 'Informed consent' is therefore an impossibly tough requirement if these two words are taken literally. However, 'half-informed consent', although more realistic, does not have much of an idealistic ring about it. Social researchers obviously cannot be permitted to bug their way round London, like the spycatchers. But, on the other hand, there is an element of dissimulation in even the most above-board social enquiry. There is a balance here which has to be struck by each researcher as an individual.

Research into deviant or marginal groups raises further considerations. There may be physical risks, for example in studying criminal gangs, and there is always the possibility that researchers may put themselves on the wrong side of the law. The main problem is one of obtaining and retaining the confidence of those with whom the investigator is working. Judith Okely describes the steps she found it necessary to take in her anthropological study of gypsies in Southern England:

> I explained that I was a student wanting to know more about the Travellers' way of life. However, many who did not ask assumed that I was ... a council employee.... There were other suspicions: that I was a journalist, a police collaborator, a foot-loose heiress, a girl-friend of the warden, a drug addict and hippy, or someone on the run from the police. I discouraged all these images except the last. (Okely, 1983:41)

The ethical problems which will be encountered in a project cannot, or certainly cannot always, be foreseen and prepared for at the start, even if some topics and methods can be seen in advance to carry greater risks than others. The mode of operation in which would-be researchers trawl the literature and then present their supervisors or funding bodies with a list of pre-cooked hypotheses which they intend to test is itself productive of a certain amount of minor fraud or self-deception, since many of the most fruitful hypotheses arise out of, or in the course of, fieldwork. So do ethical dilemmas. However institutional pressures often demand that they be pre-figured. For example, proposals for research in the health-care field involving human subjects will have to be submitted to Ethical Committees for approval.

These are local bodies, and each one is autonomous. This makes for real difficulties for researchers wishing to study nation-wide samples or to compare health authorities: there are instances of Ethical Committees reaching quite different conclusions when reviewing the same project. They have no basis in statute law in Britain, and are subject to guidelines issued both by the Department of Health and the Royal College of Physicians. These conflict in some respects: for example, the Department recommends that a lay person should be in the Chair, but the Royal College disagrees. The result is that they differ somewhat in their composition and methods of procedure. All of them, however, are oriented primarily towards clinical research, especially the drug-trial, and they therefore tend to favour a cut and dried approach which is not typical of social research (although the greater uncertainties in psychiatry are usually recognized). As Powell and Lovelock note in this volume, it would be unwise to presume that they apply more relaxed standards to non-clinical topics. If they do approve a project they will seek to agree or impose a protocol. Should the researcher subsequently run into serious problems of an ethical kind, it may be advisable to approach the Ethical Committee again.

A good example of a fairly run of the mill problem raising ethical questions which confronted a researcher during the course of fieldwork is supplied by Robert Burgess in his textbook *In the Field*. It does not appear in the chapter he specifically devotes to ethical problems, but rather is one of several passages scattered throughout the text in which he candidly discusses his experiences in carrying out participant observation in a secondary school. After observing that he had to renegotiate with the School Secretary — 'Mrs. Watson' — access to records within her charge, even though permission had already been obtained from the Headmaster, Burgess continues:

> One day when the Headmaster was out of the school she remarked, 'I bet you'd like to read some of the notes that the staff write to him (the Head) about all this'. I indicated that I had seen some notes from teachers to the Head as they were located in various files in her office. However, she claimed that I had seen relatively few as the Headmaster kept most of the correspondence from individual teachers in their confidential files in his office. 'Wouldn't you like to see those?', she asked. I reminded her that the Head had said that I could read any files except the staff's confidential records. At this she laughed, went into his office and returned with a file. She started to read bits aloud from an individual teacher's confidential record and then passed it to me to read. In the circumstances I felt that I had few options. If I had refused to read the file the secretary might have felt vulnerable as I could have told the Head about her action, but in turn I would also be vulnerable as she could claim that I had asked to read the file. There were also further problems if the Head returned while I was reading this file. . . . In this situation I was confronted with an ethical dilemma which involved my relationship with the Headmaster and the secretary, both of whom I relied on for access to different dimensions of the research situation. Here, I decided that I had few choices but to break my agreement with the Head, as I thought that if I refused to read the file the secretary might discredit me with other members of the teaching staff. (Burgess, 1984:43–4)

Other researchers might have coped with this situation differently, but it should be remembered that Burgess's reasoning was presumably split-second. Such dilemmas frequently arise without warning.

Problems with confidentiality most often occur when a report is being prepared for publication. When the names of people or places are disguised or the details of incidents scrambled in order to fulfil undertakings which have been given, or for other reasons, the results must be plausible. The research findings must also not be distorted in any significant respect. This may make for some fine judgments. Thus it would be wrong to append an English-sounding name to a quote from a Bangladeshi if his or her ethnic origin was relevant in the context, but quite acceptable otherwise.

Impenetrable concealment, particularly of research locations or of persons in particular roles or positions, is probably virtually impossible to attain. Nevertheless the effort to provide it should usually be made. Let us revisit two of the examples given earlier to see how individuals may have been damaged through disclosure, inadvertent or otherwise. First, Burgess was very careful in his main report, *Experiencing Comprehensive Education: A Study of Bishop McGregor School*, to maintain confidentiality (Burgess, 1983). However, either the Head or other members of the teaching staff or the school secretary herself might have displayed a continuing interest in his career, even to the extent of reading a methodological textbook. The revelations contained in the passage quoted above might then have come as something of a shock. Secondly, when the furore broke out over Laud Humphreys' research, many of the spouses of the men involved in 'tearoom trade' (a large number of whom were married) might have recalled that their husbands had some time earlier participated in a 'health survey'. The consequences for marital harmony can be imagined.

One measure of the concern in the academic community about these matters is the energy which has been expended in drawing up codes of ethics by the associations bringing together the members of the various social science disciplines. These bodies have no teeth — unlike the Market Research Association where the threat of expulsion may be an effective sanction. The codes which have been issued are, in any case, usually far too general in their content to supply the fine discrimination which is essential if they are to be applied in practice. There has been reluctance, too, notably in the British Sociological Association, to move towards a more professionalized model, with licensing of practitioners and the like. This may be justified. There is some evidence that professional bodies have not always been very concerned with protecting their own members from improper pressures (an important aspect of ethics) so it is difficult to see them effectively protecting research subjects or 'citizens' *from* their own members. Berry and his associates record that the response of the Institute of Chartered Accountants in England and Wales to their article was to set up an enquiry into how it came to be published. The authors were not apprised of the terms of reference and were not permitted to make their views known to the Enquiry Panel, which appeared to be much influenced by an ICAEW council member who was also the member of the National Coal Board with responsibility for finance (Berry *et al.*, 1986:91).

In his conclusions to *Tearoom Trade*, Humphreys throws down a gauntlet to his critics: 'Concern about "professional integrity", it seems to me, is symptomatic of a dying discipline. Let the clergy worry about keeping their cassocks clean: the scientist has too great a responsibility for such compulsions!' (Humphreys, 1970:168). In fact, social investigators are quite powerful in relation to their subjects — and Humphreys himself later acknowledged that the men involved in his researches could have been harmed (Bulmer, 1982:222). Facts are not inert: they can be put to a variety of purposes, malign as well as benign. Fears on this score underlie the controversies about the inclusion of questions on racial background in the British decennial censuses. On occasion, too, the rights of social researchers need to be upheld against sponsors, gatekeepers, and even groups of citizens. Unfortunately there can be no manual which can tell the apprentice researcher exactly how to do it from a moral point of view. As we have seen, many of the issues are closely contested; all the parties involved in the research process have some legitimate claims; and there are no substitutes for common-sense, sensitivity, overt negotiation concerning disputed matters, and close normative reasoning. It may be taking it a little too far to say that concern over ethical issues is, *pace* Humphreys, a sign of maturity, but it is all to the good that the view he expresses has become unfashionable.

Further Reading

For those who would like further reading in this area, Barnes's (1979) book is a thought-provoking general study and discussion. Bulmer's (1982) collection, despite its apparently comprehensive title (*Social Research Ethics*), is almost entirely concerned with covert participant observation, but on that it is an indispensable source-book. Most methodological text-books, like Burgess's, contain a chapter on ethics: these also tend to be primarily concerned with those more extreme research designs and procedures which have deceitfulness built in. Catherine Marsh's (1982) useful book on the survey method rather neglects the ethical dimension, but it does include an interesting discussion of political bias in opinion-poll questionnaires. Finally, textbooks in cognate fields may be helpful; works on the relationship between medicine and the law, for instance, will contain discussions of informed consent and of research ethics — see for example Mason and McCall Smith (1987).

References

BARNES, J.A. (1979) *Who Should Know What? Social Science, Privacy and Ethics*, Harmondsworth, Penguin.

BELL, C. (1977) 'Reflections on the Banbury restudy' in BELL, C. and NEWBY, H. (Eds), *Doing Sociological Research*, London, Allen and Unwin.

BERGHE, P. VAN DER (1964) 'Research in South Africa' in SJOBERG, G. (Ed.), *Ethics, Politics and Social Research*, Cambridge, Mass., Schenkman.

BERRY, A.J., CAPPS, T., COOPER, D., HOOPER, T. and LOWE, E.A. (1986) 'The ethics of research in a public enterprise', in HELLER, F. (Ed.), *The Use and Abuse of Social Science*, Beverly Hills, Sage.

BERTHOUD, R. (1983) 'Transmitted deprivation: The kite that failed', *Policy Studies*, 3, pp. 151–69.

BULMER, M. (Ed.) (1982) *Social Research Ethics*, London, Macmillan.

BULMER, M. (1982) 'The merits and demerits of covert participation observation', in BULMER, M. (Ed.) *Social Research Ethics*, London, Macmillan.

BURGESS, R.G. (1983) *Experiencing Comprehensive Education: A Study of Bishop McGregor School*, London, Methuen.

BURGESS, R.G. (1984) *In The Field: An Introduction to Field Research*, London, Unwin Hyman.

CHERNS, A. (1986) 'Policy research under scrutiny', in HELLER, F. (Ed.), *The Use and Abuse of Social Science*, Beverly Hills, Sage.

COHEN, S. and TAYLOR, L. (1972) *Psychological Survival: The Experience of Long-Term Imprisonment*, Harmondsworth, Penguin.

GALLIHER, J.F. (1982) 'The protection of human subjects: A re-examination of the professional code of ethics', in BULMER, M. (Ed.) *Social Research Ethics*, London, Macmillan.

HEARNSHAW, L.S. (1979) *Cyril Burt, Psychologist*, London, Hodder and Stoughton.

HOLDAWAY, S. (1982) '"An inside job": A case study of covert research on the police', in BULMER, M. (Ed.) *Social Research Ethics*, London, Macmillan.

HOMAN, R. and BULMER, M. (1982) 'On the merits of covert methods: A dialogue', in BULMER, M. (Ed.), *Social Research Ethics*, London, Macmillan.

HOOD, R. (1970) *Sentencing the Motoring Offender: A Study of Magistrates' Views and Practices*, London, Heinemann.

HOROWITZ, I.L. (1967) (Ed.) *The Rise and Fall of Project Camelot*, Cambridge, MA, MIT Press.

HUMPHREYS, L. (1970) *Tearoom Trade: A Study of Homosexual Encounters in Public Places*, London, Duckworth.

MARSH, C. (1982) *The Survey Method*, London, Allen and Unwin.

MASON, J.K. and McCALL SMITH, R.A. (1987) *Law and Medical Ethics*, 2nd ed., London, Butterworth.

MILGRAM, S. (1974) *Obedience and Authority*, London, Tavistock.

OKELY, J. (1983) *The Traveller-Gypsies*, Cambridge, Cambridge University Press.

PUNCH, M. (1977) *Progressive Retreat*, Cambridge, Cambridge University Press.

PUNCH, M. (1986) *The Politics and Ethics of Fieldwork*, Sage University Paper series on Qualitative Research Methods, Volume 3, Beverly Hills, Sage.

SMITH, D.J. and GRAY, J. (1983) 'The police in action', *Police and People in London*, Vol. 4, London, Policy Studies Institute.

VIDICH, A.J. and BENSMAN, J. (1958) *Small Town in Mass Society*, Princeton, NJ, Princeton University Press

WILLIAMS, P.M. (1979) *Hugh Gaitskell*, London, Jonathan Cape.

Chapter 13

Equal Opportunities and Higher Degree Research

Joan Orme and Ian Forbes

Whether you are interested in or committed to equal opportunities or not, a postgraduate research degree necessarily calls for justifiable and defensible scholarship. You are required to demonstrate knowledge of the subject area and provide a critical evaluation of the research of others, available literature and relevant data. This cannot be done without an awareness of the way that an equal opportunities approach impinges upon all research activities. Ideally this approach should inform all writing about research. Since it has not, it is necessary to be explicit in this chapter, by crystallizing the issue and providing broad guidelines to adopt in conjunction with the advice and practical wisdom in other chapters.

Equal opportunities aims to combat discrimination against disadvantaged groups and individuals. Legislation to achieve this includes the Sex Discrimination Act (1975), the Equal Pay Act (1970 and 1983), the Race Relations Act (1976) and the Disabled Persons Employment Act (1944 and 1958). Taken together, these Acts, subsequent case law and the development of good practice amounts to the constructive promotion of equality of opportunity in all aspects of society. Codes of practice from the Commission for Racial Equality (CRE), the Equal Opportunities Commission and the Manpower Services Commission recognize three forms of discrimination — direct, indirect and victimization. In the education sector, these documents are augmented by the CRE's 'Code of Practice for the Elimination of Racial Discrimination in Education' and 'Words or Deeds? A Review of Equal Opportunity Policies in Higher Education'. Professional bodies, such as the British Sociological Association, the British Psychological Society, and the Political Studies Association are producing guidelines for best professional practice on issues relating to equal opportunities, especially with respect to language and ethical research. Such guidelines typically advise external examiners of the standards that can be demanded of completed research work.

In effect, there is already a legal and professional framework within which research students must work, placing firm requirements upon them to achieve certain standards. Failure to do so may jeopardize the chances of obtaining a higher degree, not just because equal opportunities principles have been violated but because these principles provide guidelines for rigorous, unbiased professional research.

The best principles of equal opportunities impinge upon research practice at each stage of the research process. These stages normally involve selection of research topic, methodology, analysis, write-up and conclusions. However, in an equal opportunities framework, good practice includes two additional factors: the aims of the research; and the intended use of the results. This means that justification and destination also need to be addressed in any discussion of higher degree research.

Selection of Topic

Equal opportunity, as it affects the implementation of any plan — research or otherwise — requires the practitioner to analyze, record, and evaluate the programme of activity to ensure that there is no inherent bias or discriminatory activity, whether intentional or unintentional. This means that good research will always be consistent with equal opportunities principles. Before starting, the aims and assumptions of the research need to be clarified, closely examined and spelled out. Are they relevant to the research? Are traditional assumptions, without any real foundation, being unwittingly imported? Is it presumed that change will occur, and that the research may be a causal part of that change?

An equal opportunities approach to research requires that perspectives on race and gender are considered at the design phase of every piece of research undertaken. This does not mean that research cannot be undertaken unless there is a specific race and or gender component. Cries of academic freedom arise at any such suggestion (CRE, 1989). What it does mean is that there has to be a specific admission and assumption that the general population is at least 50 per cent female and multi-cultural in composition. These factors have important ramifications for contemporary research. For many years research was either biased or gender-blind. Only male populations were researched or theorized, or women were included only as an adjunct to men. This was compounded by the universalist conclusions that were subsequently drawn. Moreover the core texts in all the social sciences are dominated by male writers, and their androcentric and usually eurocentric assumptions and principles are inevitably carried over into the present. Over the past decade, awareness of gender bias has improved and the balance is beginning to be redressed (Roberts, 1981; Stanley and Wise, 1983; Harding, 1987; Eichler, 1988), but a similar development is still required in ostensibly 'colour-blind' research (Banton, 1987; Gaine, 1988). In Britain, where ethnic minorities constitute 6 per cent of the total population but much higher proportions in certain areas, it should not be possible to publish research which makes no mention of ethnicity as a factor in the experience of research subjects.

The commitments to equality and justice require that groups other than white undisabled men are recognized in research activities. This does not amount to a complete challenge to traditional research practices: there is nothing inherently sexist (or, we would argue, racist) about empirical enquiry as long as it is understood that the outcomes of such enquiry are different if we take into account gender and race (Roberts, 1981). Unfortunately the definitions of social groups have usually been based on the white male as the norm, thereby threatening the validity of the research exercise by the crude exclusion of any groups defined along more precise and unambiguous lines. A critical examination of the routine assumptions is necessary — much more than just a breaking down of numerical data 'by sex' and 'by race'. Matched samples reflecting the composition of the population may be appropriate, or if it is relevant to have a sample of, for example, all white males then the reasons for and the implications of this decision need to be documented and justified.

The requirement to treat race and gender perspectives as socially important variables of *all* research is only a first step. The second is to increase the amount of primary research into these areas. Attempts to encourage such research sometimes offends the views of some traditional academic researchers, this time on the grounds of subjectivity and bias. But these critics have not objected to studies where white male experience was taken to represent the norm. Furthermore the decision to study the thoughts of a group of white men is too often accompanied by the assumption that their ideas constitute the major body of knowledge. This privileges their thought at the expense of other groups and discounts alternative histories and knowledge.

The view that men, or man, can be taken to be a generic group, representative of the whole of humanity, cannot be sustained in literary, psychological, political or sociological terms. The assumption that the concerns of men, or the majority ethnic group in society, are the best guide to the proper concerns of society or research is equally unacceptable. It is because of the process of universalizing from the specific that we have concentrated on issues of race and gender in this section. When research is carried out into age, class, religion and disability, it is not automatically assumed that the findings are valid for the total population. Indeed, the essential differences of the experiences are often the rationale for the research. Such sensitivity to difference should also be afforded to women and people of colour.

Methodology

Equal opportunities can present a challenge to as well as enhance the relevance of higher degree research. The key issues are: the status and nature of agents in society; the existence of differentiated groups in society; the reality of power relations between agents and groups; and the possibilities for change at all levels. All research makes assumptions about agents, groups, power and change. An empiricist approach presumes that fact and value are distinct, and that measurement and analysis can render truth and objectivity. Other approaches — phenomenological, critical theoretical, feminist — deny that the fact/value distinction exists in any straightforward sense. All methodology is imbued with value assumptions, and all analytical, quantitative, observational and experimental practices will reflect key assumptions, either by omission or commission. In practice, research should be sensitive to the way that social science disciplines have traditionally and systematically disguised crucial differences between the experiences of social agency for women as distinct from men, blacks from whites, the disabled from the undisabled, and so on.

It is important to translate some of the aspects of critical and qualitative methodologies into traditional research practices. What such methodologies bring is an appreciation of the way that the research process impinges upon the subjects of the research and how this in turn influences the results. This is true of all research but has particular significance when undertaking research into the personal and private experience of particular groups. Hence Ann Oakley (Roberts, 1981) documents the experience of interviewing pregnant women and points out that to gain full accounts of their experience she had to be something more than an impersonal researcher administering a 'neutral' questionnaire. Similarly, sensitivity to religious and cultural norms are needed when researching aspects of ethnic minority experience. When to interview, with respect to times of the day and days of the year which may have religious significance, are obvious factors often overlooked by researchers imbued with an anglocentric approach. Choice of subjects and interview method is also significant. For example, research into the views of Muslim women requires careful organization since male researchers and even white female researchers would be unacceptable, and interviews would probably have to be conducted in the presence of a third person.

Language

Language is critical in several respects. In terms of selecting data collection instruments, the literacy and spoken language of the group under research must first be discerned, and questionnaire design must include a check for colloquialisms or anglocentric assumptions. For analytical and theoretical research, the language of key texts and authorities will contain a host of embedded assumptions and prejudices that are no more valid for being venerable. Therefore such texts must be critically analyzed in order to detail the nature and function of those assumptions.

Whatever the language and sources used, your writing should avoid racist and sexist terms. This may require some research into words which are new to the language or whose meaning has changed. The most common, and incorrect, assumption in the literature and in practice is that white male experience can be used to provide descriptors for all experience. This is vividly demonstrated in the use of gendered language in questionnaires, in documentation about the research and in writing up the research. In theoretical theses and even in work where samples have been drawn equally from males and females the male pronoun has been used to describe the subjects, regardless of the actual population being dealt with in the research. It is becoming much more widely recognized that precision and accuracy is accompanied by gender-neutral and appropriately gender-specific language. In the first place ambiguity is avoided. More importantly, the implicit assumptions to be found in official documents, previous research and in everyday usage can then be challenged and their impact analyzed as part of the research exercise. These are reflected in such jargon as 'the rational man' of economics and politics, sociology's 'man in the street', and 'the nature of man' in everything from anthropology to zoology. The use of language which avoids the traditional stereotypes of sex, race and class is, at the very least, best professional research practice and can make a significant contribution to the development of the discipline (Spender, 1980; Hearn, 1987).

Justification

The presumption of all research is that it will be of benefit to society in general and to the individual researcher. It is therefore incumbent upon the researcher to ensure that harm is not caused through that research. Ultimately equal opportunity is about resources, whether that be money, or goods, or influence, or the exercise of power. Opportunities to benefit from these things should be distributed fairly. Research in social sciences is one such opportunity distributed to just a few; your research can result in further opportunities among those who are the potential targets of research, either in terms of a feeling of involvement and importance, or perhaps as beneficiaries of improved information for themselves and policy-makers alike.

Equal opportunity practice and philosophy is ethically significant in research, especially with regard to responsibility to the agent or subject.

These points have been thoroughly analyzed by feminist researchers and writers in particular, and they have in the process recognized that oppression is a general phenomenon in society, affecting especially black people and those from lower socio-economic groups. Since these are the people who are so frequently the subjects of research in the social sciences, it is important to ensure that disadvantage in society is not exacerbated by research activity.

This applies to all categories of subject, from research on, for example, theories of human nature to empirical work on specific groups and individuals. In involving subjects and researching part of their personal experience, it is necessary to recognize the impact on them, whatever the method of investigation. Essentially the experience is theirs, but, as Croft and Beresford have documented (1986), researchers often proceed to gather the information, reinterpret it and make it public, and in doing so take over ownership of the research and thereby the experience of others. There is a close congruence between good equal opportunities practice and best research practice here. A lack of understanding or a distrust of research aims and methodologies can lead to a recording of expected rather than real behaviour, requiring complex and sometimes unreliable processes of validation and verification, and vitiating the justifications of the research in the first place. If equal opportunities is to be a state of mind of the researcher in the social sciences, then researchers will be alert to the involvement of their 'subjects', and will contract to give regular and accurate feedback. In practice, therefore, researchers should identify and make public the way that their subjects will be informed both of the results and the interpretation of the results. Completing the thesis directly affirms the time, commitment and importance of the subjects of research and meets the responsibility of the social science researcher to contribute to and expand a body of knowledge which will ultimately contribute to change and policy decisions on behalf of those who have participated.

Destination

The equal opportunities approach recognizes the inherent power bases within the research process. As Mies (1983:123) puts it: 'Research, which so far has been largely an instrument of dominance and legitimation of power elites, must be brought to serve the interests of the dominated, exploited and oppressed groups.' The purpose of all research is that it can be used to challenge and develop existing knowledge; that it can be replicated and its methodologies transferred to other situations is a way in which this challenge can occur. For this to occur, for it to be meaningful to groups other than those who have access to university libraries, means that there has to be some commitment to disseminating the results. Traditionally such dissemination has been via research reports or articles in specialist journals which have a limited and specialist readership.

A further concern must be the uses to which the research is to be put. There are specific prohibitions against material in the public domain that will incite racial hatred and violence, so it is clear that our society has legitimized the concept and practice of limits to that which is published. The researcher must therefore pay attention to the effect of his or her own work in the public realm. A commitment to simple impartiality and 'truth' does not suffice, because every piece of research inevitably involves the construction of particular standards of evidence and proof, and creates a discourse rather than a definition of truth in the way that the contexts of theory, practice, justification and intention are combined with the raw material of the study in question. In other words, the wider context of the research must be taken into account. The conclusions reached should avoid introducing irrelevant considerations, or seek to apply specific findings outside the area of competence. It is the responsibility of the researcher, and of the supervisor, to guard against the misuse of data and findings by being aware at the outset of the potential for uncritical and superficial interpretations. This may require specific disclaimers about the application of the findings.

The research has to be accessible so that it can be questioned, challenged and accepted. Ideally it should be available in such a form which could encourage others, who might not necessarily perceive themselves as researchers, to participate in the process, for example by helping to formulate new research agenda.

Summary

The equal opportunity approach to research has legal, ethical and practical dimensions. It constitutes an agenda which all researchers in common must address — this may be your one point of contact with others doing markedly different research! There are four key points. First, there is the need for awareness of the social and political construction of knowledge in respect of women, ethnic minorities and disadvantage and the scope for research into these areas. Second, it is the responsibility of the researcher to question and not replicate traditional assumptions and practices where appropriate, especially with regard to unjust and unequal treatment, and to examine the construction and design of research methods. Third, the development of a research and writing style which is accurate, relevant and unambiguous rather than racist and sexist by default is vital. Finally, the research topic should be validated by appropriate means, such as completion of the thesis and dissemination of interpretations, findings and results, in order to contribute to change in society.

References

BANTON, M. (1987) 'The battle of the name', *New Community* **14**, pp. 170–5.

BRITISH SOCIOLOGICAL ASSOCIATION (1989) *Anti-Racist Language: Guidance for Good Practice*, London, BSA.

BRITISH SOCIOLOGICAL ASSOCIATION (1989) *Gender Neutral Language Guidelines*, London, BSA.

COMMISSION FOR RACIAL EQUALITY (CRE) (1989) *Code of Practice for the Elimination of Discrimination in Education*, London, CRE.

CROFT, S. and BERESFORD, P. (1986) *Whose Welfare: Private Care of Public Services?*, Brighton, L. Cohen Urban Studies Centre.

EICHLER, M. (1988) *Non-Sexist Research Methods*, London, Allen and Unwin.

GAINE, C. (1988) *No Problem Here — A Practical Approach to Education and 'Race' in White Schools*, London, Hutchinson.

HARDING, S. (1987) *Feminism and Methodology: Social Science Issues*, Bloomington, Indiana University Press.

HEARN, J. (1987) *The Gender of Oppression*, Brighton, Wheatsheaf.

MIES, M. (1983) 'Towards a methodology for feminist research' in BOWLES, G. and KLEIN, D. (Eds) *Theories of Women's Studies*, London, Routledge and Kegan Paul.

ROBERTS, H. (1981) *Doing Feminist Research*, London, Routledge and Kegan Paul.

SPENDER, D. (1980) *Man Made Language*, London, Routledge and Kegan Paul.

STANLEY, L. and WISE, S. (1983) *Breaking Out: Feminist Consciousness and Feminist Research*, London, Routledge and Kegan Paul.

Part 3

Research Strategies in the Social Sciences

Chapter 14

Introduction:
Research Strategies and Decisions

Jon Clark and Gordon Causer

Introduction

The aim of this chapter is to provide a general framework for carrying out postgraduate research, illustrated where appropriate with examples. In talking of research strategy we wish to emphasize the need for a planned and systematic approach; however, this needs to be paired with the flexibility to cope with unforeseen developments. The key to successful research lies in combining a flexibility of response to changing circumstances with the maintenance of a coherent overall strategy.

For analytical purposes, we have divided the research process into seven elements:

* objectives
* design
* methods
* management
* data collection
* analysis
* presentation

We would recommend that all students should attempt to construct an outline strategy — incorporating the first four elements — as soon as they can. Data collection, analysis and presentation will come at a later stage and are likely to vary substantially according to research design, methods and academic discipline. For this reason, we will concentrate in what follows on objectives, design, methods and management.

Research Objectives

The Importance of 'Problem-finding'

The setting of objectives is of overriding importance; they guide the whole research process. Most research aims to provide answers or solutions to some kind of research 'problem'. Before a problem can be answered or solved, though, it has to be adequately formulated. Problem formulation or, in the words of the American social scientist, Robert Merton, 'problem-finding' (1959, p. ix), plays a vital role in the initial stages of setting research objectives.

Merton has suggested that problem-finding can be broken down into three main components: originating question(s), i.e. what you want to know; research rationale, i.e. why you want to know it; and specifying questions, i.e. which particular questions you need to investigate in order to provide the answers to the originating question(s) (1959, p. xiii). In this section of our chapter, we will discuss the various components which constitute the process of establishing research objectives. Our presentation of research objectives will have three main sections:

— identifying a topic area;
— defining the research question(s) and research rationale;
— identifying key concepts.

Identifying a Topic Area

Problem-finding is often preceded by the identification of a broad topic area of research, such as technological change, divorce, labour productivity, road-traffic planning, pre-school education, demographic change, or child abuse. Alternatively, students may choose a subject as a result of a general interest in a broader academic discipline or sub-discipline, such as political philosophy, labour economics, child psychology, urban geography, economic history, or the sociology of law. This choice may derive from a purely intellectual interest, from the academic context in which the student is working, from their own domestic, work or leisure experience, or from a wider public policy debate.

However a topic area does not in itself make a research project. For this the topic area needs to be converted into a specific 'problem'. This is one of the stages at which it is advisable to call on the experience and guidance of the supervisor!

Defining Research Questions and Rationales

In defining research questions it is important to remember that they need to be 'scientifically consequential'. Some questions are unlikely to lead to 'original' research findings or a major increment in understanding. In deciding whether research questions are likely to be scientifically consequential, the key is to identify the rationale behind them, to say what of significance is likely to happen to our present state of knowledge or our current practice as a result of answering the questions.

We will now give some examples of different types of research questions and rationales. In practice many research projects involve a mixture of these types.

Fact-finding/filling gaps in knowledge. In a sense this is a tautology — there would be no point in doing research if we already knew the facts under investigation.[1] In many cases, however, the 'facts' of a given situation may not be known. This may be because the area in question has been under-researched in the past (e.g. certain forms of child abuse in the 1980s) or because the phenomenon of concern is itself a new development within society (e.g. the development of micro-electronic technologies in the late 1970s). In other cases, conventional academic or popular wisdom may hold that certain facts are well-established, but a review of the evidence for such claims may suggest the need to examine the area afresh. In such cases, establishing the facts and thus filling a gap in knowledge can be both the originating question and the rationale of a research project. What then needs to be done is to specify the more detailed questions to be investigated in each case. This may involve one or more of the objectives outlined in the next three sections.

Hypothesis testing. Testing a hypothesis is an objective common to both the natural and the human/social sciences. Many pieces of social science research, and many of the opinions and views we express in our everyday lives, have underlying hypotheses at their heart (e.g. 'If I do A, then X is likely to react in way B, which will have the outcome C'). In everyday life hypotheses are often hidden or simply hunches. In the social sciences, in contrast, hypotheses need to be stated in explicit form, and specifying questions identified which will enable their validity to be tested. The general objective of such research is to provide an improved knowledge-base on the basis of which hypotheses may be confirmed, modified or refuted.

Establishing a relationship between variables. In some senses, establishing a relationship between variables is a weaker, more open-ended, variation of hypothesis-testing, but a more specific focus for research than simply fact-finding or filling a gap in knowledge. Whereas hypothesis-testing is normally concerned with ascertaining the validity of a particular proposition, establishing a relationship between variables is concerned with finding links of a more general nature between certain phenomena. For example, a study of the relationship between the level of unemployment and the level of wage settlements is likely to be based on the assumption that there is some kind of causal relationship between these two variables. However the objective of the research may be to clarify the precise nature of the relationship rather than to test a specific hypothesis (e.g. that the level of unemployment determines the level of wage settlements). As this example suggests, the line between hypothesis-testing and establishing a relationship between variables is not a clear-cut one, for the very identification of potentially relevant variables entails the prior assumption (or hypothesis) that a link of some such nature is likely to exist.

Testing the adequacy of models or theories. Some research has as its primary objective the development or modification of more general models or theories, i.e. integrated sets of propositions which are held to have explanatory power. Even where research is not directly concerned with testing a model or theory, it is likely that it will entail the use of some kind of analytical or conceptual framework to order and make sense of the data being collected and analyzed. Much postgraduate research is therefore likely to involve, at the very least, a critical discussion and definition of 'key concepts', and often the development of a distinctive 'conceptual framework'. For this reason we will look now at the importance of identifying such key concepts — in some senses the lowest order of analytical abstraction — in the process of establishing research objectives.

'Key Concepts'

Concepts are propositions which suggest that a phenomenon should be viewed in a certain way.[2] Whereas hypotheses can, at least in principle, be subjected to empirical confirmation or refutation, it is not possible to prove empirically that concepts are 'right' or 'wrong'. Rather concepts are normally evaluated in terms of their utility in helping to answer the problems under investigation. In the words of the British social scientist, John Goldthorpe:

> Since concepts are tools, they must be judged essentially in terms of their utility. What we should ask are questions such as how well

particular concepts help us to set out substantive problems that are of interest to us, and whether they lead us to pose rewarding questions and to collect illuminating information relevant to these problems. (Goldthorpe, 1990:417)

All researchers, then, need to identify the key concepts in their research, to show awareness of, and to examine critically, the most important definitions of the concepts in the existing literature, and either to adopt one of the existing definitions or develop an original definition because it is best suited to analyzing their particular problem. The development of a conceptual framework and the definition of 'key concepts' are matters which will need to be worked on throughout a thesis. However, preliminary choices and decisions will need to be made at an early stage in the process.

As we have indicated, an important aspect of this process will be the analysis of the existing literature on a chosen topic area, using it as a means of clarifying conceptual questions and as a benchmark of the existing state of knowledge. Indeed, identifying the relevant literature or debates to which the research will contribute, and showing satisfactory knowledge of the background and context of the research problem, are an important part of the research rationale and also one of the main criteria which will be applied in assessing the merits of the eventual thesis.[3]

Research Objectives: Conclusion

Many pieces of research contain a mix of the types of objective outlined above. In addition, some researchers may wish to use the findings of their research to develop solutions to practical 'problems' in, for example, particular organizations or in society at large. This may be an important additional objective, or even the primary one, but in order to achieve it it will still be necessary to define research objectives in the way outlined above.

If you have worked through this section in connection with your own research, it might be useful to attempt to answer the following questions (some of which may overlap):

* What is my broad topic area and/or academic discipline?
* What are the main originating and specifying questions to be investigated?
* What is the rationale of the research (what debates/areas of knowledge does it aim to address/extend, what is 'at stake')?
* What are the key concepts?

We should emphasize that these are not easy questions to answer. Indeed it is our view that research supervisors have a major role to play in assisting the student to find answers to them, both in the light of their own past experience of conducting research and the collective wisdom of previous researchers in the topic area or discipline.

Research Design

Having established the research objectives, the next stage is to design a project which will enable you to attain them. This is the question of 'research design', which Bryman defines as 'the overall structure and orientation of an investigation' (Bryman, 1989:28). In designing a piece of research there is unlikely to be 'one best way'. Normally, though, some research designs will be more appropriate to achieving defined objectives than others (for further details see Hakim, 1987).

In this section, we will look at design principles, the operationalization of concepts, the choice of 'raw materials' for research, questions of access, the use of pilot studies and the need to keep research projects within manageable limits.

Design Principles

The most obvious question of design principle concerns the broad type(s) and mix of research methods to be used. For example a researcher concerned with explaining why a particular religious belief exerts an attraction for a particular group could choose to carry out a sample survey of believers, an examination of the writings of selected believers, direct observation of the activities of the religious group in question, or a mix of all three. Each method will generate different types of data, all of which may contribute in distinctive ways to the understanding of the phenomenon in question.

The broad choice of the type(s) and mix of methods to be used raises a further set of questions of design principle. In survey research the type of design choices to be made include, for example, decisions about whether to carry out a one-off 'snap-shot' survey at a particular moment in time or whether to conduct a series of surveys (or a main survey and a more selective follow-up survey) at different junctures. In laboratory-based experimental research, decisions have to be made about whether a single type of experiment or a set of related experiments are most appropriate to provide data to answer the questions which are being posed. In case-study research decisions have to be made about whether to focus on a single case or a set of cases. These are questions of design principle.

Operationalization of Concepts and the Choice of 'Raw Materials'

We have already stressed the importance of developing a conceptual framework for the conduct of research. Of equal importance, however, is the specification of what empirical phenomena are to be taken as instances of particular concepts, which we may loosely term 'operationalization'.[4] While not all social science research entails the use of formal measurement instruments, it is always necessary to specify how the central concepts are being applied to concrete social phenomena. For example, in a study of 'high technology' industry it is necessary to specify the defining characteristics which will be used to decide whether or not a particular firm will be treated as belonging in this category.

A related issue is the question of choosing the 'raw material' which will provide the subject matter for the research in question. In the case of documentary research, this involves the choice of the most appropriate documents to be studied. With survey research decisions have to be made as to the choice of population to be surveyed. In the conduct of case studies, decisions concern the choice of site(s) for empirical investigation and the criteria according to which they will be chosen. When a preliminary choice of research materials has been made, students should then be able to justify why they have chosen this particular material and, above all, to show how it helps them answer their research questions in the light of their overall research rationale.

Access to Material

Choice of 'raw materials' will in many cases be influenced by issues of accessibility. Researchers will need to ask, for example, how the required documents are to be obtained and studied, or how access is to be secured to the desired population sample or to appropriate research sites. In some cases access to relevant materials may prove problematic. Appropriate documents may have disappeared or been actively suppressed, suitable organizations may deny access to the researcher, and so on. In such circumstances it may be necessary to modify the research design in the light of what material is available and accessible. This in turn may have implications for the achievement of the original research objectives.

The Use of Pilot Studies

This is a particular design issue for empirical investigations and is closely related to issues of research methodology. However, in designing a piece of empirical research, a 'strategic' decision has to be made about whether and to what extent to 'pilot' or 'test drive' particular research methods in a separate study prior to the main research. In certain cases — e.g. research based on the large-scale use of structured questionnaires — it will almost certainly be necessary to conduct such a study to test out the research instruments being used. In others — e.g. the conduct of case studies based on less formalized observation — a pilot study may be less appropriate, although even here there is still a need to be reflexive about the process of data collection and to ask oneself pilot-type questions of the data being gathered, especially early on.

Feasibility

In constructing a research design the question of feasibility is central. By 'feasibility' we mean not simply whether a project is feasible in principle, but also whether it is feasible within the constraints of time and resources available to the student. This may appear obvious, but we would suggest that one of the main reasons why a proportion of research students fail to complete their theses in good time is that their project, and particularly the research design chosen, is far too ambitious. The choice of research design (and, of course, the associated research objectives and methods) should take account of these considerations. The project as a whole should be practicable and 'do-able' within an agreed time span, which will of course differ according to whether the student is full-time or part-time, a masters or doctoral degree student, and so on.

The Interaction of Research Design and Research Objectives

Research objectives are necessarily cast in somewhat abstract terms. Research design, in contrast, is concerned with the practicalities of achieving these objectives. While a research project should be designed in such a way as to facilitate the achievement of the research objectives, we need to recognize that this is an ideal which may not always be fully attained. In particular, the need to keep a project within manageable proportions, and problems of access to source materials, may lead to departures from the research design which one would ideally like to employ. For example, a study of companies' recruitment policies towards particular types of employee might ideally be conducted on a national basis, so as to take account of regional and local variations in labour market conditions. In practice resource constraints may lead to a concentration on employers in a particular area. The research objectives would therefore be modified from a study of employer behaviour in general to a study of employer behaviour in a particular labour market context. The connection between objectives and design is thus a two-way process, with initial objectives being modified in the light of the practicalities of the conduct of research.

Research Methods

These will vary greatly depending on topic area, discipline base, research objectives and research design. However there are some general considerations which it is important to bear in mind when choosing research methods.

Appropriateness to Research Objectives

In some senses this point is an obvious one. However in practice students sometimes get caught up in philosophical or practical discussions about the technical merits of different research methods, forgetting that the ultimate test should be the utility of the methods in helping them to achieve their overall research objectives. For example, a study concerned to determine the *incidence* of experiences of sexual harassment among the female workforce might need to make use of large-scale survey techniques involving the use of relatively highly-structured questionnaires. In contrast, a study concerned with understanding the *experience* of sexual harassment, and women's re-actions to it, would probably make use of much less formally structured face to face interviewing techniques.

Single or Multiple Research Methods

Many projects use more than one research method. For example, in a large-scale project designed to study the effects of telephone exchange mod-ernization (reported in Clark *et al.*, 1988), the aim was to capture the process of technological change as experienced by those directly involved in it, and to examine to what extent work tasks and work organization changed over time as a result of the introduction of new exchange systems. In order to under-stand the differences in work tasks and work patterns before and after the change, the study used self-report work diaries over a period of a month at the beginning and end of the research. Intensive observation of work was carried out at the beginning of the project to gain a first-hand understanding of the nature of different work tasks and the interface between workforce and technology. In assessing job satisfaction, semi-structured interviews were used, which provided some systematic 'hard' data and some 'softer' data which could be used illustratively in presenting the material. Basic data on the age, career histories, education and training of the respondents were collected separately by means of standardized questionnaires. In addition, various types of documentation (such as job descriptions, technical standards and targets, and collective agreements) were used as a benchmark to examine how far managerial requirements and jointly agreed rules were actually implemented in practice.

In a case such as this, where multiple research methods are chosen, it is important to make some preliminary decisions about the relative importance of the different methods, which ones are primary, which are secondary, and so forth. The crucial point is to choose methods according to how far they enable you to achieve your research objectives and to implement your particular research design. If it is practicable within your resource constraints the use of a number of different methods does have distinct advantages. However we should stress that the project discussed above was far more ambitious than a postgraduate project, involving two full-time post-doctoral research fellows over a period of three years as well as at least two days a week for two full-time university teachers. This example, then, is used for illustrative purposes, not as a model for postgraduate research.

Cross-checking Results Within and Between Methods

In much research in the human and social sciences, the reliability of data may well be enhanced if they are subject to cross-checks and corroboration. This cross-checking may be within a particular method (e.g. asking a range of different questions on the same issue within a questionnaire) or between methods (e.g. using biographical and autobiographical accounts to complement official documents in historical research).

Cross-checking results within and between methods can sometimes be crucial in dealing with apparently contradictory findings. For example, when asked about their general attitude to strikes, the majority of trade unionists express opposition. However when given specific examples of situations in which groups of workers are on strike, or when they themselves are on strike, they tend to express more positive attitudes. These two different 'results' illustrate the influence of the choice of research question on the eventual research findings. They also draw attention to the issue of potential contradictions and discrepancies between different types of data collected and types of question asked. Such discrepancies may reflect the fact that different methods may elicit different responses. But equally they may reflect the fact that individuals' opinions and responses are not necessarily internally consistent. Ambivalence and ambiguity in research findings do not always need to be 'resolved' one way or the other, but may accurately capture the reality of the situation at the time of the research.

Some Concluding Thoughts on Objectives, Design and Methods

As we have already indicated, researchers need to be pragmatic as well as principled in the choice of research design and methods, always keeping one eye on what is feasible within the available resources of time, money and accessibility of source material. Limitations on access, or the opportunity to secure access via an unanticipated source, may well necessitate going back to the research objectives and modifying them in the light of constraints and opportunities. However it is important to be wary of allowing 'outsiders' (whether supervisors or external agencies!) to exert undue influence on research objectives. The publication of research, and the award of a higher degree, represent a recognition of the ability of the individual researcher to identify significant research problems, to set research objectives and to conduct original, independent research in order to achieve them.

Research Management

Success in research depends to some extent on the way it is managed. A strategy for research management is therefore highly recommended.

Project and Time Management

This involves drawing up a timetable of research at an early stage, with clearly identified targets to be achieved (papers or chapters written, field-work/primary research completed, etc.) at clearly identified time points. These should be agreed with the thesis supervisor, serving as a source of self-discipline for the student, and a regular agenda point for discussion at meetings between supervisor and student.

Liaison with Organizations/Agencies

If research is carried out in outside organizations or agencies (see on this, Bryman, 1988a; Powell and Lovelock, this volume), it is very important to establish a prime contact within the organization who has formal responsibility for your research. This person can give you legitimacy within the organization and also facilitate initial contacts with other staff. In addition, there are bound to be times when problems arise, and it is good to have someone who has the authority to deal with the situation. It is best to anticipate such events by establishing procedures and lines of authority in advance rather than having to manage contingencies in an *ad hoc* fashion as and when they arise.

Finally, and depending on the research topic and objectives, it may be useful to establish a 'liaison team' (including your prime contact) which meets at regular intervals (say six monthly) to review progress, discuss general problems, and where appropriate, for you to provide feedback on provisional results. Agreeing to establish such a liaison team and to feed back provisional results as they arise can be very important in securing access to an organization and in maintaining its interest in the research.

Feedback

It is vital to gain regular feedback on progress, as this can help confirm the original objectives, design or methods, or alternatively suggest the need for modifications. Your supervisor is clearly most significant here, but supervisory committees and liaison meetings, as outlined above, can be particularly valuable too. Feedback can give encouragement to pursue a particular line of inquiry or, alternatively, suggest other avenues of research.

Conclusion

In the previous sections we have examined the first four elements of research strategies — objectives, design, methods and management. Work on each of these four can (and should) begin as soon as the project starts, prior to the collection of the data which will provide the core of your research. Different ways of collecting data will be discussed in other chapters of this volume. In this section, we will conclude by giving some advice on data analysis — in particular when to begin it! — and the overall presentation of the research in the thesis.

On the question of data analysis — whether the data takes the form of historical documents, survey data, the results of experiments, case studies, or whatever — there is a great and understandable temptation to try to collect all the data before beginning to analyze any of it. Try to resist this temptation! As soon as you have gathered enough data to begin analysis (and this is again where you may well need to take your supervisor's advice), we would advise attempting a preliminary analysis in some form. Developing a research strategy and carrying out and reporting on research are not simply elements in a consecutive, linear process, but part of a seamless web: topic area —

problem — aims — design — methods — management — data collection — analysis — findings — presentation. Advances made in any of these areas will necessarily affect the others to a greater or lesser degree. For this reason we suggest beginning research analysis sooner rather than later. It is vital that you present your ideas and frameworks and findings at regular intervals in front of different interested parties. These range from your supervisor and supervisory committee (which in most institutions now conducts an annual review of progress) to postgraduate and staff research seminars in your own or other institutions of higher education.

The presentation of the findings in the form of a thesis is, of course, the end product of the whole research process. It follows from our discussion above that we would recommend the following headings as a guideline for structuring the first chapter of a thesis:

— research objectives (topic area, originating and specifying questions, rationale, key concepts)
— research design
— research methods (including research management where appropriate)
— structure of thesis (how the research findings are to be presented, chapter by chapter, in order to achieve the stated objectives).

Further Reading

Many of the issues raised in this chapter are taken up in other parts of this book. For a useful general introduction to research methodology we would recommend Alan Bryman's *Quantity and Quality in Social Research*, and for students carrying out empirical research in organizations, we would recommend the same author's edited collection *Doing Research in Organisations*. Students interested in a more detailed discussion of design questions should consult Catherine Hakim's *Research Design*.

Notes

1   Our formulations in this section obviously beg the question of how far 'facts' can be said to exist independently of the methods used to establish them. While recognizing that methods of data collection and analysis do influence the findings of a study, we nonetheless hold to the position — fundamental to any empirical research — that it is in some sense possible to establish factual data on a relatively objective basis through the use of appropriate research strategies and techniques.
2   Concepts are therefore distinct from hypotheses, which suggest that a phe-

nomenon or the relationship between phenomena is of a certain kind. (See on this whole area Goldthorpe, 1990:412–4.)

3 One of the first pieces of analysis most social science research students complete is a review of the existing relevant literature. Some such review of relevant debates is necessary at an early stage, but it is important to stress that it should not be allowed to take off to the point where it dwarfs everything else and diverts attention from becoming involved in the conduct of substantive research. However it is valuable to have an identifiable 'product' out of the first six months of research, and the literature review often fulfils this function.

4 The classical positivist position sought to define concepts by the operations through which they were measured, and hence became known as 'operationalism' (Bridgman, 1927; for a discussion see Bryman, 1988b:16–17). Our usage here is a somewhat looser one in that we assume neither that all concepts are amenable to measurement nor that concepts are reducible to operational procedures of this type.

References

BRIDGMAN, P. (1927) *The Logic of Modern Physics*, New York, Macmillan.

BRYMAN, A. (Ed.) (1988a) *Doing Research in Organizations*, London, Routledge.

BRYMAN, A. (1988b) *Quantity and Quality in Social Research*, London, Unwin Hyman.

BRYMAN, A. (1989) *Research Methods and Organization Studies*, London, Unwin Hyman.

CLARK, J., MCLOUGHLIN, I., ROSE, H. and KING, R. (1988) *The Process of Technological Change*, Cambridge, Cambridge University Press.

GOLDTHORPE, J.H. (1990) 'A Response' in CLARK, J. *et al.* (Eds) *John H. Goldthorpe — Consensus and Controversy*, London, Falmer Press.

HAKIM, C. (1987) *Research Design*, London, Unwin Hyman.

MERTON, R.K. (1959) 'Notes on Problem-Finding in Sociology', in MERTON, R.K., BROOM, L. and COTTRELL, L. (Eds), *Sociology Today: Problems and Prospects*, New York, Harper.

Chapter 15

Qualitative Research

Graham Allan

Many have questioned whether the contrast between qualitative and quantitative research is a particularly constructive one, arguing that the best research in social science contains elements of both. Nonetheless of all the methodological distinctions that have been concocted, it is the quantitative/ qualitative one which has proved most durable and which, to be fair, most accurately reflects the customary division of practice in social science. The intention of this chapter is not to argue that qualitative research is necessarily superior to quantitative approaches — it is for some problems but not for others — but to indicate some of the strengths and weaknesses of qualitative methods and lay some of the groundwork for the chapters on case studies and qualitative interviewing which follow.

Much documentary research in political studies, history and social policy is necesarily qualitative. As discussed in Chapter 10, appraising the pertinence and validity of this type of secondary material requires both prudence and skill. The focus in this chapter however is on the use of 'qualitative' approaches to collecting and analyzing *primary* data. The two main methods of qualitative data collection are participant observation or ethnography, as it is now more commonly called, and qualitative, depth or unstructured interviewing. Issues to do with both these methods will be discussed below, but first it is worth saying briefly what it is that sets such methods apart from those which are normally subsumed under the rubric of 'quantitative' methods.

One aspect of the contrast between 'qualitative' and 'quantitative' concerns the mode of data analysis used. Quantitative approaches assume interval or ordinal data which are amenable to statistical manipulation. Data from qualitative methods typically require a different mode of exposition. However the contrast runs deeper than data-processing procedures. It reflects different theoretical underpinnings and different views as to what counts as *valid* data (Bryman, 1988a). A core feature of qualitative research methods is that satisfactory explanations of social activities require a substantial appreciation of the perspectives, culture and 'world-views' of the actors involved. As Burgess (1984a:3) notes, prominence is given to 'understanding the actions of participants on the basis of their active experience of the world and the ways in which their actions arise from and reflect back on experience'. Thus within these approaches the researched are not seen as objects with given properties — attitudes, norms, behavioural characteristics — which can be readily measured given due care, but as actors whose own frame of reference needs detailed investigation before their actions can be adequately interpreted and explained. The essence of the approach is well expressed in Evered and Lewis's (1981) categorization of it as 'inquiry from the inside' rather than 'inquiry from the outside' (cited in Bryman, 1988a:3).

What this requires is fuller and more flexible involvement by the researcher with those from or about whom data is being collected than is typical of more quantitative approaches. But this greater involvement does not just stem from the researcher's abstracted notions of what counts as valid data. It is also a consequence of the way that the research question is selected and then translated into a research agenda (see Chapter 14), although this in turn will be influenced by the researcher's prior theoretical and methodological orientations. Here, of course, it is important to recognize that often the researcher may not appear to have to make a real decision about whether a qualitative or quantitative approach is adopted. The way the research problem is formulated and the research agenda specified gradually makes it 'obvious' what approach is most suitable.

Consider, for example, the way in which variables like ethnicity, gender and class affect children's educational performance. There are clearly questions here which are best answered using quantitative methods which allow for large, representative samples. For instance, examining the extent to which parental economic circumstances influence the qualifications children obtain would seem to lead 'naturally' to a quantitative approach involving statistical controls and correlations, once measures for the main variables have been identified. On the other hand, if you are interested in *how* and *why* it is that children from certain backgrounds do less well than others, you are more likely to take a qualitative approach and focus, say, on the ways in which children experience schooling and become committed to education. This may, for example, involve examining in some detail and over time how different children are actually treated by teachers, peers and others in the school system.

Although simple, this example can be used to highlight a number of important aspects of qualitative research. First, if you were to investigate how children were treated within schools, you would most likely recognize the need to rely on a range of different research methods. For instance, observation of classrooms and play areas is likely to be an important element; but so too are depth interviews with teachers and parents; discussions with individual, or groups of, children; examination of school records and reports; possibly an analysis of some children's written stories about their feelings towards schooling etc. While with depth interviewing there is less variety of method used, informants may still be asked to keep diaries, or participate in group interviews, in addition to being questioned individually. Different methods may be appropriate in providing answers to different research issues. In addition, using different methods may also offer some possibility of triangulation — that is, using different methods cumulatively to compensate for the biases of any one (Denzin, 1970). However the problems of combining diverse results derived from different methods should not be underestimated (Fielding and Fielding, 1986).

Second, qualitative research is often concerned with social processes — in the above case, for example, with how different types of educational commitment are generated. In some instances it is reasonable to ask people for retrospective accounts of changes that have affected them. Often though, as in the above illustration, there are grounds for thinking that recollections are likely to be incomplete or unreliable, or indeed that those involved are actually not in a position to recognize easily the factors that influenced their behaviour. In such cases observation or detailed questioning of different actors over time is probably the only way in which adequate data can be collected.

A third related point is that since much quantitative data is collected through surveys, such data necessarily reflects individual knowledge and consciousness. Yet much social science research is concerned with interaction and relationships. Thus, as in the case of seeing how schooling operates, the unit of the research may not be the individual but a form of social organization, like a school or a workplace or a residential home. Depending on the questions being posed in the research, it may be that a holistic approach to the organization is required which makes using the more standard quantitative techniques in isolation less suitable.

One further point to make from this example concerns the relationship between qualitative and quantitative approaches. Quite frequently limited qualitative research is seen as a precursor for more quantitative methods. The former is held to be useful as a kind of insightful pilot stage, capable of generating interesting ideas and hypotheses that can be 'properly' tested by more systematic and thorough quantitative investigation. While this relationship may be useful in some studies, as a general stance it misrepresents the part that qualitative methods can play in developing social scientific knowledge. As in the example above, the reality is far more complex as quantitative methods usually pose genuinely different questions. Indeed, in the example above the relationship was the other way round. The correlation between structural characteristics and educational performance can be established, but what this does is then open up questions about why the correlations are there and what the processes are that generate them. Qualitative methods — a view from the inside — may be particularly suitable for examining such matters.

At the same time qualitative approaches can rightly be regarded as 'exploratory'. Their aim is to use informants' own understandings of events in analyzing social settings. Rather than assume that world-views are already known, there is acknowledgment that much has to be learnt before the right questions can be posed, let alone answers found. Attempting to keep an open mind, to foster new lines of enquiry, is thus a central tenet of qualitative work. But this does not mean that as the research evolves, it is appropriate to transfer to a quantitative mode. It may be in some instances, but more likely the researcher will want to continue as before because alternative methods would not generate such appropriate or valid data.

Criticisms of Qualitative Research Methods

The major criticisms made of qualitative methods are that they are impressionistic and non-verifiable. Let us consider each in turn. Clearly, as recognized above, qualitative methods are impressionistic, at least in the early phases of the research. In a sense, this is the other side of the coin to their being flexible. In general the researcher initially attempts to adopt a naive pose with respect to the topic being studied. Of course, they will already have spent much time in the library reading as widely as possible around the research topic. Nonetheless, whether doing interviews or some form of case study, in the early stages of the data collection phase the researcher will try to be especially open and sensitive to new ideas, new suggestions, new relationships that are evident in what respondents are saying or doing. The point of this sustained effort at naivety is to facilitate the researcher's receptivity to the respondents' perceptions and understandings and, in ethnographies, to the social organization and dynamics of the research setting.

Inevitably, then, in the early phase of qualitative research good practice is for the research to be impressionistic — this is one of its hallmarks. It will also normally be quite 'messy'. Ethnography especially does not usually have the tidy, relatively linear progression of discrete stages common in experimental or questionnaire survey design (see Chapter 18). However this does not mean that 'anything goes' and that rigour has no part to play in qualitative methods. While the researcher will certainly want to keep an open mind and be reflective about the processes and action being observed or discussed, at the same time the collection of data and the testing of ideas need to become as systematic as possible. Platt (1988) has stressed the importance of selecting case studies on explicit and systematic criteria so that they properly address the research issue being investigated (see Chapter 16). Equally, allowing for the constraints of fieldwork, the qualitative researcher needs to be as systematic as is feasible in every other aspect of the research, while of course still remaining receptive to new issues and undercurrents emerging in the study. Thus in qualitative interviews the same topics must be covered for all respondents; every effort should be made to explore in similar detail each occurence of significant phenomena. In ethnographies, researchers must be mindful of observing action at different times; they must ensure that they talk with and interview a full range of people; the researcher needs to check out what key informants report through systematic observation of the actions they mention; and so on.

So too in analyzing data being systematic is crucial to good research. Whether the data be interview transcripts or fieldnotes, they must be examined thoroughly for each and every incidence of a phenomenon. Flexibility remains an advantage of qualitative research here — the categories of action developed for analysis are not rigidly fixed, nor is analysis restricted to a stage when the data has already been collected. As the research progresses the researcher develops ideas about how the material fits together, and about the relationships it encompasses. A major part of this is generating new conceptualizations which link together different episodes of action previously not seen as similar. Thus what counts as an example of a phenomenon, and indeed what phenomena are worthy of note, changes as the research progresses and the researcher develops a better, fuller understanding of the issues involved. Yet as this happens the researcher must be particularly on guard to be systematic and to ensure that all potential examples of the (new) phenomenon have been considered. It is easy to recognize those cases which fit in with one's current conceptualization and theorizing; it is much more difficult not to gloss over episodes or events which run counter. It is here that the need to be systematic becomes paramount. It is most important that the researcher continues to search out disconfirming incidents from his or her data; that she or he positively seeks contradictory evidence either through discussion with informants in later interviews or observations, or by trawling carefully through field-notes and typescripts. These can then be used to generate new categories and modify one's current theorizing. The processes can then be repeated anew. Through such systematic iteration the researcher can go a long way towards ensuring that the analysis generated is more than just impressionistic.

Let us now turn to the question of whether qualitative research methods are verifiable. Clearly verification is a central tenet of science: empirical investigation should be capable of being replicated by others so that the results of a study can be confirmed or refuted. The difficulty that qualitative methods pose, be they ethnographically or interview based, is that the precise procedures used to achieve the data cannot be repeated in all their detail. The point of qualitative methods is their flexibilty: the fact that the researcher can develop themes with respondents as they emerge and follow through activity that seems pertinent to the inquiry without being constrained by the need to adhere rigidly to a previously set formula. But if this is so, how can another researcher ever know whether she or he is genuinely replicating a previous study? Indeed there are famous examples of ethnographic re-studies which failed quite spectacularly to arrive at similar conclusions to the original project (e.g. Lewis, 1951; Freeman, 1984).

The reasons for this, however, are not solely to do with the feasibility of replication. First, changes can obviously occur in a community, organization or whatever in the time between first and later studies. Equally, novelty rather than repetition is called for in publications, so there is some disincentive to look for duplicate results. More importantly there is also the strong possibility that the researcher's own assumptions affect what she or he perceives, records and reports. Different researchers with their different outlooks, priorities and theoretical perspectives will 'see' different episodes as significant in their fieldwork and consequently produce analyses based upon these different visions. Similarly, researchers with their individual personalities and dispositions will open themselves up to different experiences in the field and thus be in a position to observe or listen to distinct episodes of action. Such variation in access to data is likely to have some influence on the consequent analysis.

However, note that this criticism of qualitative approaches — i.e. that the researcher's perspective colours the data generated — does not rule out verification. If anything, it highlights the need for replication in order to test and develop the analyses generated in qualitative studies. Crucially, those who favour qualitative approaches would accept that the perspective a researcher brings to the research does influence the resultant 'findings', but that the flexibility of the methods, their time-span and the quality of data collected allows for far greater reflexivity about the theoretical and conceptual assumptions being made than do those methods which produce apparently more reliable, highly structured data. For clearly all data collection requires some presuppositions. In social science, just as in other disciplines, 'facts' do not stand alone but are theoretically informed. Thus the difference between structured and unstructured data collection does not lie in the purity of the questions asked or the actions followed, but rather in the degree to which others can follow exactly the same procedures. This begs the question of whether all respondents actually experience and interpret such procedures in an equivalent way. If not, can we claim uniformity and hence essential replicability? However the more important issue here is whether the game is worth the candle. If the method is not producing valid data — in other words does not generate data which adequately addresses the research questions being posed — then replicability is hardly a matter of much significance.

In any case, in terms of contributing to social scientific knowledge, studies based on qualitative methods can be replicable, in purpose if not in detailed procedures, and cumulative. That is, while no two qualitative researchers will ask the same questions in the same order or observe exactly the same action, they can both study the same range of phenomena and generate analyses which can each inform the other and of course lead to new studies which themselves may result in further modification to our understanding. For example, the recent explosion of ethnographic studies of schooling has added a great deal to our knowledge of how schools operate in practice (Burgess, 1986, Chapters 7 and 8; Hammersley, 1985). Each study differs in the detail of the analysis it provides, each addresses a more or less different phenomenon, yet it is possible to see them collectively as a body of work that informs us about the social relations of schooling. Some may be concerned with gender inequalities; others with racial discrimination; still others with sexual harassment; yet together they indicate the processes by which advantage and disadvantage within the school system are sustained. Similarly there has been a growth in the number of intensive interview surveys concerned with women's domestic and mothering roles (e.g. Oakley, 1980; Boulton, 1983; Sharpe, 1984; Brannan and Wilson, 1987). Each has a somewhat different focus and asks different questions. Nonetheless what we now possess is a range of research in broad agreement about the social circumstances, the satisfactions and dissatisfactions, the ambiguities and contradictions women with these responsibilities typically experience, as well as the prime influences shaping them. It is doubtful if either body of knowledge could have been generated using more quantitative approaches. More importantly, these examples illustrate that with systematic data collection and analysis it is quite possible for qualitative approaches to generate analyses which are in general terms replicable and cumulative.

Research Problems

Qualitative approaches require quite a different personal stance from the detached, rather dry approach often associated with more quantitative methods. To the extent that qualitative methods represent 'inquiry from the inside' with researchers seeking more flexible involvement with their respondents, the demands made on and skills required of the researcher are different from those associated with, say, structured surveys or laboratory experiments. As Carol Jones indicates in Chapter 17, the accomplishment of systematic data through qualitative interviewing is a much more complex activity than collecting data using structured schedules. This applies even more with ethnography where the demands made on the researcher are particularly large, indeed greater probably than in any other form of data generation in the social sciences. At issue here are not just matters of convenience — such as the need to observe activities at times which clash with domestic or other personal obligations — but also the management of relationships during the fieldwork.

For example, ethnographic fieldwork requires that the researcher be politically aware and sensitive to the impression she or he is making on others. In surveys what goes on in one interview will usually not have repercussions on the relationship the researcher develops with other respondents. In ethnographic work, the opposite is true. The fieldwork normally occurs within a closed setting — a school, a workplace, a locality, a hospital, or whatever — where those involved are in routine contact with one another and where the activities of the researcher are likely to be a subject of gossip. One needs to be conscious of the cliques that exist and try not to be seen to side too heavily with any interest group. This of course may not be possible in some contexts where battle lines are heavily drawn and, as in some industrial settings, institutionally supported.

Attempts at not siding, at remaining marginal, can be extremely difficult, especially early on in the research before you have a chance to become aware of what the divisions are. In the early phases of the research, simply establishing some 'rapport' with those in the research setting can appear a massively daunting task. As a 'stranger' trying to make contact, the pressure is to grab enthusiastically at any hand of friendship proffered if only to fill the void of uncertainty and reassure yourself that the 'real' research is under way (see, for example, Whyte, 1955). Moreover not taking sides can be difficult psychologically, particularly if, as is likely, you find some people more congenial and compatible than others. Herbert Gans (1982) has described these and other psychological tensions that fieldwork induces particularly well.

Ethnographic work also requires novel recording skills. Data from interviews is comparatively easy to record either in written form or else on tape. With observation, it is both harder to decide what should be recorded — i.e. what counts as data — and to find ways in which it can be logged. Only rarely will it be feasible or worthwhile to use video-recordings which can be analyzed later. Typically the fieldworker has to rely on notes taken at the time and expanded as soon as possible after leaving the field for the day. In this respect, as well as ethically, overt fieldwork easily outscores covert approaches. Being open about the research allows you to ask questions without arousing suspicion, to examine records and documents, to gain access to people at different levels of the organizational hierarchy, and write as copious notes as you need. In comparison, the apparently common practice in covert research of frequently going to the toilet to write up notes clandestinely leaves much to be desired!

Analyzing Qualitative Material

Although a great deal has been written in the research literature about the practicalities and politics of qualitative research, there is surprisingly little information on how to analyze such qualitative data. Sometimes it appears that there is an almost magical transition from notes to analysis. Given the standard criticisms about the idiosyncrasy and unreliability of qualitative methods, this dearth of guidance on procedures for analyzing data is strange. On the other hand it is actually quite difficult to discuss the different stages of qualitative analysis because, as mentioned earlier, they are more fluid and less clearly delineated than is usual in quantitative work. Indeed, some ideas about significant relationships within the data generally emerge — in a creative fashion that is difficult to pinpoint or predict — during the fieldwork. These new ideas may then gently shift the focus of data collection, which in turn leads to the uncovering of new ideas. And so the process continues.

Generally by the time the fieldwork is finished, the researcher will have some more or less clear ideas about the significant issues that have emerged in the fieldwork and about the way in which they are to be presented and analyzed. It is probably worth emphasizing here that not all the data presented requires qualitative analysis of a particularly profound form. Aside from descriptions of the settings in which the research was conducted, it is likely you will want to include some quantitative material. For example, examiners and other readers of a thesis will want to have some idea of the frequency with which particular events occurred or what proportion of respondents expressed a given view. Equally you may have collected some quantitative data as well as more qualitative material in your study — a questionnaire survey of some issue, for instance, or a statistical analysis of changes in an organization — and want to include the results of these inquiries in the thesis. Just because the data collection is defined as qualitative does not mean that you should eschew all quantitative elements in your analysis. You will find that incorporating appropriate descriptive and quantitative material into the thesis supports the qualitative arguments being made rather than detracting from them.

However ultimately the success or otherwise of your thesis is likely to rest on how well you analyze your qualitative data. Be warned: this is not an easy task. You should certainly not underestimate the amount of time analysis takes. It is likely to be a long and often difficult process. Putting things simply, the main task is to categorize the varied data you have so that links can be made between them which explain the events which are the focus of the thesis. As already said, by the time you start the analysis phase proper you will have ideas about these. However you need to ensure that your ideas and the categories you are constructing are investigated and scrutinized methodically. You need to be systematic in ensuring the conceptual adequacy, and the comprehensiveness of the boundaries, of the categories you are constructing. A standard reference here is Glaser and Strauss (1967), *The Discovery of Grounded Theory*. In this they describe a process by which analytical categories can be developed inductively from the data through a careful scrutiny of all the different interview or observational accounts gathered in the fieldwork. The essence of the approach involves 'stripping' particular episodes of action/speech into their essential component elements. Other episodes in the fieldnotes are then scrutinized to see if they contain similar or different elements. Where there is similarity and overlap, modified categorizations can then be generated which encompass and 'bridge' a wider range of phenomena, ones which previously perhaps did not seem to have much in common (Turner, 1981).

In the past researchers almost invariably used file cards to record the different episodes of action or talk that seemed significant. These could then be physically shifted into different piles representing the emerging links between different empirical phenomena. Some still find being able to move cards around into piles is a helpful process for making connections between apparently disparate themes or events. However there are now computer programs available, for example *Ethnograph*, which are very helpful for sorting out data. The basis of these programs is a flexible coding and sorting system that allows easy collation and manipulation of data blocks — episodes of talk or action — that are marked or coded as similar. Written accounts — typescripts of interviews or descriptions of observed episodes — can be coded line by line or section by section according to whatever categories have been created. All the passages sharing a given coding can then be assembled together, compared, sorted again, recoded as required, until the researcher feels that all the instances of a given phenomenon have been ordered together and appropriate relationships generated. Those who have become familiar with these programs have found them extremely helpful for analyzing their material and ensuring that all pertinent episodes of data are incorporated.

As well as differences in analysis, qualitative research often raises problems of data presentation. How can you portray all the richness of the material you gathered in a structured, systematic written form? In quite large part, the answer to this lies in the clarity of the analytical framework you have devised in systematically working through the material time and time again. Once you have this right, once the ordering is clear in your own mind, then presenting the material in a suitable way becomes far less problematic. Equally, though, pay heed to the form of data presentation and analysis produced by other qualitative researchers. See how they have incorporated quotations from respondents or descriptions of action from their fieldwork into their analysis. And do not be afraid of using what Gluckman (1961) calls 'social situations' as a means of highlighting key social processes (see Mitchell, 1983). A carefully selected example of action or interview data can be used to portray the issues or themes which are core to the analysis, either as a way of illustrating a particular sub-theme within the overall analysis or as a vehicle for indicating the way a range of issues come together. A classic example of this is given by Elliot Liebow (1967) in *Tally's Corner*, where he gives a pretty routine-seeming description of early morning events on a ghetto street-corner. However he then uses this to inform his subsequent analysis which shows superbly the structural constraints under which male black ghetto-dwellers make their choices. Thus provided they are supported by other forms of data and tie in clearly with other aspects of the analysis, using individual episodes can provide a powerful means of getting a hold on the problems of presenting complex qualitative data. Provided the data analysis has been systematic, which itself will be evidenced in some part by the way in which the 'apt illustration' relates to other parts of the data, this technique can prove a very useful device for portraying the social complexity revealed by the fieldwork.

Further Reading

Suggestions for reading about case studies and qualitative interviews are given in the next two chapters. Bryman (1988a) provides a very good discussion of the nature and merits of qualitative and quantitative research. Those interested in participant observation and ethnography will find Hammersley and Atkinson (1983) very helpful. It provides a discussion of all the main phases of doing ethnographies. Burgess (1984a) is also a very useful text. His companion set of readings (Burgess, 1982), contains a number of important papers giving advice about different phases of field research. Although now slightly dated, Filstead (1970) also contains some important papers. In a well-written and entertaining book, Punch (1986) discusses many significant aspects of doing ethnography on the basis of his own experience of researching both schooling and police work. Notwithstanding its title, it offers a wide range of insights that make it a valuable source for any research student interested in qualitative research. The classic account of sociological fieldwork is Whyte (1955, Appendix 1). His more recent discussion of different aspects of doing participant observation studies (Whyte, 1984) is also well worth consulting. Gans (1982) provides an informative and revealing account of the personal dilemmas of doing fieldwork. The subject that has seen the greatest growth in ethnographic research in Britain in recent years is education. There is now a substantial body of literature which considers the problems presented by doing ethnography in schools. See for example Hammersley (1983), and Burgess (1984b; 1985). The collection of papers edited by Bryman (1988b) is also worth consulting, and not only if you are planning on doing research in organizations.

Acknowledgments

I would like to thank Chris Shilling for help and comments on a draft of this paper.

References

BOULTON, M.G. (1983) *On Being A Mother*, London, Tavistock.

BRANNAN, J. and WILSON, G. (1987) *Give and Take in Families*, London, Allen and Unwin.

BRYMAN, A. (1988a) *Quantity and Quality in Social Research*, London, Unwin Hyman.

BRYMAN, A. (Ed.) (1988b) *Doing Research in Organizations*, London, Routledge.

BURGESS, R.G. (Ed.) (1982) *Field Research: A Sourcebook and Field Manual*, London, Allen and Unwin.

BURGESS, R.G. (1984a) *In the Field: An Introduction to Field Research*, London, Allen and Unwin.

BURGESS, R.G. (Ed.) (1984b) *The Research Process in Educational Settings*, London, Falmer Press.

BURGESS, R.G. (Ed.) (1985) *Field Methods in the Study of Education*, London, Falmer Press.

BURGESS, R.G. (1986) *Sociology, Education and Schools*, London, Batsford.

DENZIN, N.K. (1970) *The Research Act in Sociology*, Chicago, Aldine.

EVERED, R. and LEWIS, M.R. (1981) 'Alternative perspectives in the organizational sciences: "Inquiry from the inside" and "inquiry from the outside"', *Academy of Management Review*, **6**, pp. 385–95.

FIELDING, N.G. and FIELDING, J.L. (1986) *Linking Data*, Sage University Paper series on Qualitative Research Methods, Volume 4, Beverly Hills, Sage.

FILSTEAD, W.J. (Ed.) (1970) *Qualitative Methodology*, Chicago, Markham.

FREEMAN, D. (1984) *Margaret Mead and Samoa*, Harmondsworth, Penguin.

GANS, H.J. (1982) 'The participant-observer as a human being: Observations on the personal aspects of field work', in BURGESS, R.G. (Ed.) *Field Research: A Sourcebook and Field Manual*, London, Allen and Unwin.

GLASER, B.G. and STRAUSS, A.L. (1967) *The Discovery of Grounded Theory*, Chicago, Aldine.

GLUCKMAN, M. (1961) 'Ethnographic data in British social anthropology' *Sociological Review*, **9**, pp. 5–17.

HAMMERSLEY, M. (Ed.) (1983) *The Ethnography of Schooling*, Humberside, Nafferton Books.

HAMMERSLEY, M. (1985) 'From ethnography to theory: Programme and paradigm in the sociology of education', *Sociology*, **19**, pp. 244–59.

HAMMERSLEY, M. and ATKINSON, P. (1983) *Ethnography: Principles in Practice*, London, Tavistock.

LEWIS, O. (1951) *Life in a Mexican Village: Tepoztlan Revisited*, Urbana, University of Illinois Press.

LIEBOW E. (1967) *Tally's Corner*, Boston, Little, Brown and Co.

MITCHELL, J.C. (1983) 'Case and situational analysis', *Sociological Review*, **31**, pp. 187–211.

OAKLEY, A. (1980) *Women Confined*, Oxford, Martin Robertson.

PLATT, J. (1988) 'What can case studies do?', *Studies in Qualitative Methodology*, **1**, pp. 1–23, Greenwich, CT, JAI Press.

PUNCH, M. (1986) *The Politics and Ethics of Fieldwork*, Sage University Paper series on Qualitative Research Methods, Volume 3, Beverly Hills, Sage.

SHARPE, S. (1984) *Double Identity*, Harmondsworth, Penguin.

TURNER, B.A. (1981) 'Some practical aspects of qualitative data analysis: One way of organising the cognitive processes associated with the generation of grounded theory', *Quality and Quantity*, **15**, pp. 225–47.

WHYTE, W.F. (1955) *Street Corner Society: The Social Structure of an Italian Slum*, 2nd ed., Chicago, University of Chicago Press.

WHYTE, W.F. (1984) *Learning from the Field: A Guide from Experience*, Beverley Hills, Sage.

Chapter 16

Case Studies

Howard Rose

Considering the Case-study Approach

Planning to embark on fieldwork-based research can be a troublesome matter. This may be so particularly when traditional research methods like the survey questionnaire seem to be inappropriate. Difficulties may be compounded by the belief that the options can only be framed in terms of a dichotomy of quantitative versus qualitative approaches. In one direction it seems are scientific sampling and statistical inference, while in the other direction lies participant observation and ethnographic interpretation. You might feel that the former fails to recognize adequately the complexity, richness and subtlety of the world you want to examine. Yet you do not want, nor are you able, to dispense entirely with methods which can yield 'hard facts' and thoroughly tested hypotheses.

The theme of this chapter is that there is an approach — the case-study approach — to doing social research which, by virtue of its flexibility, may be adaptable to your needs. What follows aims to open up the case-study approach to the research student and the novice field researcher, encouraging self-discovery while promoting self-criticism and self-evaluation. The intention is to explore some of the diversity of the case-study approach, to indicate its benefits and problems and to identify some of the methodological pitfalls. The discussion will draw on examples of case-study research, primarily from the fields of work and organization studies with which the author is familiar. Overall it is hoped that some of the general issues raised will commend the case-study approach to those researching in a much more diverse range of disciplinary fields. Of necessity, in a piece of this length, the illustrative examples will be brief and therefore the reader will be invited to follow up relevant accounts of case-study research. While there is no substitute for actually doing case-study research as a way of learning about these issues, sampling some of the fruits of others' endeavours can nevertheless offer considerable enlightenment.

Characterizing the Case Study

Seeking to define the case-study approach in a formal sense is somewhat unsatisfactory because it may result in a closing off, rather than an opening up, of the potential variety and diversity of the approach. While some reference will be made to definitions that have been attempted, the primary concern here will be to try to identify the distinctive or at least the typical features of the case study. Brief descriptions of case-study research will be used to examine specific methodological points and highlight the main features of the approach. The specific studies to be described are by Pollert (1981), Goldthorpe *et al.* (1969), Gallie (1978), Buchanan and Boddy (1983), Littler (1982), Pettigrew (1973) and Clark *et al.* (1988). Together these studies should give a fair representation of the potential flexibility of the approach.

In Anna Pollert's *Girls, Wives, Factory Lives*, we find an account of the working lives and experiences of women factory workers employed by the Churchman's tobacco company in Bristol, based on informal interviews and observation on the shop-floor. The study sought to construct a dynamic interpretation of women workers' consciousness in which the relationship between factory experience and domestic experience was an important issue. As the author explains, two themes were explored throughout: 'the common areas of wage labour for men and women, and the way being a woman alters this' (1981:5). Much of the ensuing discussion is framed in terms of ideas drawn from both Marxism and feminism. In terms of the structure of the book these theoretical concerns are interwoven with contextual material about the company and details of the womens' experiences, extensively supported by extracts from the interviews.

This study by Pollert brings out several features of the case-study approach. One significant feature is the concern with placing the womens' workplace experiences in a specific social, economic and historical context. Hence we are given details of the development of the factory and the company, as well as socio-economic data about Bristol and the composition of the workforce itself. The relationship between the womens' experiences inside and outside work is accorded particular importance and the author is at pains to explain how the study tackled this aspect, in the light of her lack of direct involvement with their home, community and social lives. Implicit in this approach is the focus on a 'bounded system' (Adelman, Jenkins and Kemmis, 1984) in which the relationship between the system and its context may be as important as the relationships and interactions within the system. This emphasis on the wholeness of the case accords with the view expressed by Goode and Hatt (1952) that the case-study approach is 'a way of organizing data so as to preserve the *unitary character of the social object being studied*' (quoted in Mitchell, 1983:191, original emphasis).

Another important feature of this study is that the unit of analysis is women workers in this particular factory. There is no suggestion that this is a representative sample of the female working population of Bristol, nor that this is a typical factory. Indeed, the author points out that this could be considered a 'women's factory', since: 'in general men and women never worked alongside each other on the same job. The men's departments were separate.' (1981:32) The other aspect of this matter of representativeness is that the findings from a study such as this are clearly not intended to be generalized in a statistical sense to a defined population of women workers. These aspects of the case-study approach — representativeness and general-izability — are often viewed by its detractors as major weaknesses. However to advocates of the approach these methodological points can be answered and, moreover, turned into a positive virtue.

It can be argued that much of the criticism directed at the case-study approach over these issues is based on a degree of methodological confusion (Mitchell, 1983; Yin, 1989). Under the influence of quantitative method, representativeness has come to mean typicality in the sense of a statistically reliable random sample from a population. Similarly, generalizability has come to mean the ability to extrapolate with statistical confidence from that sample to the population from which it was drawn. It should be noted, however, that survey samples are frequently taken from strategically selected localized populations not national populations, so that even here problems of generalizability exist (Bryman, 1988:35). In case-study research, by contrast, it is considered more appropriate to treat representativeness in terms of a qualitative logic for the selection of cases for study, rather than a quantitative logic of sampling from a population. In this vein Hakim refers to case studies taking for their subject matter 'one or more selected examples of a social entity' (1987:61). From a broader perspective, Burgess (1984) discusses the use of non-probability sampling in field research and refers to the need for selection strategies to be theoretically directed (pp. 54–6). Mitchell specific-ally develops this theoretical theme by characterizing the case-study approach in terms of 'a detailed examination of an event (or series of related events) which the analyst believes exhibits (or exhibit) the *operation of some identified theoretical principle*' (1983:192, emphasis added). The implication is that cases may be deliberately chosen *because* they are atypical, but correspondingly possess greater explanatory power (Mitchell, 1983; Platt, 1989). As we will see shortly, this can be a critical feature of a research study designed to test a theoretical proposition. The point here is that typicality in the statistical sense is not a major concern for case-study research. This is not to suggest, however, that representativeness ceases to be an issue. On the contrary, where more than one case is used the issues of selection criteria and qualita-tive representativeness can be of considerable importance.

The implication of this theoretical orientation to representativeness is that a similar logic should apply to generalizability. The underlying principle is rooted in the distinction between statistical and logical inference (Mitchell, 1983). Whereas the survey approach depends on the typicality of the sample for making valid statistical inferences about the parent population, the case-study approach depends on the 'cogency of the theoretical reasoning' for the validity of any logical inferences from a case or cases (Mitchell, 1983:207). A similar argument is made by Yin, who likens the case study in this respect to the experiment, since it does not represent a statistical sample and the goal of the investigator is to 'expand and generalize theories (analytical generaliza-tion) and not to enumerate frequencies (statistical generalization)' (1989:21) The practical consequence for extrapolation from case studies is that gener-alization depends upon the adequacy of the underlying theory and related knowledge, and must be qualified by the relevant contextual conditions (Mitchell, 1983).

In Pollert's study the principles of qualitative selection and logical inference tend to be more implicit than explicit, although the characterization of the Churchman's factory as a womens' factory suggests the qualitative selection of a case most favourable to demonstrating the theoretical concerns. By contrast, in the study by Goldthorpe *et al.* (1969) these aspects are a clearly articulated feature of the study design. This study was specifically concerned with testing the thesis of working-class *embourgeoisement*, which put simply suggested that as a consequence of acquiring incomes and living standards comparable to white-collar workers, manual workers were adopting new social outlooks and norms and thereby becoming assimilated into middle-class society.

In designing the study the researchers were faced with limited resources and a somewhat ill-defined phenomenon. The approach decided upon envis-aged a single case study of 'one "population" of manual workers in one particular context at one particular time' (1969:30). Significantly, the re-searchers set out to select a case that would be '*as favourable as possible* for the confirmation of the *embourgeoisement* thesis' (1969:31, original emphasis). By doing so they saw themselves as utilizing a critical case, as a test for the theoretical proposition that among the more advantaged sections of the working class a process of embourgeoisement was occurring. To put that strategic decision into practice the researchers sought to specify on a theor-etical basis the required attributes of the critical case, and then set out to find a real-life approximation to the resulting model case.

In the event the researchers were unable to find an exact match, but were able to find a 'population' that was close enough to constitute their critical case:

> The population in question was one located in the town of Luton in south-west Bedfordshire and was made up of workers in a number

of selected high-wage occupations who were employed at the Luton
plants of three major manufacturing concerns. (1969:36)

As Goldthorpe *et al.* go on to explain, the sample taken from this population
was not a random one since the occupational categories were selected to
cover those doing work central to the main production systems in each plant,
and confined to certain major departments in each firm. Recognizing the
problems which this entails for generalization, the researchers conducted
checks which to their satisfaction indicated no grounds for supposing that
those in the excluded departments were qualitatively different from those
studied.

While the primary interest of the researchers was focused on the *process*
of embourgeoisement, the research as implemented was, as they concede, a
'snapshot' picture. However, as they carefully argue, the research design used
is an appropriate test for the proposition that embourgeoisement has already
occurred among certain 'advanced' groups of manual workers (1969:51).
The main research method used was the interview, supplemented by workplace observation. Like Pollert's study, it involved no direct observation of
the respondents' out-of-work lives, despite the importance of this for the
theoretical proposition. Rather the researchers relied on the interviews for
this data and used appropriate validity checks where possible. On the basis of
thier findings, Goldthorpe *et al.* concluded that the thesis of embourgeoisement breaks down decisively at several points.

In this example of case-study research we can recognize those features
that we have already seen in respect of the study by Pollert. There are
however, a number of features that are distinctive about this particular study.
First, the deliberate choice of a critical case provides a clear example of the
opportunity for testing theoretical propositions which the principle of qualitative selection of cases offers. Second, this example illustrates the potential
for a relatively complex research design while retaining the unitary character
of the case. At first sight the unit or units of analysis appear somewhat
ambiguous. Are we focusing on the selected high-wage occupations of
Luton, the three manufacturing plants, or the major production departments
within those plants?

The ambiguity can be resolved with reference to what Yin calls 'embedded units of analysis' (1989:49–50). In the study by Goldthorpe *et al.* we have
an example of a single case in which at two levels, the plant and the
department, there are embedded units of analysis. The significant point is
that these are not statistical samples, but represent the application of the
principle of qualitative selection to the construction of a manageable research
design. It is also noteworthy that in this study there is no logic of comparison
or logic of diversity in the selection of these units of analysis. As we shall see,
it is possible to use this design element of embedded units of analysis in

single and multiple case studies, to enable the construction of a wide variety of research designs to meet a broad range of theoretical and practical requirements.

Whereas the studies by Pollert and Goldthorpe *et al.* are based on single cases, the study by Duncan Gallie (1978) offers an example of a multiple case study. Like Goldthorpe *et al.* Gallie uses a research design which is deliberately constructed to facilitate the testing of a theoretical proposition. In this example, however, a logic of comparison is built into the design. The thesis to be tested by Gallie was one which took divergent forms, but whose underlying argument was that contemporary advances in production technology have decisive consequences for working-class consciousness. In one version the argument was that advanced automation resulted in greater social integration of the worker into the enterprise. In the other version automation was believed to generate new forms of class conflict. On inspection Gallie concluded that both versions of the thesis were based on evidence of poor quality (1978:29).

Further consideration of the theoretical arguments led Gallie to the view that the basic explanatory assumptions of these theories might be fundamentally flawed and that an alternative view of the implications of automation would be worth considering. This alternative view was that while automation might have decisive effects on the objective work situation, its effects on social integration and class consciousness are indeterminate. Rather, Gallie hypothesized:

> The degree of social integration in the highly automated sector will more probably depend on the cultural values prevalent in the wider collectivity to which workers belong, and on the nature of the institutional structures characteristic of the society in which the automated sector emerges. (1978:35)

In order to test this hypothesis Gallie adopted a cross-cultural research strategy and set out 'to examine the implications of advanced technology in two societies — France and Britain' (1978:37).

The final design of Gallie's study comprised four oil refineries, owned by the same multi-national company, two of which were in France and the other two in Britain. The design was governed by three requirements: similarity of technology; regional diversity; and institutional systems that were capable of close comparison. Oil refining was chosen because it represented the most highly automated sector of industry and was therefore theoretically favourable to the thesis being tested and also offered the likely advantage of technological similarity between countries. As Gallie explains, the refinery was chosen as the basic unit of analysis in order to 'take into account the institutions of industrial relations at a detailed level' and consequently this entailed 'the sacrifice of breadth of coverage within the industry in favour of intensiveness' (1978:40). Regional diversity was incorporated in respect of the location of the refineries in each country, to make it 'possible to single out the factors that could be attributed to local conditions from the factors that were more widely prevalent in the society' (1978:40–41).

Three methods were used for the study: 'a survey of manual workers in each refinery, a study of documentary material relating to industrial relations, and longer and deeper interviews with a certain number of key participants' (1978:45). It is noteworthy that Gallie took the total set of operators and maintenance workers in each refinery as a sample population, stratified the workforce into two main categories of workers, and then took sampling fractions from each category. This usefully illustrates an important aspect of the flexibility of the case study. Whilst qualitative selection of cases is a characteristic feature of the approach, it does not rule out the use of quantitative methods within such a design. Another distinctive feature of Gallie's study is the logic of comparison which enabled the testing of the particular theoretical proposition. In fact, Gallie's main conclusion was that the findings of his study supported the hypothesis that technology *per se* is not the primary determinant of social integration in the workplace and that the wider cultural and structural patterns of specific societies are of critical importance.

The logic of comparison is one of several logics that can be used in the design of multiple case studies or single case studies with embedded units of analysis. For example, Hakim (1987) refers to the opportunity to achieve replication through multiple cases. Somewhat restrictively, Yin (1989) argues that a replication logic is the only logic for multiple case studies. A broader view is taken by Platt (1989), who suggests a third logic for multiple case studies, the logic of diversity. The logic of diversity can be useful for multiple case study designs, not only where cases are sought for their explanatory power, but also where they are intended to be descriptive or exploratory. This broader range of uses for the case study approach is discussed by Hakim (1987) and by Platt (1989). The logic of diversity can be illustrated by two examples of case study research that are not oriented towards such specific theoretical propositions as the studies by Goldthorpe *et al.* and Gallie.

Our first example is the seven case studies of applications of computing technologies reported by Buchanan and Boddy (1983). The authors point out that the case-study approach was chosen to enable 'fresh insights into new and poorly structured problems', and 'to collect data that was rich and interesting, rather than rigorous, and to generate ideas and hypotheses for further research' (1983:33). The case studies were selected from a varied set of organizations 'in the belief that the common features of new computing technologies would have similar effects in different settings' (1983:33).

Elsewhere Buchanan and Boddy have explicitly advocated an 'opportunistic' approach to locating cases for fieldwork (Buchanan, Boddy and McCalman, 1988). In this regard, it should be noted that Hakim is of the view that 'convenience samples are not acceptable in case study research' (1987:64). In practice, opportunism as discussed by Buchanan, Boddy and McCalman is probably a valid approach for certain types of study, providing the approach adopted is made explicit.

Buchanan and Boddy therefore offer one example of a simple use of the logic of diversity, guided by a relatively unsophisticated theoretical schema, for the purpose of carrying out exploratory studies which might generate hypotheses for future research. A slightly different use of the logic of diversity is illustrated by Wilkinson, who reports on four detailed case studies of 'innovations based on microelectronics in batch engineering' (1983:24). These four studies, Wilkinson reveals, were preceded by an original set of twenty-seven studies. The latter, based on an interview with at least one manager in each case, 'served largely as a pilot study for the four more detailed case studies' (1983:23). Several points arise from this brief example. First, it indicates that the logic of diversity may be applied to the design of a pilot study. Second, it suggests that it is not necessary for all uses of the case-study approach to be based on intensive involvement. Third, the four cases reported by Wilkinson were not snapshot studies, but were longitudinal studies of events over a period of time.

This brings us to consideration of another important dimension of case-study design, that of the longitudinal structure. Apart from the studies by Wilkinson, all of the studies described so far have been snapshot studies of one type or another. The longitudinal study exhibits many of the features of snapshot studies, but has the additional facility to be able to handle both historical and processual aspects. Many of the features of the case-study approach that we have gleaned so far are summarized in the definition proposed by Yin (1989:23):

> The case study is an empirical enquiry that: investigates a contemporary phenomenon within its real life context; when — the boundaries between phenomenon and context are not clearly evident; and in which — multiple sources of evidence are used.

The point that we should note here is the emphasis on investigating contemporary phenomena in their real-life context. Here Yin is seeking to distinguish the case study from the experiment and the history. While we may welcome the demarcation from the former, it is perhaps less satisfactory to exclude the latter.

A good example of the case-study approach applied to historical phenomena, although not strictly a longitudinal design, is the study by

Littler (1982) of management and labour relations in two contrasting companies in Britain in the 1930s. The theoretical focus of Littler's work is the labour process debate concerning the nature, origins and processes of transformation of work organization. An influential exposition of the labour process approach by Braverman (1974) put forward the view that the development of the labour process under capitalism could be characterized as a unilinear trend of deskilling. This trend was considered to be strongly associated with the application of ideas of scientific management, epitomized by the work of F.W. Taylor in the USA at the beginning of this century. A major concern of Littler's study is to assess the theoretical proposition that the transformation of work organization under capitalism can be explained by a simple model of craft deskilling based on Taylorism.

The distinctive feature of the research design used by Littler for the empirical evaluation of this theoretical proposition is the use of archive material. Here, the archives of the Bedaux company, a US management consultancy promoting neo-Taylorist ideas in Britain in the 1930s, offered a unique source from which the two contrasting case studies were drawn. Within the framework of a comparative case-study approach, the archive data was supplemented by contemporary newspaper reports and present-day interviews with trade union officials involved at the time. A major conclusion reached by Littler is that: 'A simple model of craft-deskilling with F.W. Taylor as the devil incarnate is not tenable' (1982:187). Rather, the empirical investigation of the implementation of Taylorism in Britain, particularly through the 'acid test' of one of the case studies, leads to a more complex picture. Like Gallie, Littler also considered it important to incorporate an international comparative dimension, to explore the question of whether Britain was an archetypal example of industrialization. Hence, in addition to the two British case studies, briefer studies of developments in Japan and the USA were undertaken. These showed that national differences were important to the extent that in Japan, for example, the ideas of Taylorism were 'filtered through the sieve of prevailing ideology' (1982:194).

In passing, we should note the features of Littler's study which correspond to features of the case-study approach that we have already encountered. We should note, for example, the use of a logic of comparison, the qualitative selection of contrasting cases and the use of multiple methods of data collection. A distinctive feature of this study, as Hakim (1987) notes, is that it illustrates how the case-study approach can be applied to historical research. An historical element is also an important part of Andrew Pettigrew's (1973) study of decision-making and specialization with regard to computerization in a single firm, referred to by the pseudonym of Brian Michaels.

The longitudinal design adopted by Pettigrew for this study comprised a direct study of the ongoing decision process and an historical study of the preceding period of computerization in Brian Michaels. The methodological principle underlying this design is Pettigrew's belief that theoretical concerns of a processual form require a longitudinal research design, thereby enabling a social system to be explored as 'a continuing system with a past, a present and a future' (Pettigrew, 1973:55; 1979:570). The direct study was carried out by Pettigrew occupying a participant-observer role (his description) within Brian Michaels for a period spanning almost two years. The choice of this role as the principal research method arose from the theoretical perspective on decision-making as a political process. The corresponding aim was 'to penetrate the veil of formal position in order to determine, as far as possible, who *really* had the power' (1973:56; original emphasis). In this respect we find in Pettigrew's study the use of the case-study design in a context where problems of bias and validity take a high profile.

A notable feature of this study is that Pettigrew tackles these methodological problems directly and in a thorough-going way (1973, Chapter 4). In particular he notes the difficulties faced by the single observer and the dangers of becoming too much identified with the perspectives of particular informants. In addressing these problems Pettigrew adopts a strategy of multiple triangulation (Denzin, 1970), using 'multiple methods, multiple data sources, multiple observers, and multiple levels of analysis' (1973:53, 65). Several writers have noted the tendency for case-study research to use a variety of data collection techniques (Nisbet and Watt, 1984; Hakim, 1987; Bryman, 1989; Yin, 1989). One aspect of this use of multiple methods, as illustrated by Pettigrew, is that it may help to overcome a potential methodological weakness of the case-study approach. Another aspect of the use of multiple methods, illustrated by Gallie, is that the methods used in case-study research may be either qualitative or quantitative, or a combination of them. Indeed, case-study method is not synonymous with qualitative method and need not even require its use at all (Yin, 1989).

An example of the longitudinal design which uses the strategy of multiple methods in both of the senses outlined is the study by Clark *et al.* (1988) of the process of technological change with respect to telephone exchange maintenance. Here the authors were not only concerned with process studies, like Pettigrew, but also with a comparative dimension. As Clark *et al.* point out: 'The research design envisaged an in-depth longitudinal study of the process of exchange modernization in two exchanges in two different telephone regions' (1988:5). The original intention was to follow the conversion of these two exchanges for a period beginning prior to exchange installation and ending a few months after each exchange had been brought into service. However, it became apparent to the researchers that such a 'neat' design was unlikely to be realizable in practice and consequently a number of exchanges at different points in their conversion were monitored for varying periods of time. Additionally, the comparative dimension was enhanced by the study of two further exchanges, one being an example of the 'old' technology and the other an example of the 'new' technology.

In the actual implementation of their research design Clark *et al.* studied eight exchanges in two British Telecom regions and three separate telephone areas. A significant point about this study for our present purposes is that it illustrates an application of the qualitative selection of cases as part of a longitudinal design, in order to construct a representative example (in the sense discussed earlier) of the process of exchange conversion. In other words, even where time constraints make the desired longitudinal design unachievable, qualitative representativeness may be adapted to the purpose of selecting embedded cases representative of the entire process. A further point of interest about this study is the use of multiple methods and, in particular the use of both qualitative and quantitative methods. As the authors point out, semi-structured interviews were a major source of data. However, various other methods were used including self-report diaries, completed by the maintenance engineers to record the amount of time spent on various tasks. The latter offer an interesting illustration of the use of quantitative methods in case-study research, whereby statistical analysis of this data was an important piece of evidence in Clark *et al.*'s argument that fault diagnosis was significantly influenced by the nature of the exchange technology (1988, Chapter 4).

Conclusion

In this chapter I have tried to demonstrate the flexibility and versatility of the case-study approach. It must be said that some of the research designs described here would be too complex or resource intensive for a research student to contemplate adopting them in detail. For example, the studies of Goldthorpe *et al.* and Clark *et al.* were large-scale studies involving several researchers working in the field over a long period of time. However, what I have tried to do is to draw out from these examples the main principles and features of the case study approach, which can be applied to a variety of research needs. In this regard it is worth noting the following characteristics. First, the case study design may comprise single or multiple cases and these may consist of snapshot or longitudinal studies. Second, where the design comprises multiple cases, the choice of cases may be based on a logic of comparison, of diversity, or of replication. Third, the notion of embedded units of analysis can be used as a design element to add greater versatility and enable the basic design to be adapted to meet various theoretical and practical requirements.

While indicating the principal design features of the case-study approach, I have also tried to draw attention to a number of methodological problems and issues. In particular it is worth noting the case-study approach to representativeness and generalizability, rooted in theoretically directed principles of qualitative selection and logical inference. It is also worth reminding the reader of the propensity for the case-study approach to use multiple methods which, in their most methodologically self-conscious man-ifestation, are oriented towards strategies of multiple triangulation for dealing with problems of validity and bias. Finally, the methodological issues asso-ciated with the case-study approach are as much matters of conduct as they are matters of principle. It is therefore left to the researcher who adopts the case-study approach to do so in a spirit of self-critical endeavour.

Further Reading

The most definitive text on all aspects of the case-study approach is probably that by Yin (1989), which deals comprehensively with the whole process of doing case-study research, from design through to reporting findings. Sound advice can also be gleaned from Hakim (1987) which contains a chapter providing a concise summary of the case study as a research design and is particularly useful in setting this approach into the context of a wide range of alternative designs. Another similar summary which also places the case study approach alongside other approaches is to be found in Bryman (1989). While the latter is more specifically oriented to research in the area of organization studies, it does offer consideration of the link between the case study and action research.

Beyond these suggestions, the reader is recommended to pursue matters in two principal directions, depending upon requirement and preference. First, the broad matter of methods and practical issues should be pursued with guidance being taken from Burgess (1982; 1984) and from the appropriate chapters else-where in this volume. On the methodological front the articles by Mitchell (1983) and Platt (1989) are both strongly recommended. Second, the researcher's consideration of case-study design and implementation issues should be extended by 'sampling' some of the published case studies in his or her discipline or field of interest. There are also a number of edited collections available, focused on specific disciplinary areas, which include discussions of various aspects of doing case-study research. For example, in the field of research in organizations Bry-man (1988) contains useful contributions by Bresnen, by Buchanan, Boddy and McCalman, and by Crompton and Jones. In the field of educational research, the contributions by Nisbet and Watt and by Adelman, Jenkins and Kemmis in the collection edited by Bell *et al.* (1984) are worth pursuing.

References

ADELMAN, C., JENKINS, D. and KEMMIS, S. (1984) 'Rethinking case study', in BELL, J. *et al.* (Eds) *Conducting Small-scale Investigations in Educational Manage-ment*, London, Harper and Row.

BRAVERMAN, H. (1974) *Labor and Monopoly Capital*, New York and London, Monthly Review Press.

BRYMAN, A. (Ed.) (1988) *Doing Research in Organizations*, London, Routledge.

BRYMAN, A. (1988) *Quantity and Quality in Social Research*, London, Unwin Hyman.

BRYMAN, A. (1989) *Research Methods and Organization Studies*, London, Unwin Hyman.

BUCHANAN, D. and BODDY, D. (1983) *Organizations in the Computer Age*, Aldershot, Gower.

BUCHANAN, D., BODDY, D. and McCALMAN, J. (1988) 'Getting in, getting on, getting out, and getting back', in BRYMAN, A. (Ed.) (1988) *Doing Research in Organizations*, London, Routledge and Kegan Paul.

BURGESS, R.G. (Ed.) (1982) *Field Research: a Sourcebook and Field Manual*, London, Allen and Unwin.

BURGESS, R.G. (1984) *In the Field: An Introduction to Field Research*, London, Allen and Unwin.

CLARK, J., McLOUGHLIN, I., ROSE, H. and KING, R. (1988) *The Process of Technological Change: New Technology and Social Choice in the Workplace*, Cambridge, Cambridge University Press.

DENZIN, N.K. (1970) *The Research Act*, Chicago, Aldine.

GALLIE, D. (1978) *In Search of the New Working Class: Automation and Social Integration within the Capitalist Enterprise*, Cambridge, Cambridge University Press.

GOLDTHORPE, J., LOCKWOOD, D., BECHHOFER, F. and PLATT, J. (1969) *The Affluent Worker in the Class Structure*, Cambridge, Cambridge University Press.

HAKIM, C. (1987) *Research Design: Strategies and Choices in the Design of Social Research*, London, Allen and Unwin.

LITTLER, C.R. (1982) *The Development of the Labour Process in Capitalist Societies: A Comparative Study of the Transformation of Work Organization in Britain, Japan and the USA*, London, Heinemann.

MITCHELL, J.C. (1983) 'Case and situation analysis', *Sociological Review*, **31**, pp. 187–211.

NISBET, J. and WATT, J. (1984) 'Case study', in BELL, J. *et al.* (Eds) *Conducting Small-Scale Investigations in Educational Management*, London, Harper and Row.

PETTIGREW, A. (1973) *The Politics of Organizational Decision-Making*, London, Tavistock.

PETTIGREW, A. (1979) 'On studying organizational cultures', *Administrative Science Quarterly*, **24**, pp. 570–81.

PLATT, J. (1988) 'What can case studies do?', *Studies in Qualitative Methodology*, **1**, pp. 1–23, Greenwich, CT, JAI Press.

POLLERT, A. (1981) *Girls, Wives, Factory Lives*, London, Macmillan.

WHYTE, W.F. (1955) *Street Corner Society: The Social Structure of an Italian Slum*, 2nd ed., Chicago, University of Chicago Press.

WILKINSON, B. (1983) *The Shopfloor Politics of New Technology*, London, Heinemann.

YIN, R.K. (1989) *Case Study Research: Design and Methods*, rev. ed., London, Sage.

Chapter 17

Qualitative Interviewing

Carol Jones

Interviewing is rather like marriage: everybody knows what it is, an awful lot of people do it, and yet behind each closed door there is a world of secrets. (Oakley, 1986:231)

Qualitative interviews are distinguished from survey interviews in being less structured in their approach and in allowing individuals to expand on their responses to questions. Trevor Lummis (1987:62) has commented:

the art of good interviewing lies in being able to keep most of the interview conversational while following various digressions, re-membering which questions the flow of information has answered and yet being prepared to question more deeply and precisely when necessary.

Interviewers use their knowledge of the topic to enable them to probe beyond the 'yes' or 'no' responses more common in survey interviews.

Textbooks dealing with interviewing techniques have increasingly been noted by researchers to be at variance with their own experiences in the field (Burgess, 1984; Measor, 1985; Oakley, 1986). The public recognition of this fact has coincided with a critique of interviewing techniques which has highlighted the complex factors which affect the interview process (Oakley, 1986; Finch, 1984; Lather, 1988; Ribbens, 1989; Devault, 1990). Informed by feminist perspectives, the approaches emerging from this debate seek to define a more egalitarian base for research relationships than the stress on control and detachment which figure heavily in older textbooks. The gradual departure from stressing the interviewer as objective observer (a detached 'outsider'), has led to a recognition of the possibilities for researchers to be 'insiders' in the research relationship, interacting rather than merely estab-lishing a 'rapport' with the people to whom they are speaking and observing.

The result of these developments has to some extent been an individualizing of interviewing techniques (see Devault, 1990). Indeed in their introduction to Carol Warren's book *Gender Issues in Field Research* (1988:5), Van Maanen *et al.* comment that 'increasingly fieldwork is regarded as a highly and almost hauntingly personal method for which no programmatic guides can be written'. Similarly, Linda Measor (1985:55) notes frankly that her own interviewing practice was one that 'developed intuitively and without methodological rigour'.

The presence and personality of the interviewer are thus acknowledged as variables in the research process, and there is a recognition of the fact that 'all researchers operate from within a theoretical overview and ... affect the data at all stages' (Scott, 1985:74). However, while these developments have benefited those already involved in qualitative interviewing, to the new researcher they can often appear daunting, complex and bewildering in their diversity and implications. The intention here is to suggest guidelines which may be useful to the research student and to consider some of the issues raised by more recent analyses of the social relations underpinning the qualitative interview.

Groundwork and Access

In moving away from a highly structured format it is sometimes difficult to know what approach to take in order to produce effective interview material (see Burgess, 1982, section 4; Burgess, 1984, Chapter 5). Is it better actually to write the questions down? Will prompts be sufficient? What about a simple key-issues approach or an *aide-mémoire*? Qualitative interviews have sometimes been described as unstructured or 'non-directive', but as William Foot Whyte points out, neither of these approaches are appropriate for research, and 'open-ended' may be a more appropriate description (Whyte, 1982:111; Hammersley and Atkinson, 1983:113–4).

In conducting interviews it is obviously necessary to retain a critical awareness of what is being said and to be ready to explore some issues in greater depth — what Linda Measor calls 'listening beyond' (Measor, 1985:63). However, this sensitivity also needs to be employed by the researcher at the stage of drawing up the interview format. We need to ask ourselves how we are actually going to uncover information about the topics we have selected to research and what approach will be the most suitable. In my current research on the career and employment experiences of women engineers, I use a semi-structured approach and have found it helpful to begin by writing out the questions in full. Although I may not use the questions as written, this exercise allows me to think about the way I might phrase questions to enable me to discuss with women their experiences of working in a male-oriented environment in relation to gender and sexuality in the workplace.

It is also necessary to think carefully about words that we might use. For example, in oral history research it is unhelpful to ask 'Did your mother work after she was married?' because this focuses on paid work outside the home as opposed to unpaid domestic labour, and also can fail to uncover details of casual or temporary periods of employment used to supplement the family budget. Dale Spender has demonstrated that men and women engage in conversations and listen differently, and that women are using a language that is essentially 'man made' to describe their experiences (Spender, 1985; Devault, 1990). Thus a project exploring women's accounts of work and leisure would require careful thought about what the terms 'work' and 'leisure' actually mean to someone whose time is spent in full-time childcare and domestic responsibilities in the home (Devault, 1990). In my own research I am aware that sexual harassment is very broadly defined in the literature (Rubenstein, 1989), but that if I asked women 'Have you ever been subject to sexual harassment at work?' most would say 'No'. It is more appropriate to discuss with them their experiences of pin-ups, calendars, joking and bantering in the workplace, and to allow them to provide their own definitions of unacceptable behaviour and their strategies for dealing with this.

After having thought about the phrasing and wording of questions and considered how they might occur in an interview, I use this to produce an open-ended and flexible interview schedule which forms the basis for the interviews. For my own convenience this is divided into topic areas (in my case on education and family background, career and employment history, social relations at work, and domestic situation) in which key questions are supported by words or phrases prompting me on what to probe for in the conversation which follows. Thus rather than have several questions dealing with the range of occupational choices open to women engineers as they pursue their careers, I have one key question: 'How do you see your career/working life developing over the next five years?', followed by '(probe — technical, managerial, technical management, lateral career move)'. I also have a separate set of pointers for those considering a career break. I feel comfortable with this combination and of the fact that it will ensure I have comparable data, but it is necessary to devise for yourself a format that meets your own requirements.

It is important, particularly in the early stages of the interviewing period, to reflect upon the questions which you are asking and to amend them if necessary. In an earlier piece of research undertaken by the New Technology Research Group at Southampton University into technical employment in the electronics industry, we asked employers the question, 'How many engineers do you employ?'. It quickly became clear that what constituted 'an engineer' varied enormously between firms and we amended the section to read, 'How does the company classify an engineer?' following this with, 'Using that classification, how many engineers do you employ?'. This two-stage approach was also of assistance in highlighting any contradictions between the criteria companies said they used to classify an engineer, and the actual qualifications and experience they were seeking when they recruited — that is to distinguish between the theory and the practice in the light of the actual labour market situation.

In putting together an interview schedule it is wise to leave sensitive or more complex issues until rapport and trust have been established, perhaps for later interviews if more than one is to be conducted with each individual (Measor, 1985). For example, in my own research I try to leave questions dealing with women's experiences of harassment until well into the interview. In discussing certain topics it is sometimes helpful to adopt an approach called 'sanctioning' (Lummis, 1987:54–5). This is where the question is prefaced in such a way as to enable the individual to feel that their experiences are shared by others and thereby encourage them to talk more openly. Thus Lummis suggests that an oral historian wishing to discover more about corporal punishment within families (which people might be reluctant to admit occurred within their home) might say: 'In those days many parents used a strap or cane to punish their children, what did your parents do?' (1987:55). Janet Finch considers the use of vignettes (that is questions which ask people for their responses to situations involving hypothetical third parties) as a means of eliciting information about values and beliefs (Finch, 1987).

Access to individuals and organizations is often hedged with restrictions for which the interviewer needs to be prepared (Hammersley and Atkinson, 1983; Burgess, 1984; Bryman, 1989). Negotiating access often takes both skill and time and should be accounted for in the research design (see Chapter 11.) Once access has been negotiated the amount of time available to see each individual should inform the interview format. Thus there will be very different considerations to take into account, both in the design of the interview format and the potential access factors, by the person conducting life-history interviews with retired textile workers to researchers interviewing young mothers or female engineers.

I always ask people if they mind being taped and people quickly forget that the tape is there (see Devault, 1990 and Lummis, 1987, for a discussion of taping as opposed to other techniques), but the interview setting also needs to be taken into account (Hammersley and Atkinson, 1983). It is well known among oral historians that the greatest problems in using tape recorders are often the chiming clock or the talkative budgerigar! A colleague conducting interviews with women about obesity and pregnancy was surprised to find that although she had made an appointment to visit the women in their homes at a particular time various friends and relatives (including husbands) were also likely to be present. In offices telephones and tannoys can often interrupt the flow of the conversation and also present problems when transcribing the tape.

It is natural to worry that the tape recorder may malfunction or that the tape will run out and miss a crucial sentence. Although there is some debate about the possible reduction of eye-contact which might result from note-taking, this can combat the fear that the batteries in tape recorder have run down and provide a good back-up in the event of technical problems (including loud or persistent background noise or people who speak very softly).

Field notes should in any case be made to supplement taped interviews, even where this does not involve participant observation (Burgess, 1982; Hammersley and Atkinson, 1983:144–62). In my current research with women engineers I note what they wear because I ask them questions about 'image management' in the workplace, and I also note facts about the working environment, such as posters on 'Great Men in Mathematics' adorning the corridors down which female engineers walk. Some researchers also keep notes which reflect their own reactions to situations and to the fieldwork as it progresses (for example, see Devault, 1990:104–15).

If you are seeking quantitative or biographical data as well as qualitative material you might consider sending a questionnaire ahead to be completed prior to the interview. The usefulness of this approach was brought home to me during my interviews with managers regarding the number of technical staff which they employed. In one large electronics company I asked the question, 'How many technicians do you employ?'. The two personnel staff to whom I was speaking spent the next fifteen minutes pouring over computer listings which became more confusing as the time progressed and it eventually proved impossible to provide a concrete figure. When the Personnel Manager finally asked in exasperation, 'Why did we agree to see this lady!', I tended to sympathize with him! With hindsight I should have sent details of any quantitative information that I required in advance to enable them to extract the data before I arrived. In my current project, I ask the women engineers to fill in details about their education and career histories prior to the interview, allowing me to take them through the material and expand on moves and choices relevant to the research.

Conducting the Interview

The relationship which is established between the interviewer and those being interviewed is important in determining the quality of the data

(Measor, 1985:57). Given the short amount of time available for most interviews it is useful to be aware of strategies for establishing and maintaining this relationship.

The interviewer is required to interact with the person being interviewed, 'entering another person's world, and their perspective' (Measor, 1985:63). Older textbooks suggested that the interviewer adopt a pleasant and business-like nature, and maintain a neutral, value–free and uninvolved role, lest they contaminate the situation (Oakley, 1986; Scott, 1985: 76). In some research it is difficult to see how this position could either be adopted or maintained, as for example in Liz Stanley and Sue Wise's (1979) account of their experiences as the recipients of obscene phone calls. Trevor Lummis (1987:68–9) acknowledges that he would now be more challenging and more willing to press informants when information appeared contradictory, although he rightly points out the need to be aware of the line between discussion and intrusion.

As Jane Ribbens suggests, a much neglected quality for the researcher is the ability to listen (Ribbens, 1989:586). In this respect the interview is very different from the usual conversation in which both parties endeavour to obtain equal time for their views, opinions and comments, and to feel that silences denote 'failure'. In an interview setting silences and the spaces they create are important in allowing the person being interviewed to think about what has been asked rather than simply to respond.

A less obvious strategy for establishing a rapport is an awareness of the appropriate clothes to wear for an interview, paying attention to 'image management' (Measor, 1985:58–61; Hammersley and Atkinson, 1983:78–88). Carol Warren describes how the fieldworkers on a 1960s project into the use of police records in America had to cut their hair, shave, and wear jackets and ties in order to be accepted by the police who viewed long hair, beards and frayed jeans as indicative of disaffected students and draft dodgers (Warren, 1988:27). Measor also suggests using shared interests to stimulate rapport, again differentiating between the music, football and fashion which she discussed with pupils, from the interest in gardening which she shared with retired teachers (Measor, 1985:61–2). However, this should not be forced or contrived, rather reflecting a sensitivity to the overall situation (Measor, 1985:61; Hammersley and Atkinson, 1983:79–80).

The emphasis on rapport and interaction tends to ignore other considerations and can lead the researcher to feel that an unsuccessful interview is an indication of their failure as an interviewer. Even the most experienced interviewer will encounter people with whom it is very difficult to establish a basis from which to conduct a conversation, and there can also be equal problems with 'over-rapport' (Hammersley and Atkinson, 1983:98–104). As Oakley notes, 'Interviewees are people with considerable potential for sabotaging the attempt to research them' (Oakley, 1986:252). In comparing one's own interviews with those appearing in completed pieces of work it is often possible to feel dispirited when the latter appear to have an internal structure and coherence that seems beyond reach. However, it should be borne in mind that these are highly selected extracts and that the amount of post-hoc rationalization and editing which can occur is another of the secrets behind the closed door (Stanley and Wise, 1979; Devault, 1990).

The material which is collected during an interview may often be very personal and even in more 'organizationally' based research there are issues of confidentiality. Unlike Burgess's schoolboys, who were keen to see their names in print, most people would not relish this idea (Burgess, 1984:108). It is essential, therefore, to stress that participants and any organizations in which they might work will not be identifiable, and to explain carefully not only the background to the research, but also the use to which it will be put. There is always a problem in interviewing employees in a work situation in that access is negotiated through 'gate-keepers' (usually managers) and that this may set up a conflict of interests, with the employee feeling obliged to participate and the gate-keeper believing that they will be kept informed about what is said (McNeill, 1990; Hammersley and Atkinson, 1983:63–8). I gained access to one company's female engineers via the Personnel Department and was surprised, in view of the project-based nature of much engineering work, to find that the interviews could be arranged in working hours and in the Personnel Department's offices. Since there were only eight women employed as engineers by the company I felt there may be pressure on them to be involved and therefore made a point of confirming with them individually that they were happy to be interviewed, making clear that no one would know if they were not. It became apparent that some of them had felt obliged to attend under pressure from Personnel, but once I had explained the research and assured them of confidentiality they all agreed to continue. Some time later the Personnel Manager rang me to ask me if I could give her information gained in the interviews for a paper which she was writing for her manager on women in engineering. I refused, explaining that the material was confidential, but I sent details of existing studies which fulfilled the same function. Gatekeepers thus need to understand the confidentiality of the research at an individual as well as an organizational level.

Finally, although the issue is raised by Lorna McKee and Margaret O'Brien in relation to their experiences of interviewing lone fathers (McKee and O'Brien, 1986; also Warren 1988:33), the personal safety of the interviewer is mostly neglected in the literature. If you are going to interview people in any situation in which you feel vulnerable (including in people's homes, later in the evening, in a part of town with which you are unfamiliar) it is sensible to make sure that a friend or colleague knows where you are and at what time you expect to return.

After the Interview

Once the interview has been completed I always write to thank the person for agreeing to speak to me. I inform them that I will be transcribing the tapes over the coming weeks and ask permission to contact them again should it be necessary to confirm any details with them. Ideally interviews are transcribed verbatim. However it might be feasible for a lone researcher, working without secretarial support, to transcribe only sections of tapes, noting topics, themes and categories as they emerge (Hammersley and Atkinson 1983:167–72). If it will be some time before a tape can be transcribed, an index card containing a summary of the points covered in the interview may be a useful aid. In some research how things are said and what is left unsaid is as important as what is said (see, for example, Devault, 1990; Thompson, 1978; Humphries 1984). If this is the case there should be no tidying up and editing of transcripts and dialect and personal patterns of speech should be retained.

As Devault points out (1990:110): 'Social scientists have become increasingly aware during the 1980s, that writing is not a transparent medium with which researchers simply convey "truths" discovered in the field, but itself constructs and controls meaning and interpretation.' Some researchers have become increasingly concerned about the potentially exploitative nature of their activities in relation to those being interviewed (Stacey, 1988). Lonely or distressed people may be eager to talk, and women are particularly used to being asked to give details of their personal lives (McNeill, 1990; Ribbens, 1989). Feminist researchers interviewing women are particularly concerned about this. Janet Finch has commented (1984:78): 'The ease with which one can get women to talk in the interview situation depends not so much on one's skills as an interviewer, nor upon one's expertise as a sociologist, but upon one's identity as a woman.' She notes that she left interviews 'with the feeling that my interviewees need to know how to protect themselves from people like me' (p. 80). There may be cases in which comments cannot be used and considerations other than the research need to be given primacy. Sue Scott describes how this was brought home to her during survey research in a hospital when she encountered a very distressed woman who had survived a suicide attempt and who needed someone to talk to rather than to be interviewed (Scott, 1985:68–9).

Researchers, it is argued, have the ability to walk away and use the material in ways that may conflict with the interviewees' own perceptions and values (Lather, 1988; Ribbens, 1989). It is certainly interesting to speculate how we might analyze or present material differently if we knew that we had to 'report back' to those whom we have interviewed.

Ann Oakley has raised the question of whether it is possible to have real interaction, leading to friendship, with some interviewees (Oakley, 1986).

She notes that she did not follow advice on how to parry requests for information but rather gave it freely and retained contact with several of the people she interviewed after the research was completed. Ribbens (1989) has questioned the extent to which Oakley did more than give information, but in my own research I have answered questions which women engineers have asked in relation to my own experiences and background and I have explained why I am asking certain questions in relation to existing data. When women have expressed an interest in joining groups like the Women's Engineering Society I have sent them information after the interview, and as a result of my interviews in one company the women engineers are intending to establish a network of professional women. Several researchers have noted the therapeutic and counselling role of some interviews, and I have also noticed that people are likely to say that they had enjoyed the interview and that it had given them the opportunity to take a broader perspective (see Measor, 1985; McKee and O'Brien, 1983). It also enhances one's faith in the validity of the answers.

Social Relations as Factors in Qualitative Interviews

Once it has been accepted that there is a complex relationship between the researcher and the individuals on whom their research centres, then it is essential that the researcher reflects on the nature of that relationship and on the factors, such as gender, race and ethnicity, class and status, and age, which may be important variables in that relationship.

These are important issues and lead to a consideration of the need to do more than 'listening beyond'. They lead to a recognition of the need to 'understand beyond', to be aware of how the social and cultural factors which both parties bring to the encounter affect what happens thereafter (Hammersley and Atkinson, 1983:14–19; Harding, 1987:1–14). This 'understanding beyond' or reflexivity about the research process can be witnessed in Sue Scott's interviews with research students and their supervisors (Scott, 1984; Scott, 1985). Contrary to the textbook analyses, which tend to ascribe a dominant position to the researcher, she found herself an 'insider' in the academic world (interviewing peers and women), but at a disadvantage in terms of gender and status when interviewing both male students and male academics. Her experiences of the men she was interviewing attempting to control the situation and of being conscious of a difference in the quality and structure of cross-gender interviews, is echoed elsewhere (for example, McKee and O'Brien, 1986).

As has been noted, female researchers often note their enjoyment and ease in interviewing women. In some research relating to masculinity it is interesting to speculate on how different the results may have been had the researcher been attempting cross-gender interviews;[1] for example, contrast David Collinson's account of humour in the engineering workplace where much of the joking and banter centred around women as sexual objects, with Linda Imray and Audrey Middleton's attempts to research the male preserve of village cricket (Collinson, 1988; Imray and Middleton, 1986). Indeed, in his doctoral research in a northern factory, David Morgan notes that he was 'disadvantaged' by virtue of his sex (the people he worked with were women while supervisors were men), his background (middle-class compared with the working-class labour force), his age, and his marital status. He concludes: 'gender differences in fieldwork are not simply a source of difficulties such as exclusion from important central rituals or, in my case, exclusion from all-important interactions in the toilets, but are also a source of knowledge about the particular field' (Morgan, 1981). The 'participant observer' and the interviewer both have other identities which they bring to the research situation.

The question of the extent to which it is possible to be an 'insider' merely by virtue of shared gender identity, race or ethnicity remains open to debate. Joe Styles' reflections on moving from observation to participation in the activities associated with the gay baths which he was studying, question the assumption that participation as an insider reveals truths: 'I did not possess any special access to the life of the baths merely because I am gay' (quoted in Warren 1988, pp. 32–3). Similarly, Tony Larry Whitehead, a black American anthropologist, found that during his field work in Jamaica his speech (standard English as distinct from dialect English), and his colour (defined by locals as 'brown' and carrying particular cultural and economic connotations), meant that low income males were unwilling to talk to him other than monosyllabically (quoted in Warren 1988:26–7).[2] As Warren notes, 'maleness alone may not ensure access to all male worlds', and the points of difference, as well as the similarities, in any situation need constantly to be borne in mind and recognized as factors both in the research and in the analysis (Warren 1988:17; Ribbens, 1989; Morgan, 1981).

Suggestions for Reading

The most useful general book on interviewing is Trevor Lummis (1987) *Listening to History*, which provides an excellent introduction for researchers of many disciplines, and can be read in conjunction with Robert Burgess (1984) *In the Field: An Introduction to Field Research*, Measor (1985) and Martin Hammersley and Paul Atkinson's *Ethnography Principles in Practice*. Although Robert Burgess other methodology textbooks appear to relate to educational research, much of what they say has general applicability.

The paper has focused on feminist analyses of interviewing because these have often been the most critical of existing methodologies and the most constructive in their suggestions for how we might proceed in the future. Oakley (1986), Finch (1984) and Ribbens (1989) all consider the issues raised in women interviewing women, while Scott (1984, 1985), McKee and O'Brien (1986), and Morgan (1981) consider gender more generally as a factor in interviews. Carol Warren's (1988) *Gender Issues in Field Research* essentially takes an anthropological perspective, but this reflects the close links between qualitative interviewing and ethnography generally. Speech and language are central to interviewing and Dale Spender's (1980) pioneering analysis in this area can be supplemented by Devault (1990).

Notes

1 Hammersley and Atkinson noted in 1983 that where gender is acknowledged in research it is usually the female gender. Apart from David Morgan's article there is still a paucity of reflective work on masculinity in the research process (p. 84).
2 See also Patricia Hill Collins (1986, 1989) on the diversity of black women's experiences in relation to issues of race, ethnic orientation, gender and class.

References

BRYMAN, A. (1989) *Research Methods and Organization Studies*, Hemel Hempstead, Unwin Hyman.
BURGESS, R. (Ed.) (1982) *Field Research: A Sourcebook and Field Manual*, Hemel Hempstead, Allen and Unwin.
BURGESS, R. (1984) *In the Field: An Introduction to Field Research*, Hemel Hempstead, Allen and Unwin.
CLINE, S. and SPENDER, D. (1988) *Reflecting Men at Twice Their Natural Size*, London, Fontana.
COLLINS, P.H. (1986) 'Learning from the outsider within: The sociological significance of black feminist thought', *Social Problems*, **3**, pp. 14–32.
COLLINS, P.H. (1989) 'The social construction of black feminist thought', *Signs*, **14**, pp. 745–73.
DEVAULT, M.L. (1990) 'Talking and listening from women's standpoint: Feminist strategies for interviewing and analysis', *Social Problems*, **37**, pp. 96–116.
FINCH, J. (1984) ' "It's great to have someone to talk to": The politics and ethics of interviewing women' in BELL, C. and ROBERTS, H. (Eds) *Social Researching: Politics, Problems, Practice*, London, Routledge and Kegan Paul.
FINCH, J. (1986) *Research and Policy: The Uses of Qualitative Methods in Social and Educational Research*, London, Falmer Press.
FINCH, J. (1987) 'The vignette technique in survey research', *Sociology*, **21**, pp. 105–14.
HAMMERSLEY, M. and ATKINSON, P. (1983) *Ethnography: Principles in Practice*, London, Tavistock.

HARDING, S. (Ed.) (1987) *Feminism and Methodology*, Milton Keynes, Open University Press.

IMRAY, L. and MIDDLETON, A. (1986) 'Public and private: Marking the boundaries' in GAMARNIKOW, E., MORGAN, D., PURVIS, J. and TAYLORSON, D. (Eds) *The Public and the Private*, Gower, Aldershot.

LATHER, P. (1988) 'Feminist perspectives on empowering research methodologies', *Women's Studies International Forum*, **11**, pp. 569–81.

LUMMIS, T. (1987) *Listening to History*, London, Hutchinson.

MCKEE, L. and O'BRIEN, M. (1986) 'Interviewing men: "Taking gender seriously"' in GAMARNIKOW, E., MORGAN, D., PURVIS, J. and TAYLORSON, D. (Eds) *The Public and the Private*, Gower, Aldershot.

MCNEILL, P. (1990) 'Ask nicely', *New Statesman and Society*, 9 February 1990, p. 29.

MEASOR, L. (1985) 'Interviewing: A strategy in qualitative research' in BURGESS, R. (Ed.) *Strategies of Educational Research: Qualitative Methods*, London, Falmer Press.

MORGAN, D. (1981) 'Men, masculinity and the process of sociological enquiry' in ROBERTS, H. (Ed.) *Doing Feminist Research*, London, Routledge and Kegan Paul.

OAKLEY, A. (1986) 'Interviewing women: A contradiction in terms?' in OAKLEY, A. *Telling the Truth About Jerusalem*, Oxford, Basil Blackwell.

RIBBENS, J. (1989) 'Interviewing — An "unnatural situation"', *Women's Studies International Forum*, **12**, pp. 579–92.

RUBENSTEIN, M. (1989) 'Preventing sexual harassment at work', *Industrial Relations Journal*, **20**, pp. 226–36.

SCOTT, S. (1984) 'The personable and the powerful: Gender and status in sociological research' in BELL, C. and ROBERTS, H. (Eds) *Social Researching: Politics, Problems, Practice*, London, Routledge and Kegan Paul.

SCOTT, S. (1985) 'Feminist research and qualitative methods: A discussion of some of the issues' in BURGESS, R. (Ed.) *Issues in Educational Research: Qualitative Methods*, London, Falmer Press.

SPENDER, D. (1985) *Man Made Language*, London, Routledge and Kegan Paul.

STACEY, J. (1988) 'Can there be a feminist ethnography?', *Women's Studies International Forum*, **11**, pp. 21–7.

STANLEY, L. and WISE, S. (1979) 'Feminist research, feminist consciousness and experiences of sexism', *Women's Studies International Quarterly*, **2**, pp. 359–74.

THOMPSON, P. (1978) *The Voice of the Past: Oral History*, Oxford, Oxford University Press.

WARREN, C. (1988) *Gender Issues in Field Research*, Newbury Park, Sage.

WHYTE, W.F. (1982) 'Interviewing in field research', in BURGESS, R. (Ed.) *Field Research: A Sourcebook and Field Manual*, Hemel Hempstead, Allen and Unwin.

Chapter 18

Quantitative Research

Chris Skinner

Introduction

The aim of this chapter is to amplify some of the general discussion from Chapter 14 in the specific context of quantitative research, to introduce some key terms of quantitative research with references for further reading and to provide links to the following chapters on Survey Methods, Secondary Analysis and Statistical Analysis. Two broad types of quantitative research may be distinguished: *primary research* in which you both collect and analyze data, and *secondary analysis* in which you analyze data from secondary sources, such as government surveys (discussed in Chapter 20). This chapter focuses on primary research, although much of the discussion will also be relevant to secondary analysis.

In Chapter 14 the process of primary research was divided into the following elements: objectives, design, methods, management, data collection, analysis and presentation. In this chapter we concentrate on just the first two of these: objectives and design. Chapter 19 is devoted to *survey methods*, probably the most widely used form of quantitative data collection in the social sciences. Other methods of data collection such as laboratory experimentation and educational testing are not covered in this book, being more discipline-specific and less amenable to general discussion; see Nachmias and Nachmias (1981, Part 2) for an introduction. The analysis and presentation of quantitative data involves the use of statistical methods and these will be considered in Chapter 22.

Traditions of quantitative research and debates about its role and relation to qualitative research vary widely between disciplines and raise philosophical issues (Bryman, 1988) beyond the scope of this chapter. Relative to qualitative research, the *design* of quantitative research can be more difficult in the sense that it requires more explicit prior specification of what data are to be collected, in terms of variable definitions and so forth. However once this is done and the data are collected, the *analysis* of quantitative data, via, for example, tabulations of the pre-specified variables, can be more straight-forward. As a consequence, while at the early stages of research you may find it somewhat daunting to translate your research objectives into a quantitative research design, at the analysis and writing-up stages you may be surprised at the value you attach to your quantitative data.

Research Objectives

In the Chapter 14 four types of research question were discussed:

* ascertaining facts
* hypothesis testing
* establishing relationships between variables
* modelling

Each of these can be an objective of quantitative research. In statistical terminology the first of these questions may be termed *descriptive* and the remainder *analytical*. The use of quantitative data from secondary sources for descriptive purposes is very common in thesis work, for example it would be natural to accompany a discussion of the prevalence of a certain crime by appropriate Home Office statistics. On the other hand, the use of primary quantitative research solely to 'ascertain facts' for descriptive purposes is less common because the constraints on sample size faced by research students imply that population characteristics can only be estimated very approximately. Thus primary quantitative research is usually directed at the other analytical questions. Exceptions do, of course, occur. For example, research students in historical demography might attempt to ascertain from historical records numbers of individuals migrating between different regions or countries.

For analytical questions it is often useful to distinguish *dependent variables* Y, which constitute the main focus of the research, and other *independent*, *explanatory* or *background variables* X. Research questions often relate to how the independent variables influence the dependent variables. Sometimes it will be natural to view this influence in a *causal* sense. At other times a looser *comparative* sense may suffice. Thus, if X is a variable defining different categories, for example different types of schools children may attend, and Y is, for example, a measure of educational attainment, then the dependence of Y on X may simply be viewed as a comparison of levels of attainment between different school types.

The objective of quantitative research may either be specified prior to data collection in the form, for example, of *hypotheses* to be *tested*, or else the research might be viewed as more open-ended and *exploratory* with relationships between variables expected to reveal themselves at the analysis stage. The latter approach can, however, be risky for postgraduate students conducting primary research since the necessarily small sample sizes achievable are likely to make it difficult to distinguish real effects from sampling variation. This separation of 'signal' from 'noise' can be achieved much more effectively if it is planned for at the design stage. For example, suppose that the object of study is a learning process and that at most sixty children can be studied. Suppose further that, in fact, a key variable affecting this process is whether English is the normal language spoken at the child's home. If a random 'exploratory' sample of sixty children were selected and only four of these turned out to be from homes where English was not normally spoken it would be very unlikely that anything could be usefully inferred statistically about the effect of this variable on the learning process. On the other hand if the study were designed to compare thirty children from such homes with thirty other control children from English-speaking homes, matched on age, sex and measures of educational background then a useful statistical assessment of the effect of the language variable on the learning process is much more likely to be achievable.

A difficulty with the prior specification of research objectives is that your ideas and objectives will inevitably change during the course of your research and this can lead to a mismatch developing between your theoretical perspective and the data which you eventually collect. For example, Newby (1977) describes how his ideas evolved during a PhD study of deference in farm workers. His concept of deference changed from being a set of attitudes possessed by an individual to being a characteristic of the relationship between two individuals. For this reason, data he collected from individual farm workers to construct attitudes scales of deference were eventually discarded. It is, of course, desirable to maintain as far as possible the relevance of your data to your theoretical research objectives as your research progresses. The classical model allows for evolution of both theory and data via iteration of the cycle of hypothesis specification/design/data collection/ analysis. This model may work for some students, notably in psychology, who conduct a series of experiments, each one building on lessons from previous experiments, and perhaps for students doing secondary analysis. But the majority of students will only have the time and resources for one major piece of quantitative data collection. In this case, thorough preparatory pilot work is essential not just to test your 'measuring instruments' but also in order to make sure that you have clarified and refined your research objectives before you begin your main data collection.

Types of Research Design

Research design involves the translation of the research objective into a specified plan for data collection. The objective will be taken here to be analytical and to concern the investigation of how a dependent variable Y is affected by an independent variable X, where for simplicity X is assumed to be dichotomous, representing the presence or absence of some condition.

A key distinction in quantitative research is between *experimental* and *non-experimental (correlational, naturalistic)* designs. In an experimental design you (the researcher) can control which units (e.g. individuals) are exposed to the condition represented by X. Experimental designs arise in various settings. For example, in educational research, the researcher may be able to decide which children are assigned to which teaching method. More generally in *evaluation research* (Rossi and Freeman, 1985) the researcher may be able to decide which individuals are subject to some *programme* or *intervention*. In a *clinical trial* (Abramson, 1984) the researcher can control which individuals/patients receive which form of care or treatment. In *single case experimental designs* (Barlow and Hersen, 1984; Morley, 1989), which arise particularly in clinical research, the researcher (who is often also the clinician) can control whether and when a subject experiences different interventions or treatments. In a *psychology experiment* the researcher can control which subjects receive which *stimuli*. Further examples of experimental designs in the social sciences are presented by Hakim (1987:Chapter 9).

On the other hand in non-experimetal studies the presence or absence of the condition represented by X will be outside the control of the researcher. For example, in an *epidemiological study* (Abramson, 1984) comparing the health (measured by Y) of persons working in a nuclear power station with that of persons working elsewhere, the researcher will not be able to control values of the X variable i.e. whether or not an individual works in a nuclear power station. Similarly most survey research is non-experimental. Frequently practical or ethical considerations will prevent you from being able to decide whether or not units are exposed to the condition represented by X and hence prevent you from using an experimental design. The main problem with non-experimental designs is that you cannot know whether you are comparing 'like with like' so that you cannot be sure that any measured effect of X on Y cannot be attributed to pre-existing differences. For example, in the study of the health risks of those working at nuclear power stations the kinds of persons who work at nuclear power stations may differ systematically from the general population according to variables such as age, sex or education, so that any measured difference in health status Y may simply reflect the effect of these *confounding variables*. Experimental designs usually employ *randomization* (Cox, 1958:Chapter 5) to determine which units are exposed to which experimental conditions. This method protects against the effects of known or unknown confounding variables by creating groups which are 'equivalent' with respect to these variables.

When it is not possible to determine which units are exposed to which condition, various *quasi-experimental designs* may be used to control for the effects of confounding variables (Campbell and Stanley, 1966). When the condition involves a temporary intervention, such as a 'treatment' pro-gramme for young offenders, a *premeasure* of the dependent variable may be taken before the intervention and then the effect of the intervention can be mea-sured in terms of differences in a *postmeasure* of the dependent variable relative to pre-existing differences in the premeasure. Even better control may be obtained by taking repeated measures over a period of time in a *time series design* (Cook and Campbell, 1979).

These designs imply the need for *longitudinal data*, i.e. data which refer to more than one point in time for each unit or individual. Such data may be collected prospectively, i.e. contemporaneously, or retrospectively, usually by asking respondents to recall information. Prospective studies (often also called *longitudinal studies* or *panel studies* in the survey context) could stretch your resources as a research student, although a simple *follow-up study* involv-ing interviewing individuals before and after some programme or interven-tion should be feasible. Also studies involving intensive data collection from a small number of individuals over a short period of time (Alexander, 1989) are of 'research student scale'. Retrospective studies require fewer resources but are much more restricted in the kind of information which can be collected with reasonable accuracy (Groves, 1989:Section 9.4).

Sometimes the conditions represented by X are not temporary and no sensible premeasure is possible. For example, in a comparison of the experi-ences of British students and overseas students at a British university the variable X = British/overseas might be viewed as 'permanent'. In this case one way to attempt to control for the effects of confounding variables such as sex and age is to use *matching*, for example by selecting pairs of students (one British, one overseas) each sharing the same sex and age (Moser and Kalton, 1971:Section 9.3; Anderson *et al.*, 1980, Chapter 6). Matching is also used in *case-control studies* in which two groups defined by the dependent variable Y — the *cases* who experience a given outcome (usually a disease in medical studies but it may be any outcome such as delinquency) and the *controls* who do not experience the outcome are compared with respect to one or more independent variables (Schlesselman, 1982).

The above discussion has focused on the simple case with just a single independent variable X, representing two alternative conditions. Often, however, it is of interest to study how several independent variables jointly influence a dependent variable. In experimental designs this raises the ques-tion of which combination of values of the independent variables should be studied. This is a complex question involving various technical issues (Cox,

1958; Kirk, 1968; Keppel and Saufley, 1980), but a question which is worth considering carefully since different designs may differ greatly in their associated precision (see p. 221).

Evaluating Research Designs

Lists of alternative research designs, such as in the previous section or in research methods texts, can appear abstract and daunting and may tempt you to pick out just one 'recipe' which appeals and to proceed with this design as given. Such an approach is inadvisable. First, you will need to justify your choice of designs against alternatives in your thesis. Second, it is essential to evaluate at the outset whether a given design really is capable of providing useful answers to your research questions. It is not uncommon for students to start with over-ambitious research objectives for which *no* design could provide useful evidence within the resource constraints they face.

In order to evaluate any proposed research design it can be helpful to conduct a thought experiment in which you visualize all stages of the research which flow from the design right through to the stage of analysis and even to the way you will present the results in your thesis. The aim of this 'experiment' is to assess whether the results you will obtain from the proposed design really will provide relevant answers to your research questions and whether there are characteristics of the design which might threaten the validity of the conclusions you hope to be able to draw. Campbell and Stanley (1966) present a useful checklist of threats to validity for evaluating research designs in relation to the analytical objectives described in the previous section. Cook and Campbell (1979) expand their checklist of threats under the four headings below. The application of the following criteria to any given design will, of course, depend partly on factors such as non-response rate, which will themselves be outcomes of the research and not known beforehand. Pilot work plays a vital role in the assessment of the likely magnitude of such factors when choosing a design.

Internal Validity

A design is 'internally valid' if the measured effect can be attributed only to the effect of the independent variable X. A variety of threats to internal validity exist. Probably the most important reason why measured effects may not properly reflect the 'true' influence of X is because of the effect of confounding variables described above for non–experimental designs. But other threats also exist. For example, even in experimental studies if subjects are lost in a way systematically related to the response variable Y then the measured effect may not properly reflect the 'true' effect.

Precision

Closely related to the criterion of internal validity is that of precision or sampling variability of the estimated effect. An important alternative explanation which needs to be considered for any measured effect is that it only reflects the sampling variation arising under the *null hypothesis* that no real underlying effect exists. For the small sample sizes typically used by research students this can place important limitations on what kind of effects can usefully be studied. Thus, even if X does affect Y, limited sample sizes may mean that the difference between the measured effect and zero is not 'statistically significant'; (see Chapter 22). Such a finding is of very little use to you because it could mean that there is no effect or it could mean that there is an effect but that not enough data has been collected to detect it. Therefore, if a main objective of the research is to study certain effects or to investigate certain hypotheses about such effects, it is worth attempting to select a research design for which these effects can be estimated with sufficient precision. The determination of the sample size needed to achieve a given precision involves some technical calculations (e.g. Cox, 1958: Chapter 8; Kirk, 1968:9–11, 109–110; Guilford and Fruchter, 1973:185–197). These calculations will depend on various aspects of the design (e.g. a within-group repeated-measures design can be more precise than a between-group design) and on the size of the potential effect (a larger effect can be more easily detected). While such calculations are not simple, the cost of not thinking about precision in advance is that you run the risk of discovering at the analysis stage that all the effects you are most interested in are statistically insignificant, which would be a very frustrating outcome to your research.

Construct Validity

Construct validity refers to how well the measured variables Y and X represent what they are intended to measure. A necessary condition for a variable to have high validity is that it has high *reliability* (i.e. stability of responses over repeated measurement) and so this is often investigated first. Reliability may be measured in various ways, for example using test-retest correlations under repeated measurement or in terms of *internal consistency* for variables constructed as scales from multiple items (Kerlinger, 1973: Chapter 26).

General construct validity is more difficult to measure than reliability but various approaches are available (Kerlinger, 1973:Chapter 27). One important potential threat to construct validity in X is *reactivity*, which arises when subjects react simply to being under observation, rather than just to the 'real' conditions represented by X. For example, a *placebo effect* occurs in a clinical trial when a patient reacts to the knowledge that they are being given a new treatment, in addition to responding to the actual treatment itself. In this case the measured effect of X on Y will reflect not just the 'true' effect of the treatment but also the placebo effect of the patient reacting to being part of a clinical trial.

External Validity

External validity is concerned with the extent to which the findings can be generalized. Two important considerations are the representativeness of the sample and the extent to which it is possible to generalize from the context of the data collection, e.g. a psychology laboratory, to other social settings. On the whole, theses are likely to be judged more critically with respect to internal validity than external validity. Thus it would be a major failing of a thesis if the claimed findings could be attributed to an explanation, alternative to the one you propose, when you could have avoided this alternative explanation by an appropriate design. On the other hand, it will usually be understood that the resources available to research students constrain their studies to narrowly defined populations, and the generalizability of your results will not usually be a major issue provided you have internal validity and provided you can present a sensible justification of your choice of sample and the context of the data collection.

Further Reading

General introductions are provided by Babbie (1989), Kidder and Judd (1986) and Nachmias and Nachmias (1981). Slightly more dated but still useful as a reference is Kerlinger (1973). All these books are American; Hakim (1987) is a useful source for UK research, although it tends to emphasize issues of large-scale research. For emphasis on behavioural and mental health research see Parry and Watts (1989), on health-related research see Abramson (1984), on educational research see Cohen and Manion (1989) and on organizational research see Bryman (1989). For a discussion of philosophical issues associated with quantitative research see Bryman (1988).

References

ABRAMSON, J.H. (1984) *Survey Methods in Community Medicine*, 3rd ed. Edinburgh, Churchill Livingstone.

ALEXANDER, P. (1989) 'Intensive quantitative methods', in PARRY, G. and WATTS, F.N. (Eds) *Behavioral and Mental Health Research: A Handbook of Skills and Methods*, Hove, Lawrence Erlbaum.

ANDERSON, S., AUQUIER, A., HAUCK, W., OAKES, D., VANDAELE, W. and WEISBERG, H. (1980) *Statistical Methods for Comparative Studies*, New York, Wiley.

BABBIE, E. (1989) *The Practice of Social Research*, 5th ed., Belmont, California, Wadsworth.

BARLOW, D.H. and HERSEN, M. (1984) *Single Case Experimental Design: Strategies for Studying Behavior Change*, 2nd ed., New York, Pergamon.

BRYMAN, A. (1988) *Quantity and Quality in Social Research*, London, Unwin Hyman.

BRYMAN, A. (1989) *Research Methods and Organization Studies*, London, Unwin Hyman.

CAMPBELL, D.T. and STANLEY, J.C. (1966) *Experimental and Quasi-experimental Designs for Research*, Chicago, Rand McNally.

COHEN, L. and MANION, L. (1989) *Research Methods in Education*, London, Routledge.

COOK, T.D. and CAMPBELL, D.T. (1979) *Quasi-experimentation: Design and Analysis Issues for Field Settings*, Chicago, Rand McNally.

COX, D.R. (1958) *Planning of Experiments*, New York, Wiley.

GROVES, R.M. (1989) *Survey Errors and Survey Costs*, New York, Wiley.

GUILFORD, J.P. and FRUCHTER, B. (1973) *Fundamental Statistics in Psychology and Education*, 5th ed., New York, McGraw Hill.

HAKIM, C. (1987) *Research Design: Strategies and Choices in the Design of Social Research*, London, Allen and Unwin.

KEPPEL, G. and SAUFLEY, W.H. (1980) *Introduction to Design and Analysis: A Student's Handbook*, New York, W.H. Freeman.

KERLINGER, F.N. (1973) *Foundations of Behavioral Research*, 2nd ed., New York, Holt, Rinehart and Winston.

KIDDER, L.H. and JUDD, C.M. (1986) *Research Methods in Social Relations*, 5th ed., New York, Holt, Rinehart and Winston.

KIRK, R.E. (1968) *Experimental Design: Procedures for the Behavioral Sciences*, Belmont, CA, Brooks/Cole.

MORLEY, S. (1989) 'Single case research', in PARRY, G. and WATTS, F.N. (Eds) *Behavioural and Mental Health Research: A Handbook of Skills and Methods*, Hove, Lawrence Erlbaum.

MOSER, C.A. and KALTON, G. (1971) *Survey Methods in Social Investigation*, London, Heinemann.

NACHMIAS, C. and NACHMIAS, D. (1981) *Research Methods in the Social Sciences*, New York, St. Martin's Press.

NEWBY, H. (1977) 'In the field: Reflections on the study of Suffolk farm workers', in BELL, C. and NEWBY, H. (Eds) *Doing Sociological Research*, London, Allen and Unwin.

Chris Skinner

PARRY, G. and WATTS, F.N. (Eds) (1989) *Behavioral and Mental Health Research: A Handbook of Skills and Methods*, Hove, Lawrence Erlbaum.
ROSSI, P.H. and FREEMAN, H.E. (1985) *Evaluation: A Systematic Approach*, 3rd ed., Beverly Hills, Sage.
SCHLESSELMAN, J.J. (1982) *Case-Control Studies: Design, Conduct Analysis*, New York, Oxford University Press.

Chapter 19

Survey Methods

Bryan Glastonbury and Jill MacKean

Introduction

The possibility of carrying out a social survey may be in your thoughts from an early stage, but it becomes an issue for detailed decision once you have decided exactly what information you need, and you have to choose the most appropriate method of data collection. Sometimes the information can be obtained from observation or from records, but very often the main source will be the respondents themselves. You may wish to conduct informal interviews (see Chapter 17), but to be more systematic, questions are formed and compiled into a questionnaire, which is either administered by an interviewer or given to the respondent to complete and return.

There is a logical sequence to conducting a social survey. Once the basic decision to collect data by survey has been taken, focus moves to the mechanics of putting that decision into action. Before a questionnaire can be designed, some attention must be paid to the different techniques for approaching respondents — by mail, phone or face to face contact. There will be practical concerns here, such as how far away your potential respondents live. There will also be arguments about the nature and amount of data you want to gain from each respondent, which will in turn raise the question of 'How many respondents?' and whether a sample is to be taken of your total survey population. Surveys can be used both to provide descriptive results and for what are commonly called 'evaluative studies'. A genuine evaluation (for example, of the quality of life of physically handicapped people) requires a comparison (in this instance with the lives of able-bodied people). Sometimes the basis for comparison already exists, perhaps in an earlier study, but if not then you will have to consider whether to provide such material yourself, by collecting data from your main respondents and from a *control group*. Hence your planning will need to accommodate two surveys.

Sampling is one of the areas where errors can be introduced, so you need to give it some attention. You need also to be aware of error risk throughout the planning sequence of designing questions, preparing answer blocks, especially attitude scales, and bringing together the questions into a coherent questionnaire. Once the questionnaire (or 'data collection instrument', to use a more impressive label!) is drafted, it has to be tried out (the pilot study), modified into its final form, produced in the necessary volume, and put into action. The initial exercise of getting questionnaires out to respondents or arranging interviews is an exciting point in the research process, leading to the thrill of receiving the first sets of data, and the occasional frustration of coping with too many reluctant respondents. Once the data has been collected, and ways of minimizing non-response have been pursued, the process of analysis begins. Converting the raw data from respondents into the first research results is another moment to savour. After data analysis there is the final phase of the survey, presenting the findings in the most accurate, informative and interesting way you can devise, and, if there is an 'applications' topic on your research agenda, working out the most suitable route to ensuring that your research gets the attention it deserves.

We will now turn in more detail to the sequence outlined above, moving through data collection methods, sampling, errors, question design, attitude scaling, questionnaire structuring, survey implementation, and data analysis. In much of what follows you will read about a range of methodological possibilities, or options which you can pursue. Under 'Data Collection Methods', for example, you will be told that you have to choose between questionnaires which you complete by interviewing the respondent, and those which the respondent fills in for you. The guidelines we offer you will be based first and foremost on helping you make choices which will result in your research being methodologically sound and relevant. Nevertheless we shall try to acknowledge, and you cannot afford to ignore, two other themes.

One concerns the practical surrounds of your research process. It is one matter to produce a methodologically excellent research design: it is a rather different exercise to maintain a sound method in the face of an array of practical impediments. You must work out the cost of your preferred methods in terms of printing questionnaires, travel, postage, etc., and then decide whether you can afford it. A similar calculation is needed about your time. How long will each interview take? How long will it take to complete the number of interviews you want? Do you have that amount of time? How does the timetabling for data collection fit in with the overall timetable for your higher degree? A text of this kind can inform you about methods, but only *you* can put those methods into the context of your practical circumstances.

The second theme relates to your aptitudes. A preliminary question about social surveys is: Do you want the survey approach to make best use of the skills and aptitudes you possess, or do you want it to push you into learning new skills? Coming into research as a postgraduate, possibly also with work experience in the setting that you are now to survey, you will already have some relevant skills, and know enough about yourself to be aware of your relevant weaknesses. Many social scientists, for example, will be trained and experienced in interviewing (clinical psychologists, social workers, for example); others (economists, social statisticians) will have expertise based on their numeracy. The reverse position is that some post-graduates will lack areas of knowledge and experience, and perhaps be fearful of interviewing or doing a survey which will need a sophisticated statistical analysis. It is important to take these factors into account, to 'play to your strengths' if working for a higher degree is a sufficient challenge, or choose methods which force you to learn new skills if that is your preference.

Data Collection Methods

The core issue here is the way the questionnaire is to be administered. Interviewing has some obvious advantages. The interviewer can encourage the potential respondent to participate, can keep her or his attention and can interpret complex instructions. If opinion or attitude questions are included, especially if they are open-ended, the interviewer can make sure that the respondent understands the question, and can probe or prompt if necessary, or pursue a point to ensure that the respondent is reflective rather than superficial. In some circumstances there is little alternative to interviewing because of the nature of the data sought by the researcher. If you have detailed questions about sensitive matters, like income, marital difficulties, or stressful life events, then these need to be put by a well prepared interviewer able to cope with respondents' feelings of invasion of privacy or distress.

The main disadvantage of interviewing is that the process can introduce bias, because it is difficult to treat all respondents in the same way. Interviewing is also costly of your time, and is difficult to justify if your question-naire is full of routine, easy to answer, unthreatening questions. Almost certainly you will be able to get more completed questionnaires for your money (though probably a lower percentage response rate) by not using an interview approach. Interviews are best when you want a smaller number of high quality, detailed responses.

The questionnaire can be administered by an interviewer either face to face or over the telephone. An interviewer calling at a house can choose a particular household member and collect observational data if required. However, if the sample is geographically widespread, the method can be costly in terms of travelling expenses, especially if many repeat calls are made on non-responders. Many interviews have to be carried out in the evenings and interviewers, often women, do not like to visit some areas after dark, nor do some potential respondents like opening their doors after dark to unknown callers. Face to face interview schedules also have to be planned with a range of small practical issues in mind, like possible need for and availability of public transport, times of the year when poor weather is most common, clashes with respondents' favourite TV programmes, or at times when there is a strong chance that your visit to the house will find everyone out. Telephone interviewing is uncommon in higher degree work, but if you want to check out the possibilities see Dillman (1978) and Groves *et al.* (1988).

A self-completion questionnaire can either be sent through the post or delivered directly. There is no possibility of interviewer bias but there are some disadvantages. Respondents need good literacy skills. If there are questions which test knowledge there is no guarantee that the respondent will not look up the answer. In fact there is no guarantee that the required respondent will complete the questionnaire, they might pass it to a friend or relative. For a mail survey (Erdos, 1970; Dillman, 1978) a reliable and up-to-date list of addresses is required, and if this is available a widely spread sample is possible at no extra cost.

An example of a hand–delivered questionnaire arises in surveys of school children, where a questionnaire is handed out to a group or class who complete it then and there. An advantage is that the response rate is good, usually 100 per cent, and the process very cost effective. A disadvantage is that the person who hands the questionnaire out, perhaps the teacher, could introduce a bias by their presence.

Computer-administered questionnaires are another example of a self–completion method. They are obviously limited to those with access to a computer and, preferably, computers which are networked so that the information can be transferred direct rather than by floppy disks. It is possible to have complex questionnaires with involved 'skip' questions (questions which direct groups of respondents to different questions depending on their answer), and only those questions relevant to the respondent appearing on the screen. An example here is research involving testing respondents' eligibility for welfare benefits, where several computerized assessment questionnaires are in regular use.

To summarize the pros and cons of different ways of collecting data by questionnaire, interviewing offers flexibility to react to the respondent's situation, probe for more detail, seek more reflective replies, and ask questions which are complex or personally intrusive. At the same time such flexibility can lead to bias in the way questions are asked, prompts given, and answers recorded. The various forms of self-completion questionnaire have to be more standardized and, as we shall see later, need careful structuring to make up for the fact that there is no interviewer around to offer clarification. The value of greater standardization is less bias, but it is harder to cover complex material this way.

At a practical level interviews are time-consuming and costly, especially if much travel is involved. As a result, though a good response rate may be obtained, the time and resources available to you may dictate a small sample. Self-completion questionnaires, especially postal ones, can be sent to much larger samples, even though the proportion who respond will be lower. While you might aim for a 75 per cent response rate from an interviewed sample, 50 per cent is more realistic through the post, though of course these will depend to an extent on the subject of the study and who makes up the sample. Interviewing can be a fascinating experience, but it also has its risks and inconveniences (timetable interviews for the warm months, not the depths of winter!). Self-completion processes are generally more sedentary, but will give you less of a 'feel' of your respondents. There is a 'hybrid' compromise, based on a self-completion questionnaire with straightforward questions, sent to a large sample, with a parallel or follow-up interviewed questionnaire with more complex material for a smaller group of respondents.

A rule of thumb guide is that if you are more interested in the depth and quality of your data than in having a large number of responses, then look carefully at interviewing. If your questions are fairly easy to answer and you want a lot of responses to facilitate statistical analysis, then self-completion may be for you. But, and it is an important reservation, keep practical issues well in focus — the time and resources you have for the data collection sequence, the accessibility of your sample, the administrative tasks surrounding the questionnaire, and your own interests and aptitudes.

Sampling

Sampling is not something which is confined to scientific research but, as our attitudes and opinions are based to a very large extent on sampling, it is a part of our everyday lives and is often used where resources are not available to study all possible information. The use of quality control in industry, where only a small sample of the product is examined, is a good example. The use of sampling in surveys was first introduced at the beginning of the nineteenth century and is used extensively today, not only in small surveys but also in large-scale government research such as the General Household Survey. Market research is largely dependent on sampling.

When a sample from a group of individuals or units is taken and a measure made on that sample (the proportion of individuals with a given attitude, for example) this measure is used to estimate the characteristic of the whole group. Of course, if one sample is taken from a group of individuals and some measure taken, and then a second sample taken and the measure repeated, unless all individuals in the group have identical measurements the two results will not in general be the same. An error will have been intro-duced by measuring only the sample and not the whole group. There are ways of sampling which can sometimes be used to reduce this error. To take a very simple example — suppose there was a group of people whose average height you wanted to calculate. For some reason you did not wish to measure everyone, so you decided to take a sample. You could take what is called a *simple random sample* where you select a fixed number of individuals completely at random, measure them, calculate the average and use this as an estimate of the average height of the whole group. One problem is that there might be a large variation in heights among your group and different samples would produce very different estimates. Instead you might decide to measure every other person sitting round a room (*a systematic sample*) and estimate the average height of the group in the same way. Such a sample is easier to select than a simple random sample but it might be that men and women were sitting alternately so that your sample might be composed of all men or all women, giving you a greatly over-or under-inflated estimate. If you have some prior knowledge of your group or population this can be used to improve the precision of your estimates. Here you might reasonably suppose that, on average, men were likely to be taller than women, and the variation within each subgroup of men or women would be smaller than among the combined group. So you could use *a stratified sample*. Your group would be divided into men and women and you could take a simple (or systematic) random sample from each subgroup. You would then have two estimates which can be combined to form a weighted estimate for the whole group.

Yet another form of sampling can be illustrated by considering the problem of estimating the average height of all members of a university, for example. Rather than take a simple random sample of individuals from the whole university it might be simpler to take a simple random sample of departments from the university and then include all individuals in the selected departments in the sample of individuals. This is an example of *cluster sampling* where the clusters are departments.

The methods of sampling that have been discussed so far are known as probability sampling. In these methods every individual or unit has a known chance of being selected. Another form of sampling, non-probability sam-pling, is much used in market research. Consider the interviewers who stand in the streets. They are sampling the general public, but the chances of being selected are not calculable. The method used is generally *quota sampling*, where the interviewer is given a quota and continues interviewing until the quota is filled. The quota is generally stratified, a certain number of men, women, those in different age groups, social classes, etc. Some of these stratification factors are simple to use, others such as social class, are not, as the respondent has to be questioned before being assigned to a category. Medical surveys also often involve non-probability samples — the next 100 patients on the waiting list, the patients coming to the clinic on a certain day, for example.

These techniques of sampling apply equally to studies of single groups and to studies involving a control group. However, with control data there is an alternative course to selecting two independent samples. That is to choose the main research group in the normal way, and then select the control group by matching control respondents to the research group. Such matching can be done by, for example, ensuring that the control group has the same age and gender profile as the main sample. (See Chapter 18 for references on matching.)

Sampling theory is complex and the subject of extensive literature. Any general book on surveys will have a section on sampling. For a more theoretical approach books such as Cochran (1977) are recommended. It is an extremely important subject and one which needs to be given careful thought. Advice from your supervisor (who may well pass you on to a statistician) should be sought at an early stage if there is any doubt as to method. There are four practical questions which are likely to concern the postgraduate researcher. Should a sample be used, rather than the whole potential population of respondents? What sort of sample should be used? How do you go about actually taking a sample? What size should the sample be?

From a methodological point of view the survey population (that is, all those who are potential respondents) contains anyone coming into the group being studied. This may be a narrowly defined group, such as all the residents in a named home for elderly people, or a widely ranging one, such as all single parents. Practical aspects, like your own time and the geographical spread of respondents, will affect the size of this group, because you will have to define your population in terms of what it is possible to survey. For example, if you plan to use interviews, instead of all single parents, you might designate all single parents within thirty miles of the research location.

Another factor determining the real as opposed to the theoretical survey population is identification. You may suspect that there are thousands of single parents within thirty miles, but how do you get their names and addresses? When it comes to the point, your potential respondent group is not what the Office of Population Censuses and Surveys or some other research tells you exists, but those to whom you can get questionnaires. Often a sampling frame, in the sense of a list of names and addresses of those people in whom you are interested, does not exist; or if it exists it may be confidential and inaccessible to you, like the list held by all social services departments of families in which a child is thought to be at risk of abuse. Sometimes you can negotiate access to confidential sampling frames, but it is just as likely that circumstances will force yo to accept non-probability samples or what Bryman (1989:113) calls *convenience samples*.

Once you know, in realistic terms, the size of your survey population, the question of whether or not to take a sample is answered by adding the number of completed questionnaires you would like to obtain to an estimate of the number of non-respondents. If the total is less than the survey population, then there is scope for sampling. Choosing the type of sampling from those outlined in earlier paragraphs is basically about ensuring that your sample group is as typical as possible of the whole survey population, thereby maximizing scope to make generalizations from your results. In academic research randomness tends to be favoured, while taking a quota can be looked down on as the province of market researchers. In reality a useful approach is to analyze the survey population to see how much stratification might be feasible, and aim to select as randomly as possible from within a sensible stratified framework.

It follows that the first phase of taking a sample is a careful process of selection leading to a suitable framework for the sample. The next phase may be a quota or stratification: for example, if you wanted to interview ten people of each gender, in each of several age groups, from among those attending hospital out-patient clinics, you might well opt to take the first ten who arrive in each category. In contrast you may select in a more random way if you have access to a list of names and addresses for your survey population, such as the Electoral Register. Here, depending on the size of the sample as a proportion of the total list, you can take a systematic sample of every nth name; or you can select a simple random sample by giving everyone on the list a number, and then using a computer to generate random numbers, or use random number tables.

Almost all survey researchers agonize over the issue of sample size. Often it is a matter of seeking a compromise between the researcher's resources and the need for generalizable (statistically valid) results. The larger the sample, the greater the prospect of such results, but the higher the cost in time and money. Sadly there is no easy route at a planning stage by which sample sizes and the consequent validity of results can be calculated because a crucial factor is the extent of diversity in the survey population. A more diverse group requires a bigger sample. At a practical level, keep in mind that stratification is a process of taking account of some of the diversity (controlling variables), so can influence sample size. In reality, most postgraduate researchers will take the largest sample their time and resources permit.

Designing Questionnaires

This task will focus on three topics: designing questions, slotting in answer blocks, especially attitude scales, and then putting everything together into a coherent questionnaire.

Questions

The first step in designing a questionnaire is to construct the questions. They have to elicit the information that you require and be appropriate to the form of administration that you are going to use. Before starting to form questions make certain that all objectives and important terms are clearly defined, and that you have a sensible assessment of the capacities of your respondents. Simple and unambiguous wording should be used, both to avoid confusing the respondents when they strive to answer the question, and to avoid confusing yourself when you seek to analyze and categorize the replies.

If you are going to use an interviewer-administered questionnaire then the questions must be formed in such a way as to be easily read out — as in a normal conversation. If the questions are formed in a stilted, abnormal way, then the interviewer (most often you) will be tempted to alter the wording, which may result in a change in the meaning.

There are two main kinds of questions: open-ended and pre-coded. Open-ended questions leave the answer entirely to the respondent. These have to be used when there is no way of knowing what answers the respondents are likely to give, or if you want quotable responses. Often they are used in pilot studies but translated to a pre-coded version in the main study.

Pre-coded questions have a list of answers from which to choose. In a self-completion questionnaire the respondent chooses the option or options. In an interviewer-administered questionnaire the options are either read out or shown to the respondent who chooses one or more, or are chosen by the interviewer as a result of the respondent's answer. In this type of question care must be taken that the options are exclusive and exhaustive. The category 'Other' is often added in case the list is not complete, but keep in mind that if there are possible answers which are not on your list, bias can ensue.

Two examples of questions that can cause difficulty are those involving memory and those involving a sensitive topic. The ability to remember is affected, not only by the memory of the individual, but also by the length of time since the event and, above all, by the saliency of the event, that is the relative importance of the event to the individual. It is much easier to remember the timing of a major event than a minor one, given that they took place at the same time. If memory is thought likely to be a problem then attempts should be made to bound the time interval in some way, perhaps by asking whether the event took place before or after some other major event whose timing is known.

Sensitive topics are those touching on socially unacceptable matters such as drug abuse, sexual deviance or dishonesty; private matters such as personal finance, sex or religion; or those topics which might result in an answer which would lower the respondent in the eyes of the researcher. Questions involving knowledge would come into the last category: people do not like to admit ignorance and might make up an answer if they did not know it. There are various ways in which sensitive questions can be asked which enable the respondent to feel more free to answer: for example by emphasizing confidentiality, opening the question by suggesting that everyone practises the particular unacceptable behaviour, by asking if they know of anyone who does this before asking if they do themselves, or by setting up the question so that it appears to be about a friend or neighbour rather than the respondent. Many books on surveys give a list of such alternative approaches (for example, see Payne, 1951). However there is a point of view that roundabout methods are unnecessary and that respondents are surprisingly frank when faced with sensitive questions as long as they are asked in a matter-of-fact manner. There are certain sorts of questions to avoid. The most important are questions which lead the respondent in the direction of a certain answer. These are often seen in ill-designed questionnaires and can lead to biased results. Another example of a badly designed question is one that contains more than one query but room for apparently only one answer. If only one answer is given it might not be possible to ascertain which query is being answered.

Attitude Scales

Some questions ask for the respondent's evaluation as to whether something is good or bad, nice or nasty, acceptable or unacceptable. For illustrative or quotable purposes such questions can be left open-ended, but if a composite result from the survey group is wanted, then a pre-coded answer block is necessary. In these circumstances scales have to be developed which use the most suitable evaluative terms, allow for gradations in responses, and minimize bias by covering the same range of positive and negative evaluations.

Some simple examples illustrate these points. Pretend you are conducting a survey in your local eating place, and the question is 'How do you rate the food?' Some possible answer choices might be:

Good	Good	Good	Good
Bad	Average	Variable	Bad
	Bad	Bad	Other . . .

The first principle to note is that of polar opposites: the chosen positive and negative terms are, as nearly as can be made, direct opposites of each other. 'Good' relates to 'Bad', not to 'Could be better'. Next the use of 'Average': in all attitude scales an issue is whether to mark the divide between positives and negatives by including a neutral 'fence-sitting' mid-point. In one sense this is desirable, because there may well be respondents whose views genuinely put them on the fence. On the other hand, the researcher may want to exclude such an opportunity so as to force the respondent to state a positive or negative attitude.

Getting the right terms is often most difficult for the mid-point. What does 'Average' mean? Is the food uniformly neither good nor bad, or is it 'Variable', some good, some bad? One way of allowing respondents to describe the middle ground more precisely is through an open-ended 'Other . . .' category. These examples bring in gradations:

Excellent	Excellent	Give the food a
Good	Good	mark out of 10
Average	Reasonable	
Poor	Poor	. . . .
Very bad		

The first simply extends the scale, retaining the symmetry with a neutral mid-point. The second is a recipe for bias, with its scope for three positive and only one negative response. The third introduces a new approach, by requesting a mark and so avoiding the need for a careful framework of terms. Asking for marks is useful. They are a precise measure when it comes to analysis, and respondents often enjoy themselves. At the same time, some definitions must be provided such as, 'A mark of 1/10 means you consider the food inedible: 10/10 means it is the best you have ever eaten'.

The same process can be used for comparative evaluations, perhaps between your university cafeteria and the bar food in the pub across the road. It is possible either to seek the gradations or collect the marks for both locations separately, or introduce comparative language: 'Is the food in the pub better, the same standard, or worse than in the cafeteria?'

Further possibilities exist for multiple comparisons, such as ranking: 'Please rank these dishes from the cafeteria from 1 to 5, with 1 as your favourite, 5 your least favourite', followed by a list of five dishes. At a more sophisticated level is the matrix of two-way evaluations, which seeks to probe inconsistencies and contradictions in a respondent's attitudes. An example is: 'In the following sets of alternatives underline the one which you think is more important as a charge on the tax-payer:

Heart operations	or	Hip joint replacements
AIDS research	or	Home nursing
Hip joint replacements	or	AIDS research
Home nursing	or	Heart operations
Hip joint replacements	or	Home nursing
AIDS research	or	Heart operations

235

This requests relative evaluations of any two out of four health service activities. It offers direct comparative evaluations of two items, a set of preferences relating to four items (there could be more), and shows whether or not the respondent is being logical and consistent. This latter operates by checking for logical patterns, such that, for example, a respondent who prefers heart operations to home nursing, and home nursing to AIDS research, should, if consistent, prefer heart operations to AIDS research. In reality it is noticeable how inconsistent people can be in their attitudes.

A complex development of the use of polar opposites is the *semantic differential* (pioneered by Osgood, Suci and Tannenbaum, 1957). Without going into detail, they harnessed a wide range of contrasts (good/bad, strong/weak, fast/slow, interesting/boring, introverted/extroverted, happy/sad, and many others) to a format for in-depth attitude evaluations. Through this kind of approach we have also become familiar with the sliding scale way of measuring:

Can you tell me how you feel about your partner by marking where you stand on the dotted line between the following reactions:

Dislike . . . . Like
Outgoing . . . . Self-centred
Careful . . . . Clumsy

As with the two-way matrix, the semantic differential helps build up a profile of respondent attitudes to specific subjects. Anyone wishing to pursue this path of development could be guided towards personal constructs and the repertory grid, which is outside the coverage of this section (Bannister and Fransella, 1971).

Questionnaires

A good questionnaire is more than a collection of questions: it is a coherent document which takes account of the characteristics of respondents, the nature and volume of data to be collected, the format of data-gathering, and plans for analysis.

The questionnaire, and each question within it, must be tailored to such information as the researcher has or can estimate about the respondents. Thus completing the questionnaire needs to be within the capacity of the least able respondent in the sample; otherwise results will be biased towards those who are more competent. What are the skills demanded of the respondents? To complete the questionnaire must they be able to read and write? Do they need to understand difficult or professional language? How vital are their abilities to verbalize and conceptualize? What sort of factual data, or memory of such data, do you expect them to have?

A different range of estimates relates to the motivation of respondents. How willing are they to give information or express opinions? Can anything be said about their possible interest in or boredom with the survey, and hence their willingness or ability to concentrate? How will they react to what might be an invasion of their privacy? Might they be suspicious of you or of the questions you ask?

To complete the picture you also need to look at the setting for the survey from the respondent's viewpoint. Are you coming at a convenient or inconvenient time of day? Could there be distractions, like the respondent's children seeking attention? Does the questionnaire come across as friendly, useful and worth filling in? Is allowance made for respondents who do not have English (or colloquial English) as a first language? Is the content and handling of the questionnaire sensitive to minority cultures and values?

The importance of these points, and ways to deal with them, will depend on who the respondents are and what sort of survey is being conducted. What is important is to be aware of such issues and to make a very careful analysis of respondents both before structuring the questions and in the context of the pilot study. The primary aim of using a survey is to gather data from respondents. It follows that the questionnaire must be designed to facilitate data-giving. The things to be avoided are questions or whole questionnaires which the respondent will not answer (through, for example, feelings of inconvenience, privacy, suspicion, inferiority or plain boredom); cannot answer (because of lack of knowledge or communications skills); answers with too many 'Don't know' or 'Can't understand' responses; or answers with superficial triviality. The things to be encouraged in respondents are an appreciation and understanding of what the questionnaire is seeking to achieve (more of this later), interest and commitment to giving answers, motivation to strive for accuracy and depth in those answers, and a good feeling at the end so that the respondent considers it a worthwhile job done.

Part of the respondent's reaction will be towards the nature and volume of data being sought. Feelings of suspicion and a sense of privacy are common but can be limited by a careful preliminary explanation of what the questionnaire is about and the purposes to which the results will be put. Do not expect respondents to be willing to report their secrets, whether facts or feelings, in the interests of a higher degree thesis. A more widely beneficial potential use of the research, on the other hand, might help. A visibly fat questionnaire, or the prospect that its completion might take a long time, will also deter. As a rule of thumb it is probably sensible to keep an interviewed questionnaire to a maximum of forty-five minutes for most respondents, a self-completion one to fifteen minutes, and to say at the start how long it should take.

The sequence of questions in a questionnaire warrants attention. It is worth treating this matter a bit like forming a relationship — start at a fairly easy superficial level and gradually become more intimate and sensitive. That is, begin with routine questions that relate to the subject and move gently into the harder or more personal ones, rather than launching straightaway into difficult matters. Demographic questions are often asked first because they are straightforward, but they can be sensitive (like social class or income) or be viewed by the respondent as irrelevant to the proper subject-matter. They are better kept to the end and introduced with an explanatory sentence about why they are being asked. In any event, if the questionnaire is long in relation to your estimate of the respondents' ability to concentrate, keep some easy questions for the end, when concentration has lapsed.

The questionnaire will vary according to whether it is to be presented by the interviewer or completed by the respondent. From a practical viewpoint the presentation of a questionnaire by an interviewer has two components, the questions written on paper and the performance of the interviewer. It is almost inevitable that the respondents will see the document, and it is often a helpful part of the process to show them. Hence it needs to be neat, clear and well presented. The interviewer implements the survey and guides the respondent through the questions, and thus has a role in continuity, in presentation, in the relationship with the respondent, and (possibly) in clarifying questions. Preparation for research interviewing is important, so as to be systematic and consistent: behaving differently with each respondent will lead to bias. If more than one interviewer is involved, they must work (perhaps rehearse) to achieve a similar approach.

A questionnaire sent to a respondent for self-completion, without any face-to-face contact with you, has to be totally coherent and self-contained. In practical terms this means that there has to be a written introduction, explaining the survey and trying to persuade the respondent to complete and return the questionnaire. The questions themselves have to be set out clearly, with precise instructions about how to record answers, and the conceptual as well as practical sequence of the questionnaire has to be covered by written guidance. Even when you are present self-completion questionnaires need to be self-contained, although the wider context can be handled verbally. It is common with postal questionnaires to give the respondent a phone number (possibly also a range of times when you guarantee to be available) for any queries about the survey.

The form the survey takes can also influence the extent to which the questionnaire is prepared for subsequent computer analysis. Pre-coded answer-blocks facilitate analysis, so there is a case for using them as often as is possible given the need for some illustrative or qualitative material. A compromise here is to use a pre-coded block but add some space and an invitation to write in a sentence. Whether the questionnaire itself is coded in advance for computing is more debatable. Certainly it speeds up the analysis process, but it is risky because too often changes have to be made to accommodate answers which were given but not anticipated. Computer code numbers on the questionnaire can also make the document look cluttered and unattractive to potential respondents. Some computer programs (such as SNAP) incorporate the construction and automatic coding of a questionnaires without showing coding numbers on the questionnaire document, though this approach is only really suited to questionnaires with all pre-coded answer blocks.

Care is also needed with open-ended material. A desirable feature of a survey report is illustrative or qualitative data given in the respondents' own words, but there are two risks. One is that a question seeking illustrative material will be asked and answers recorded in such a way that the responses are chaotic and cannot be categorized for tabulation. A second, more managerial risk is to obtain respondents' own words by tape-recording interviews. Handled carefully, and in conjunction with a more structured survey, this can be a most valuable source, but tape-recording must be very selective. Depending on your skills, it can take anything from four to nine hours to transcribe one hour of interview, so it has big workload implications. One approach to selectivity is to record just a few interviews, or only those comments which you feel will be useful. Some respondents may need some persuasion to give answers into a recorder (it is sensible to back away in face of any resistance), but can be tempted if told — 'What you have just said is really interesting. So that I can have your own words, would you mind saying it again on tape?'

A final practical point about questionnaires. They take a lot of rough handling from interviewer or respondent, and during the process of transfer to computer. During completion it is important for whoever is recording answers to be able to turn pages easily and have enough space. If they are being used out of doors they need to be wind and rain resistant. They are unique documents. Make them to work well and to last!

Errors

There are two main types of error in the results obtained from surveys — sampling errors and non-sampling errors. Sampling errors occur because a sample is used instead of a complete population. If a probability sampling method has been used it is possible to estimate the error, so that some idea of precision can be obtained. This can be a complex calculation and is covered in books such as Cochran (1977).

Non-sampling errors are caused by non-response, collection of inaccurate information and inaccurate coding and analysis. In most surveys there is a certain amount of non-response. There may be some outright refusals, although these are generally fairly few. The proportion of refusals will depend on the saliency of the subject and the skill of the interviewer or contextual documentation. Refusals may be total or partial (refusing to answer certain parts of the questionnaire). More common than those who refuse are individuals who are impossible to contact. Another source of non-response are those who are unsuitable, perhaps infirm, deaf or with language problems (in an interview survey) or illiterate (in a self-completion survey).

All efforts should be made to minimize non-response. Non-response cannot be ignored. If this is done and estimates are based on responders only, then one is making the assumption that the responders are like the non-responders in relevant aspects. This is very often not so. For example if the main reason that people did not respond was that they were not interested in the subject, then the achieved sample will not be representative of the whole population and a biased result will be achieved. If there is available some relevant information on the non-responders then non-response can be calculated within subgroups and the inverse of these rates used to weight the results. For partial non-response more information is often available and there are various imputation methods that can be used (see Kalton and Kasprzyk, 1982).

If it can be assumed that there is a 'true' value that you are trying to measure (a true opinion for example), then any deviation from this value is a response error. Various factors can contribute. The interviewer may be unskilled, dishonest or possess characteristics which influence the respondent (i.e. 'interviewer bias'). The respondent may give a wrong answer because they do not know the answer, do not remember, misunderstand the question, or do not wish to answer. The conditions of the survey may influence the respondent — the place of the interview (perhaps it is in a school or hospital where respondents feel inhibited), or maybe a third party is present. Other sources of error are in the coding, especially of open-ended questions, and data entry to computer. The latter must be expected and watched for.

Any survey researcher should be aware of the possible sources of error and take all means to minimize the problem. As has been suggested, it can occur throughout the survey process, and the way to prevent it is to be continually vigilant. Prevention is very much better than cure. Indeed, with a few exceptions, there is no practical way of correcting a corrupted data set.

Implementing Surveys

Once a questionnaire has been prepared attention switches to the context of the survey implementation, and to the trial (pilot) of the questionnaire itself along with the data-collection procedures. The fact of having a pilot study introduces a two-stage process. The first (pilot) stage is based on estimates of how it is best to proceed: the second stage is informed by the findings and experiences of the pilot, and so can convert earlier estimates into clear decisions.

Initial preparations include making estimates of when (from the viewpoint of researcher and respondent) it is most convenient to carry out the data collection, how long it is likely to take per respondent and for the whole sample, what practical arrangements have to be made for travel, appointments etc. and how non-response is to be handled.

If the survey is to use interviews, the interviewer will need a letter of identification (like a letter of *bona fides* typed on university headed note-paper, signed by the supervisor) to show to respondents and anyone else who might be concerned. Surveying by knocking on doors can arouse suspicion, so an official letter to the local police in advance can be useful. When appointments are to be made, a systematic process is needed for initial contacts and for follow-ups when the first attempt fails. If the questionnaire is to be sent by post for self-completion there is the letter of introduction and explanation to be written. Whatever the data collection method, there are decisions to be made about the procedure for handling non-response — the number and type of efforts to be made to obtain response, and how the reasons for non-response will be uncovered.

The rule of treating all respondents alike applies to the context as much as to the actual data collection. Thus introductions, letters or phone calls to make appointments, efforts to get a response must all be planned, systematic and evenly applied.

The first direct experience of how well all these things work will come from the pilot study. There are two approaches to the pilot study. One is to treat it as a miniature version of the whole study, from beginning through to a report on the results. This is particularly important where major, high-cost studies are being planned, and the pilot is used not just to test survey processes, but also to check whether there is justification for going ahead with the major research. The other approach is to limit the pilot to checking the data-collection instruments and procedures. Given the usual time and resource constraints this may be a more practical route for higher degree students.

If the latter approach is taken, it must be comprehensive within its set boundaries. The pilot is used to scrutinize your methods and to justify changes in questions, questionnaires, presentation and surrounds, the roles played by researcher(s) and interviewer(s), the reactions of respondents, timetable and costs. In order to achieve this it is vital that the pilot should be carried out as nearly as possible in the same way as is proposed for the full study.

There are three questions which research students regularly pose. The first asks how big (i.e. sample size) the pilot should be. There is an arbitrary and a practical answer. The arbitrary approach is to agree a size with your supervisor (say ten to fifteen) and then get on with it. The practical approach is to maintain a continuous assessment of your pilot work. Carry out two or three data-collection processes, then assess the experience, making changes where warranted. Try the revised procedures/questions and then check the outcome again. Keep this routine going until you are satisfied with every aspect of the process. This may result in a smaller overall pilot effort or a larger one, depending on how well designed and prepared the survey was in the first instance.

The second question is: 'Who should be subjects (respondents) for the pilot study?' If the survey population is large enough for a pilot sample to be taken without jeopardizing the main sample, then this should be done. There is no equivalent to testing the survey on respondents who could have been part of the main study. However, there are occasions when the survey population is small and all are needed for the main study. In these circumstances it may be acceptable to look elsewhere, either for naturally matching respondents or for a contrived match. Sometimes it is possible to find people whose circumstances are close to those of the research group, but who live in another location; or pilots who match on most but not all variables. If this does not seem feasible, then consider getting some colleagues to undergo preparation for role-playing a respondent. It can sometimes be helpful to get a friend to role-play and be as difficult as the role will permit, in the sense of trying to expose any weaknesses in the data-collection instruments or procedures.

A further possibility is to use pilot data in the main study or repeat the main study with respondents who were used in the pilot. The first of these, using pilot data for the main study, is the basis of the third commonly asked question — 'Can you do this?' In one unlikely circumstance this may be acceptable — if no substantive changes are made as a result of the pilot and the time-span between pilot and full study is short. In most instances re-using data would be fraught, because it would not be quite the same data set or would have been collected in a different way. Going back to respondents on a second occasion also risks bias unless the interval is so long that the respondent has forgotten most things about the initial contact. On balance, if the choice is between re-using data or a respondent (or even using pilot respondents from a close-knit setting where they are likely to talk to potential main study respondents), and going elsewhere for matching or role-play pilots, it is probably sensible to go elsewhere.

The pilot study gives certainty to what were previously estimates and allows the main study to go ahead. The early dealings with respondents, especially interviews, can be exciting times, but data collection palls, especially if you are looking for a large number of responses. Researcher or interviewer boredom needs to be recognized and taken into account. The greatest risks are of bias and error slipping in because procedures become sloppy and are allowed to change. Before starting the main study gather together a full set of all documents and add to it a clear written statement of the procedures you intend to use. This will be invaluable as a continuing reminder to you, as a part of the discussion of methods in your thesis, and as a guide to a substitute in the event of your falling sick. Like a long-running West End play, build in regular production reviews to make sure you are keeping the standards high! And like a good diarist, keep a log of the interesting and amusing events of data collection — there will be some, and they will enliven your thesis.

Survey Analysis

This section makes the case for using a computer to analyze your data (see also Chapter 21 on statistical analysis.) If you are planning to collect quantitative data on more than a very few individuals, it is sensible to use a computer to analyze the results. Anyone who has tried to sort out and analyze the results of a survey without the help of a computer will know that, even with a small amount of data, the job is formidable. It is perfectly *possible* to do simple analyses either by sorting questionnaires (or forms) by the answers to a particular question, and counting the various piles or by writing all the responses on to large pieces of paper. Many people who have not used a computer before feel that it would take longer to learn how to use one than it would take to do the analysis 'by hand' — and many people have realized that this was a mistake! There are several good reasons why it is advisable to use a computer to analyze data of this kind. Obviously if the number of cases is very small and the analyses required are very simple, then a simple hand-counting method might be as quick. But usually the time taken to learn the necessary basics is time well spent. For one thing you will have learnt a new skill which might very well be useful to you later on. Another reason for using a computer is that once you have the data in computer-readable form you can do as many analyses as you want to merely by using a few keys on the keyboard. It might be that you start off with the idea that it is really only a few tables that you want, but having considered these tables you realize that further and more complex statistical analyses are needed. If you have not prepared your data for the computer you might have an almost impossible task trying to do it by hand. You might then have to use the computer after all! Any analysis that involves multivariate techniques (where more than one variable is considered at a time) is much better done on a computer, not only because of the time saved but because a computer is less liable to make mistakes.

There are a few terms which are used in survey analysis which should be explained:

Case A unit about which information is collected. It is often an individual person but could also be an organization such as a school or a hospital.

Variable An item of information collected about cases. Variables can be of two kinds:

a) **Numeric variables:** taking only numeric values. These can be variables such as age, weight, height etc. where the actual value is recorded or variables where a coded value is recorded such as sex where '1' could indicate a male and '2' a female.

b) **Alphanumeric (or string) variables:** which can be either numbers or letters or a mixture of both. You might wish to record names, addresses or comments, for example.

Variable values These are the possible values taken by a variable, for example '1' or '2' for 'sex'.

Value labels These are the names, or labels, given to the values of the coded numeric variables. For example for the variable 'sex' the value '1' could be given the label 'male' and the value '2' the label 'female'.

Organizing Data for the Computer

It is important to know exactly how you are going to handle and analyze your data before you start to collect it. Your questionnaire should be designed in such a way that it is simple to key most of the information directly into the computer. You must decide how you will handle multiple response variables (those variables where you may want to record more than one value from an answer) and variables that need coding after they have been returned to you. A code book (or dictionary) must be created. The minimum information to be included will generally include the variable name, variable values, value labels, the codes to be given missing values and the maximum number of characters that the variable can take.

After the code book is written and the questionnaires checked and coded, the data is ready for input. There are various methods that can be used. A wordprocessor or editor can be used and the data saved as an ASCII (American Standard Code for Information Interchange) file which can be used by other computer packages. It is sensible to decide which package you are going to use for the analysis, as different packages require the data laid out in different ways. Fixed format is a generally accepted method — each case starts on a new line and can continue for as many lines as necessary, and each variable occupies the same column or columns for each case.

Alternatively a spreadsheet package (e.g. Lotus 123) or a database package (e.g. dBase III) can be used. These can store not only data but some data description, such as variable names, as well. They cannot produce much in the way of analysis (although Lotus 123 can produce graphics) but they can write files which can be read by other analysis packages.

Another option is to use a data-entry package such as SPSS-PC Data Entry. With this package a framework is set up containing the data description into which the data is punched. Various edits can be imposed, such as 'ranges' which only allow certain values to be punched in and 'rules' which do not allow specified inconsistency (such as someone who has an age keyed in as 5 to have three children). Another useful facility is 'Skip and Fill'. If there are some parts of the form or questionnaire which do not apply to everyone, then you might want to fill all these variables with some missing value (such as 99) and go to the next relevant variable. This can save a lot of time. Data can be entered in the form of a spreadsheet with the variable names appearing at the top of the columns or, alternatively, a form can be designed which can be set up to look like the original questionnaire (or to take any format desired). The data and the data description can be saved together for later analysis by SPSS. ASCII files can be written out to be used by other packages. The package is menu-driven and easy to use.

Analyzing the Data

The software package chosen will depend on availability and the type of analysis required. There are many packages available and a few of the most useful will be briefly mentioned. Most have mainframe and personal computer (PC) versions.

SPSS — Statistical Package for the Social Sciences. This is a widely used package and is very useful for the routine management and analysis of survey data. The PC version is particularly easy to use. One of its advantages is that it can cope with most kinds of data. This is not so with all the others. For example if you have what is called a hierarchical data set where you have, say, a record with details of a household plus records for each member of that household, then SPSS can deal with this. System files (containing data description as well as data) can be used. However it is not as versatile in more complex analyses as some packages.

BMDP — Biomedical Computer Programs. This is another general purpose statistical package. In many ways it is similar to SPSS and can be used to perform many of the same analyses. Like SPSS, it can also be used to create and save a system file.

SAS — Statistical Analysis System. This is a general purpose statistical package which can do almost everything that SPSS or BMDP can do, but is more flexible. It has a very wide range of statistical procedures. As a result it is not so easy to use as some others. There are so many things that it *can* do that the manuals are enormous and rather intimidating.

MINITAB. This is a very easy-to-use general-purpose package designed especially for people with no previous computing experience. The instructions that you type in are similar to English. The handbook is simple to follow. Its scope is limited, although for any simple calculations on simple data including not too many cases it is worth considering. It can be used interactively and is rather like using a very superior calculator.

STATGRAPHICS. This is a general interactive statistical package designed for microcomputers. It can do most general analyses. It is not very versatile for recoding and transforming variables but has one of the best graphics capabilities.

SNAP. This is a PC program for simple survey analysis. It offers tabulations and cross referencing, but few statistical tests. Its potential stems from being designed to handle a survey from start to finish. You can design questions and questionnaire on it, and have your coding done automatically and a code book printed off.

So, which to choose? It will depend on the number of cases that you have, the sort of data sets and what you want to do. If you have a small number of cases, a simple data set and want simple analyses then MINITAB might be suitable as it is so easy to use, but it is very limited. SNAP also has limitations on size (a tendency with many PC programs or PC versions where there is limited storage space on the computer), but is rather more versatile. For a larger more complex data set or for more complex analyses, SPSS, BMDP or SAS would be more suitable. It is important to decide which package you are going to use at an early stage in your project. You should have thought about what sort of analysis you want to carry out and you can consult the manuals or seek advice to see which package is most suitable for your purpose. You need to think about the analysis before you collect the data. Very often it is left until all the data has been collected which makes things much more difficult.

Further Reading

Stacey (1969) provides a good introduction for research students, placing survey design and data collection within the general context of social research. Hoinville *et al.* (1978) give sound practical advice on the planning of surveys. See also Fowler (1984). De Vaus (1986) places more emphasis on analysis and provides some useful pointers to further reading. Moser and Kalton (1985) and Rossi *et al.* (1983) serve as good comprehensive sources of advice and reference. For an examination of the theoretical criticisms which the survey method has received from sociologists see Marsh (1982).

References

BANNISTER, D. and FRANSELLA, F. (1971) *Theory of Personal Constructs*, Harmondsworth, Penguin.

BRYMAN, A. (1989) *Research Methods and Organisation Studies*, London, Unwin Hyman.

COCHRAN, W.G. (1977) *Sampling Techniques*, New York, Wiley.

DE VAUS, D.A. (1986) *Surveys in Social Research*, London, Allen and Unwin.

DILLMAN, D.A. (1978) *Mail and Telephone Surveys*, New York, Wiley.

ERDOS, P.L. (1970) *Professional Mail Surveys*, New York, McGraw-Hill.

FOWLER, F.J. (1984) *Survey Research Methods*, London, Sage.

GROVES, R.M., BIEMER, P.M., LYBERG, L.E., MASSEY, J.T., NICHOLLS, W.L. and WAKSBERG, J. (1988) *Telephone Survey Methodology*, New York, Wiley.

HOINVILLE, G., JOWELL, R. and ASSOCIATES (1978) *Survey Research Practice*, London, Heinemann.

KALTON, G. and KASPRZYK, D. (1982) 'Imputing for missing survey responses', *Proceedings of the American Statistical Association, Survey Research Methods Section*, pp. 22–31.

MARSH, C. (1982) *The Survey Method*, London, Allen and Unwin.

MOSER, C.A. and KALTON, G. (1985) *Survey Methods in Social Investigation*, London, Heinemann.

OSGOOD, C.E., SUCI, G.J. and TANNENBAUM, P.H. (1957) *The Measurement of Meaning*, Urbana, University of Illinois Press.

PAYNE, S.L. (1951) *The Art of Asking Questions*, Princeton, Princeton University Press.

ROSSI, P.H., WRIGHT, J.D. and ANDERSON, A.B. (1983) *Handbook of Survey Research*, New York, Academic Press.

STACEY, M. (1969) *Methods of Social Research*, Oxford, Pergamon.

Chapter 20

Secondary Analysis

Andy Hinde

Introduction

In Chapter 18 on 'Quantitative Research' the distinction was made between *primary research*, in which you collect and analyze your own data, and *secondary analysis*, in which you analyze data collected by someone else. This chapter deals with the latter. It begins by defining secondary analysis and listing the main types of sources of secondary data. The role played by secondary analysis in postgraduate research is then discussed. The advantages and disadvantages of secondary analysis *vis à vis* primary research are outlined, and the considerations which should influence the choice of whether or not to use secondary data are summarized. One of the most important of these considerations is the availability of readily accessible secondary data which are potentially capable of answering the questions you wish to pose. Accordingly, the chapter describes in some detail how to search for secondary data and how to select and obtain a suitable data set. There is not space in a short chapter such as this to do more than outline the main issues. In the final section a number of sources which deal with the topic of secondary analysis in more detail are reviewed. You should endeavour to familiarize yourself with at least some of these sources at an early stage in your research. Finally, this chapter does not consider statistical techniques, which are covered in Chapter 21.

Secondary Analysis: Definition and Sources

Secondary analysis may be defined as 'any further analysis of an existing data set which presents interpretations, conclusions or knowledge additional to, or different from, those presented in the first report on the inquiry as a whole and its main results' (Hakim, 1982:1). Since in an MPhil or a PhD you are expected to contribute new knowledge (it is assumed that you will not be replicating previous work) secondary analysis in the context of a MPhil or PhD thesis is simply any analysis done on data which you have not collected, or *secondary data*.

Secondary data may come from a number of different sources. Hakim (1982:5–8) lists six: population censuses, continuous or regular surveys, national cohort studies, multi-source data sets, data sets derived from administrative records, and *ad hoc* surveys. Some of these, especially the continuous or regular national surveys and national cohort studies, are typically very large, rich data sets containing many social and economic variables for large samples. A well-known example is the UK General Household Survey (GHS). This is based on interviews with more than 10,000 households, containing over 25,000 individuals, and has been conducted every year since 1971. (Note that the same households are not interviewed each year.) It contains data on topics as diverse as housing tenure, migration, participation in the labour force, and smoking behaviour (Hakim, 1982:Table 7.1, pp. 100–103). The very size and scope of data sets as large as this can present practical difficulties with the analysis. For examples of work using the GHS and other UK national surveys, see the papers in Joshi (1989).

Other sources, such as *ad hoc* surveys, may be limited in scope and may not always consist of random samples. For example, there are a number of data sets available which comprise information transcribed from the original returns of nineteenth-century censuses of England and Wales (Mills and Pearce, 1989). Usually these consist of complete enumerations of the population of particular villages and towns. The variables they contain are limited to those about which questions were asked in the censuses (relationship to head of household, age, sex, marital status, occupation and birthplace). A widely admired study using census data of this type is that by Anderson (1971).

The Role of Secondary Analysis

Most research theses make some use of previously collected data, even if only by extracting a few figures from census tables or other published sources to provide a context within which to set primary research. At an early stage in the project, therefore, you will have to decide what use you are going to make of secondary analysis.

There are, broadly speaking, two roles which secondary data might play in the project. First, they might be used *in a subsidiary role*, where your own primary research or theoretical development is the main thrust of your work. For example, in a study of gender and class differentials in the incidence of smoking amongst teenagers, for which you plan to carry out your own survey, you might wish to make use of the information on smoking behaviour collected as part of the GHS to provide a context within which to set your work. Second, secondary data might be used *in a central role*, so that you rely entirely on analyzing previously collected data in a new way. Of course, you could eschew the use of secondary data altogether — although some presentation of aggregate statistics for descriptive purposes, as described in Chapter 18 on quantitative research, is usually desirable.

Whatever you decide to do, the decision must be made early. As Chapter 19 on survey methods makes clear, it takes a lot of time to plan and prepare your own survey, so you must start planning and preparing work early in the project if your survey is to be successful. It can, however, also take quite a time to choose, obtain and set up the data for a penetrative secondary analysis. Moreover, as we shall see, the search for suitable secondary data may prove fruitless, leaving you no alternative but to undertake your own primary research (unless you are prepared to change your research topic).

Primary Research or Secondary Analysis?

A number of considerations will influence your choice of whether or not to rely upon secondary analysis. They are described in the following paragraphs (although not necessarily in order of their importance).

First, the skills you possess or wish to acquire may influence your decision. An advantage of carrying out your own survey, and analyzing the results, is that you gain a first-hand appreciation of every stage of the research process. Concentrating upon secondary analysis means that you will avoid such aspects as questionnaire design and interview techniques. On the other hand, the ability effectively to exploit large, nationally representative surveys is an important research skill in itself, and one which you will probably not have the chance to develop if you rely upon primary research.

The nature of the topic you wish to tackle may make the decision for you. If you are interested in social and economic history, or in long-term temporal trends, or in social change, it will probably be impossible for you to do your own survey. Secondary analysis also permits comparative research, and even cross-national studies (although the difficulties of these are formidable and 'cross-national research is the last place for the inexperienced secondary analyst to begin his career' (Hyman, 1972:291)). Of course, there are other topics where the availability of suitable secondary data will be critical. It may be that you cannot find any extant data sets that will allow you to achieve the objectives of your research. This is especially likely if you are seeking qualitative data, since most easily available secondary data sets are quantitative in nature. If this is the case, you have no alternative but to carry out your own survey.

You should weigh up the advantages and disadvantages of secondary analysis relative to primary analysis in the context of your own topic. These advantages and disadvantages are described more fully in the next section.

Finally, personal preference may be important. Some people like the thought of designing and implementing their own survey. Others are appalled by the prospect of carrying out a large number of interviews. Whereas personal preference should not, perhaps, be the main consideration, you should bear in mind that you will be spending many months carrying out the research upon which you will base your thesis. If you enjoy what you are doing, not only will the work seem much less onerous than it will if you are nervous or apprehensive, but the end result will probably be better!

Advantages of Secondary Analysis

Weighing up the benefits and costs of any research strategy at an early stage is essential. Since the decision concerning the role which secondary analysis is going to play in your research is so important, it is vital that you have an appreciation of the advantages and disadvantages of using secondary data compared with primary research. In this section, the benefits conferred by secondary analysis are briefly examined; in the following section, its disadvantages are summarized. For a fuller discussion of the benefits, see Hyman (1972:6–24) and for a consideration of both benefits and costs, see Dale, Arber and Procter (1988:44–60).

The advantages of secondary analysis are of four types. First, there are the considerable savings in time and cost to be made by obtaining your data directly, without having to go through the processes of designing and implementing your own survey. Since, as a research student, your time and resources are limited, this is an important advantage.

Second, there is the question of the quality of the data. Many secondary data sets are of high quality, having been produced by experts in the arts of questionnaire design and fieldwork. Their sample design is usually good, and the sample is often much larger than any you could hope to obtain in a primary survey (many contain data on several thousand individuals). By using such data, you are indirectly making available to yourself the experience and expertise of those who carried out the survey. Moreover, if there are problems with certain aspects of the data, these may well have been spotted by the authors of the initial report. Having said all this, it is worth emphasizing that you should not assume that because you are using secondary data, you do not need to check it for inconsistencies, or spend time familiarizing yourself with the data prior to embarking upon statistical analysis.

Third, the generalizability of the results of secondary analysis may be greater than those of primary research. Because many published data sets contain samples drawn at random from national populations, statistical inference becomes much more straightforward (see Chapter 21 on statistical analysis).

Fourth, there are a number of intellectual advantages. Secondary analysis, by definition, builds on previous work, and so fits naturally within the process by which new knowledge is created (Dale, Arber and Procter, 1988:44). It also opens up the possibility of replicating previous studies using new data, or 're-analysing the same data from different perspectives and within different theoretical frameworks' (Dale, Arber and Procter, 1988:54). Sometimes, it will reveal unexpected relationships between variables. Finally, Hyman (1972:23–4) points out that secondary analysis can assist in elevating and enlarging theory because the secondary analyst is compelled to rummage through data collected by other people, at other times, and 'there is at least a chance that he may broaden his theorizing and choice of problems in the light of the exotic stimulus' (p. 24).

Potential Problems with Secondary Analysis

After reading the previous section, you may be wondering why anyone goes to the trouble of carrying out their own survey (unless secondary data are unavailable). In this section some reasons will be given in the form of a summary of the disadvantages of secondary analysis when compared with primary research. Although most of these disadvantages can be overcome by effort and imagination, reflection upon them will demonstrate that secondary analysis is not without its difficulties.

One problem is that of the vanishing sample, which arises when you are interested in some well-defined minority subgroup of the population. Even though many secondary data sets are based on large samples, these samples are usually nationally representative. This means that the number of individuals in the sample who are members of the subgroup which interests you may be too small for a meaningful analysis. In such a case, doing your own survey may well be the best strategy to adopt.

The definition of secondary analysis presented at the beginning of this chapter spoke of analysis which presents results and interpretations different from those presented in the initial report on the survey. This highlights the fact that much secondary analysis uses data for purposes other than that for which they were collected. Although doing this is in many ways a good thing (for it makes efficient use of data, and renders serendipity more likely), it can create problems. The variables in a secondary data set may not be exactly those you want to answer the questions you wish to pose. You may have to transform and manipulate the data in quite complex ways to render them suitable for testing the hypothesis you wish to test. This process may require a lot of thought and care. We might term it a clash of purposes problem.

Moreover, even if there are no great intellectual problems posed by the data, secondary analysis, particularly of large sample surveys, can involve the manipulation of large data files. You must prepare for this, both by having available the computing hardware to do it (in the case of large, nationally representative surveys this usually means a mainframe computer), and by familiarizing yourself with the requisite computing software. A good knowledge of the data manipulation capabilities of a major statistical package (SPSS-X or SAS) is essential for secondary analysis of large sample surveys (see Chapter 20 on survey methods for more information about such packages). Of course, with smaller data sets you may be able to get away with using a desk-top microcomputer. A related problem may arise from the fact that many secondary data sets are made available as computer files, the exploitation of which may require knowledge of a particular statistical package. This issue is discussed further below.

Finally, because your data have not been collected by you, more will probably be expected by way of analytical content of a thesis relying entirely on secondary analysis than of a thesis based on primary research. This is especially true now that the time limit for the submission of theses is being given such priority.

Choosing a Data Set

If you decide to proceed with secondary analysis, you will have to select a suitable data set. In doing so, many of the issues discussed in the preceding sections will be relevant. However, before you can select a suitable data set for secondary analysis, you clearly need to have information about what is available, and how to obtain it. This section summarizes the main potential sources of secondary data. The following section offers some advice on how to go about the final choice.

There are a number of places where you might search for secondary data. For published statistics, for example census reports, the statistics section of your university or college library may prove useful. Almost all such libraries have a section in which published statistics are stored. You should familiarize yourself with the contents of that section. If you are planning to use secondary analysis merely to set your own survey in context, then this may be as far as you need to go in your search for data.

If you are relying exclusively on secondary analysis, then you will probably need to go further than published statistics. By far the most important source of unpublished data are the *data archives*. The use of these is described in Hakim (1982:159–76). For the United Kingdom research student, the most important data archive is that operated by the Economic and Social Research Council (ESRC) at the University of Essex. They produce a catalogue of current holdings, which may be obtained from the ESRC Data Archive, University of Essex, Colchester CO4 3SQ (Tel. 0206–872001). Alternatively, there is an online computer catalogue, access to which can be gained through the Joint Academic Network (JANET) at the address ARCHIVE@UK.AC.ESSEX (ask at your computer centre for details about how to use JANET). Approaches to the ESRC Data Archive may be made direct (to the address above), or through your department or faculty's ESRC Liason Officer (if one exists). More details about how to use it to choose a data set are given in Hakim (1982:161–3) and Dale, Arber and Procter (1988:78–97).

For data dealing with other countries, you might wish to search other data archives. The ESRC Data Archive can provide details of these; it also holds various data sets from other countries and can obtain them for you. A list of major American and European data archives is given in Hakim (1982:Table 11.1, pp. 165–7).

Finally, there are a range of other sources. Certain large data sets may only be used under special arrangements. An example is the Office of Population Censuses and Surveys (OPCS) Longitudinal Survey, which links together census and vital registration information about a 1 per cent sample of the United Kingdom population.

The Final Choice

Once you have found out what data sets are available on your chosen topic, you must obtain further information about each of them. It is unwise to go straight ahead and order the survey which seems most likely to cover the area in which you are interested.

At all points in the choice of a research strategy it is essential that you have a clear idea of exactly what you wish to achieve by your research. You should keep in mind the characteristics of the population which interests you, the questions you want to answer, and the hypotheses you want to test. This is especially important when making the final choice of a data set for secondary analysis. Although secondary analysis means that you can avoid having to implement your own survey, it does not mean that you can avoid the necessary preliminary work. When selecting a data set, you should go through much of the same procedure as if you were going to carry out your own survey (at least as far as the preliminary design of the questionnaire). New questions may emerge as your analysis proceeds, but it is best to let them arise naturally out of your previous results.

Once you have made a short-list of promising data sets, you should examine them in more detail. This may be done in a number of ways. First, if possible you should examine the questionnaires and code books (for data sets stored in computer files, the latter give details about how the responses were entered into the computer). Find out exactly what questions were asked. It may be that in a survey which, at first glance, seems very promising, questions relating to the variables in which you are particularly interested were not asked. Find out how the answers were coded to see if the coding system is appropriate for your work.

Find out whether or not you are likely to need the whole data set. Even though a particular survey may have produced an enormous amount of data, you may find that a subset of the variables available will be sufficient for your needs. If it is possible to obtain just this subset, your computing requirements (such as filestore space) may be substantially reduced. Before you go ahead and obtain just part of a data set, however, make sure that you will definitely not want other variables later. If you are in doubt about a variable, obtain it anyway!

You should, in any case, consider the computing requirements in some detail. Find out if you will have access to the hardware and filestore needed to store the data set. (Remember, some national surveys are very large indeed.) Find out, also, if you will need any special software to use the data.

Read the initial reports and other published work arising from the data set. The initial report will describe the data set in some detail and present the results of any preliminary analysis (usually of a descriptive nature) which has been done. It might also draw attention to any problems with the data which were detected at this stage. The descriptive statistics could also alert you to a potential 'vanishing sample' problem. They can also point to possible 'missing value' problems in the data. The fact that a question was asked does not mean that it was always answered. There are many examples of questions which were not answered by a majority of those interviewed. You do not want to find out, having ordered the data, that two-thirds of the replies to the critical question (so far as your project is concerned) are coded as 'missing'! Having read the initial report, you should read publications arising from previous analysis, either by the collector of the data, or by previous secondary analysts. Apart from preventing you from replicating analyses which have already been done, this might also give you additional information about the reliability of replies to individual questions.

Obtaining your Data Set

Once you have decided upon your data set, you will need to obtain permission to use it. For data published and stored in libraries, this is not usually necessary — an acknowledgment of the source in the usual way is sufficient. Data sets obtained from a data archive may fall into one of several groups. For some, this permission is routinely given by the data archive. In other cases, you may have to inform the original collector of the data (usually called the *depositor* by the data archive). In yet other cases, you will have to write specifically to the depositor, asking his or her express permission.

If your data are coming from a data archive, ordering it is usually relatively simple. Having expressed an interest in the data, you will be sent forms to fill in. Much of the information required by these forms is related to the *format* in which you want to receive the data. For some data sets there is no choice, but for others, several possibilities may exist. For example, you may have a choice between a hierarchical data file and a flat file. For more information about these and other choices you might have, see Dale, Arber and Procter (1988:88–96).

One potential difficulty which could arise at this stage has already been alluded to earlier. Some secondary data sets, especially large complex sample surveys, are stored on computers in ways which make access to the data dependent on your using specific software. For example, some data sets are stored using the hierarchical database package SIR (Scientific Information Retrieval) and you cannot extract variables from them without writing SIR programs. Unless you know someone who is able to help you do this, or are prepared to learn to do it yourself, you may encounter problems with such data sets. Usually it is possible to find someone to assist you (either at your local computer centre or at the data archive from which you are obtaining the data).

Conclusion

In this chapter I have tried to give you an introduction to the major decisions which have to be made if you are to use secondary analysis as your major research strategy. It may appear that the number of factors which you need to take into account is rather large and that if you follow all the suggestions you will never get round to doing any analysis before your grant expires! In fact, it is only in a minority of projects that you will need to think hard about all the issues raised in this chapter. In many cases, it is clear that secondary analysis is the only way forward, and that the number of potential data sets is very small, so that the decisions may be made relatively quickly. Of course, questionnaires, code books and first reports will still have to be read.

Further Reading

A classic text (probably *the* classic text) on secondary analysis is Hyman (1972), although its examples are a little dated now and are drawn almost entirely from North American research. Two excellent books which deal with secondary analysis in the United Kingdom are Hakim (1982) and Dale, Arber and Procter (1988). The latter is, perhaps, the best available practical guide to the process of secondary analysis using United Kingdom data, and covers a wide area through computing software to the conceptualization and derivation of variables. A useful short introduction to secondary analysis is provided in Kiecolt and Nathan (1985).

The ESRC Data Archive publishes a regular *Bulletin*, each issue of which contains details of recent acquisitions both to their stock and to the stock of foreign archives. The *Bulletin* also includes articles describing particular data sets, information about computer software and news about research in progress. Your department will probably have a copy; if not, you can obtain one by writing to the ESRC Data Archive at the address given earlier in this chapter. Some data sets (such as the GHS and the OPCS Longitudinal Study) also have their own newsletters.

Acknowledgments

I am grateful to Dr Ian Diamond of the Department of Social Statistics at the University of Southampton for his assistance.

References

ANDERSON, M. (1971) *Family Structure in Nineteenth-Century Lancashire*, Cambridge, Cambridge University Press.

DALE, A., ARBER, S. and PROCTER, M. (1988) *Doing Secondary Analysis*, London, Unwin Hyman.

HAKIM, C. (1982) *Secondary Analysis in Social Research*, London, Allen and Unwin.

HYMAN, H.H. (1972) *Secondary Analysis of Sample Surveys: Principles, Procedures and Potentialities*, London, Wiley.

JOSHI, H. (Ed.) (1989) *The Changing Population of Britain*, Oxford, Blackwell.

KIECOLT, K.J. and NATHAN, L.E. (1985) *Secondary Analysis of Survey Data*, London, Sage.

MILLS, D. and PEARCE, C. (1989) 'People and places in the Victorian Census: A review and bibliography of publications based substantially on the manuscript census enumerators' books, 1841–1911', *Historical Geography Research Series* No. 23, Institute of British Geographers' Historical Geography Research Group.

Chapter 21

Statistical Analysis

Tim Holt

Introduction

Many texts provide an introduction to statistics and a detailed description of basic statistical methods. Several that integrate the use of statistical computer packages such as SPSS or MINITAB are listed in the bibliography. My purpose is to provide a guide to planning statistical analyses. A detailed description of particular procedures will not be given but this chapter should help researchers to read statistical texts or to study a particular method of analysis.

As a useful breakdown, we can classify the majority of quantitative research topics undertaken by research students in the social sciences into three types:

(a) small-scale primary surveys or data collections;
(b) designed experiments;
(c) large-scale secondary survey analyses.

The classification is not rigid and issues discussed under one category have a relevance to the others. The classification is useful since it has a bearing on the types of analyses that can be undertaken and from which useful results might be expected. In the next section we will describe these categories in greater detail and in the following sections we shall describe a statistical framework in more detail.

A second form of classification which will be needed is to distinguish between the *dependent* variable, the primary focus of a particular analysis, and possible *explanatory* variables. For example, we may be interested in whether or not a person released from prison is reconvicted within five years. This is the primary focus of our interest. However we might expect that the outcome differs systematically depending on other characteristics of the subject. For example the reconviction rate may be different for prisoners who have a stable marriage or cohabitational relationship at the time of release compared to those who have not. Similarly it may vary with age and whether or not the prisoner has a trade or particular level of education. Such variables are explanatory variables that may help us to understand why some people are more likely to be reconvicted than others. Note that the generic term frequently used to describe the unit of data collection and analysis is the 'case' (see Chapter 19). In this example, and others that follow, the units of analysis are people and the term 'subject' is used instead.

A third classification which will be needed is to recognize that *discrete* and *continuous* variables often call for the use of different statistical methods of analysis. Discrete variables take a small number of specific values and intermediate values have no meaning. The values often represent categories of response to a question or the classification of a subject into one of several categories. For example, in some situations, employment status may be recorded as one of two categories (0 = unemployed; 1 = employed) or may be given a more extensive classification (0 = full-time employee; 1 = self-employed; 2 = part-time employee; 3 = unemployed; 4 = not in the labour force). The first example, when there are only two possible responses, is an important special case of a discrete variable known as a *dichotomous* variable. Note that the variable values (e.g. 0 through 4 in the second example) have no arithmetic meaning. The order of the categories and the corresponding values are arbitrary. The category self-employed, for example, does not naturally occur between full-time employee and part-time employee. This is an example of a *nominal* scale discrete variable. Sometimes the category values will follow a natural order. For example the severity of a disease (0 = absent; 1 = mild; 2 = moderate; 3 = severe). This is an *ordinal* discrete variable and the values carry some arithmetic information since the category 'mild' does fall somewhere between absent and moderate. *Continuous* variables can in principle take any value in a possible range. Examples are age and income and a wide range of statistical methods are available for analyzing variables of this kind.

In the next section we divide the basic categorization of research projects into the three types and in the following sections methods of statistical analysis will be discussed.

Quantitative Research Topics in the Social Sciences

Small-scale Primary Surveys

Small-scale primary surveys or other forms of primary data collection are common for projects in which the research student is working alone and is responsible for planning and carrying out the study including data collection and analysis. Such studies are often characterized by limited resources and fieldwork which must be completed by the student. The sample size is often of 100 subjects or less. Frequently the subjects are very varied and the researcher recognizes that a wide range of individual characteristics may affect the dependent variable. The net result is a large number of variables collected from a relatively small sample.

In such studies the emphasis tends to be on descriptive analyses and simple contrasts. Analysis is often restricted to taking one explanatory variable at a time. Consider the example of the dichotomous reconviction variable for released prisoners. Separate cross-tabulations may be obtained of the reconviction rate against the age of the offender; whether or not the person has a stable cohabitational or marital relationship and possession of a trade or particular level of education. The analysis is restricted to one explanatory variable at a time since cross-tabulations of more variables (for example reconviction, age and the possession of a trade) will result in a large table with comparatively few cases in any cell. For example if there are five age groups and two categories each of reconviction and possession of a trade, then a three-way cross tabulation will contain $2 \times 5 \times 2 = 20$ cells with an average of about five cases in each if there is a total sample size of 100. The frustration is that initial comparisons often lead to interesting social science questions but the data is not extensive enough to pursue these.

Designed Experiments

The source of the difficulty for small scale primary surveys is that any comparison may involve quite disparate groups of subjects. If we compare the reconviction rate for 20–24 year old and 35–39 year old subjects for example, the two groups may also differ in a variety of other ways apart from age. The older subjects may have different work experience, marital status, education and training. It is difficult to attribute any difference in reconviction rate to age or any other explanatory factor because the effects of each cannot be isolated reliably.

An alternative approach is adopted by experimental scientists in some situations. A very limited set of specific hypotheses is identified which are thought to hold generally or in particular subsets of the population. An experiment is designed with the express intention of making specific comparisons between groups. The basic ideas have been described in Chapter 18.

Such studies sacrifice the general representativeness of the sample to the whole population and instead deliberately select subjects who are as similar as possible. The characteristic which is the focus of the specific hypothesis to be tested can be allocated to the subjects by the researcher (e.g. alternative methods of treatment, or levels of service). The net result is that even for small sample sizes, specific hypotheses can be tested and useful conclusions drawn.

Large-scale Secondary Survey Analyses

The third category is large-scale secondary data analysis which is described in Chapter 20. Often this arises as secondary analysis of survey data held in the ESRC Data Archive. Alternatively the research student may be located in a department where a large-scale study is being undertaken. A team of researchers and research students who are familiar with the data will exist and sub-projects with more narrowly focused objectives are assigned to individual researchers.

In terms of statistical analyses, many of the restrictions and limitations of small-scale surveys are effectively removed and more extensive and more sophisticated analyses can be undertaken. The data set may comprise a few thousand cases or more. Each dependent variable may be analyzed by including a number of explanatory variables. Alternative explanations can be investigated and a much deeper understanding of the social process achieved. It would, however, be wrong to think that large scale data analysis is a panacea for social research. Often, as described in Chapter 20, the variables available are not precisely the ones which a researcher with a specific objective would have measured. Furthermore such studies are generally observational rather than controlled experiments with the usual drawbacks which this implies for exploring causal mechanisms.

Analyzing Small Scale Surveys

Data Display and Description

We begin with basic statistical description and graphical methods for displaying data. This is important because it creates familiarity with the data set and identifies the responses which are typically given and the range of responses offered by subjects. Also, unusual cases can be identified. These may be genuine or the result of errors in the data as a result of mistakes in coding and processing the data to create a computer file. Preliminary checks and reference to the original source documents is an important stage in building up confidence in the data quality.

Consider a discrete variable such as the response to an attitudinal question or a continuous variable such as scores for a reading test for schoolchildren. The *distribution* of responses refers to the *relative frequency* with which different values occur in the data. Graphical methods can be used to

Figure 1:   *Distribution of responses to statement about teamwork for 608 Nurses*

Response	Percentage	
Strongly agree	31.8	*****************
Agree	51.5	**************************
Neither agree or disagree	8.1	****
Disagree	7.3	****
Strongly disagree	1.3	*
	100.0	

Figure 2:   *Age distribution of nurses*

Age	Percentage	
20–24	7.2	*********
25–29	19.2	********************************
30–34	14.1	**************************
35–39	12.0	***********************
40–44	18.6	*********************************
45–49	11.0	*************
50–54	9.2	************
55–59	7.6	*********
60–64	1.0	**
	100.0	

display the distribution and it can be summarized into a small number of numerical values.

The distribution of responses for a discrete variable may be displayed graphically by plotting a *bar chart* in which the length of each bar reflects the number of subjects giving each response. Figure 1 shows the bar chart and corresponding percentages for responses given by 608 nurses to the statement that teamwork was a strong feature of their work environment. For many research students, their data set will be much smaller than 608 cases but this example will be used throughout this section to illustrate essential points.

There is a clear preference towards agreement with the statement since 31.8 per cent strongly agree with the statement and a further 51.5 per cent agree with it. The percentage in each category of response gives a set of numerical values which summarize the distribution. Since the categories are ordered, a number of other summary values may be useful such as that in total 83.3 per cent express some form of agreement or 8.6 per cent express some form of disagreement.

For continuous variables alternative methods of displaying the data are required since in principle every response could yield a different value. Graphical display of the data may be obtained using a *histogram* or *stem and leaf* plot which are essentially similar in their objective. Figure 2 shows a histogram for the distribution of ages of the nurses. Computer programmes display the histogram as a set of equal age subdivisions (e.g. age 20–24, 25–29, 30–34 years etc.). The number of respondents in each range is shown by the length of the corresponding plot.

The distribution can be summarized by *measures of location and spread*. For example, the *average* (or mean) age of the respondents is 38.4 years although there are nurses as young as 21 years and as old as 63 years. A measure of spread is the *standard deviation* which in this case is 10.4 years. This is described fully in statistics texts but as a rough rule of thumb most nurses will have ages within two standard deviations from the mean. Two standard deviations below the mean is 38.4 − 2 (10.4) = 17.6 years, and two above is 38.4 + 2 (10.4) = 59.2 years. Most nurses will have ages within this range.

The distribution of ages can be described more precisely by quoting the ages below which fixed proportions of the nurses occur. For example, 50 per cent of the nurses are younger than 38.5 years which is known as the *median* age. Similarly 25 per cent of nurses are younger than 29.0 years and 25 per cent are older than 46.0 years. These are the lower and upper quartiles respectively. These three values (the median and the two quartiles) can summarize the distribution of ages in a fairly informative way. A graphical display of this information is given in a box plot as shown in Figure 3:

Figure 3:   *Box plot of age distribution of nurses*

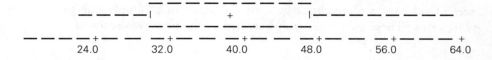

The median age is shown inside the box and the lower and upper quartiles are the ends of the box. The extensions beyond the box show the total extent of the data from the youngest nurse to the oldest. Thus in a single image an impression of the age distribution of the nurses is conveyed.

If the distribution is fairly symmetric then the mean and median will be similar in value. However if the distribution is asymmetric (skewed) then the median is unaffected whereas the mean tends to be influenced by the extreme values in the tail of the distribution. This is common for many social science variables such as income. For this reason the median and quartiles are preferred as a description of the distribution when skewness is exhibited. For statistical procedures described in the following sections the mean and standard deviation are more widely used.

In virtually all social science contexts, the subjects are known to be diverse and the researcher will wish to break down the data into identifiable subgroups for further investigation. Thus, to continue with the nurse example, we may wish to separate nurses by grade (sister, staff nurse, enrolled nurse) and to examine the responses of each group separately. The same methods of graphical display and statistical measures may be applied to each subgroup. For discrete data this leads naturally to cross-tabulations of response category by explanatory variable. Percentages should sum to 100 within each category of the explanatory variable.

Sampling Variation

The average age of the 608 nurses in the previous section was 38.4 years. Interest does not focus on these nurses for their own sake, but for what they tell us about the wider population of nurses. We seek conclusions which hold more generally than for the 608 nurses in the sample. The value 38.4 years is the sample average. Under certain conditions relating to the way the sample was selected, it is the best estimate of the average age for the more general population of nurses. However an estimate cannot be perfectly accurate and a different sample of 608 nurses would have yielded a different average. The distribution of different sample averages that occurs from one sample to another is called the *sampling distribution* and the difference between any of these averages and the true population value is called the *sampling error*.

We need to know how much reliance we can place on any estimate and whether or not any difference which we observe between the sample averages of subgroups represents a genuine difference or is simply due to sampling error. These two issues are described in the next two sections.

Testing Statistical Hypotheses

The average ages of the sample of 281 sisters and 179 staff nurses are 42.2 and 35.9 years respectively. The question is whether it is plausible that in general sisters are no older on average than staff nurses. The observed difference of 6.3 years could be attributable to the chance fluctuation resulting from a particular sample of 460 nurses being selected. This is an important question because we do not wish to over-interpret the statistical results. Before making too much of the apparent age difference we need to be reassured that it reflects a genuine difference rather than chance variation in the data.

The essential features start with the idea of a *null hypothesis* that in fact the average ages of sisters and staff nurses in the general population of nurses are the same. If this were true, the statistical procedures establish how plausible it would be to obtain a sample of 281 sisters and 179 staff nurses with a difference in average age of 6.3 years or larger. To test the null hypothesis, the observed difference of 6.3 years is compared with the range of variation that might occur simply by chance. If the age difference is small compared to

Figure 4a: Test that average age of sisters equals that of staff nurses

Sisters n = 281	average age of sample = 42.2 years	st. dev = 9.2
Staff Nurses n = 179	average age of sample = 35.9 years	st. dev = 10.7
P-value = 0.0000		

Figure 4b: Test that average age of staff nurses equals that of enrolled nurses

Staff Nurses n = 179	average age of sample = 35.9 years	st. dev = 10.7
Enrolled Nurses n = 148	average age of sample = 34.1 years	st. dev = 9.5
P-value = 0.1020		

the differences that could occur by chance alone then the null hypothesis will be accepted and we conclude that the observed difference may not reflect a real difference in average ages between the two groups. If, on the other hand, the observed difference is larger than we would expect from chance fluctuation then we reject the null hypothesis (that the two groups have the same average age) in favour of the *alternative* hypothesis that the observed difference reflects a genuine difference of some magnitude.

No statistical conclusion is ever absolutely certain and this is reflected in the way computer packages will report the test result. The essential piece of information is a *P-value* which measures the probability that if the null hypothesis is true, the observed difference in average ages for the samples from the two groups is the result of chance fluctuation. Figure 4a gives the result of one particular statistical test (known as a t-test) for sisters versus staff nurses and Figure 4b gives the corresponding analysis for staff nurses versus enrolled nurses.

The difference in average ages between staff nurses and enrolled nurses (Figure 4b) is 35.9 − 34.1 = 1.8 years. The P-value quoted is 0.102. This means that there is a 10.2 per cent chance that a difference at least as large as 1.8 years would result from chance fluctuation alone if the true average ages of staff nurses and enrolled nurses were the same. The analysis in Figure 4a is stronger since the P-value quoted is 0.0000. There is a 0 per cent chance (actually less than 0.01 per cent chance since the P-value is displayed to four decimal places) that if the average ages are the same in the two categories the observed difference of 6.3 years has occurred in the sample by chance (actually less than 0.01 per cent chance since the P-value is displayed to four decimal places) that if the average ages are the same in the two categories the observed difference of 6.3 years has occurred in the sample by chance

Figure 5: Sisters 'and staff nurses' responses to the statement that teamwork was an important component of the work situation

	Strongly agree	Agree	Neither agree nor disagree	Disagree	Strongly disagree
Sisters	95 (43.1%)	138 (49.5%)	23 (8.2%)	18 (6.5%)	5 (1.8%)
Staff Nurses	49 (27.4%)	106 (59.2%)	11 (6.1%)	12 (6.7%)	1 (0.6%)

selection of the respondents. Since it is so unlikely that the observed difference has occurred in this way we have a firm basis to reject the null hypothesis in favour of the alternative that a genuine difference in average age exists.

Earlier we noted that the median was preferred as a descriptive statistic if the underlying distribution was asymmetric. For small samples there is a corresponding preference for test procedures which are known as *non-parametric methods* and which make no assumptions about the underlying distributional properties. For hypothesis testing the most common procedures are the Mann–Whitney test and the Wilcoxon test although there are a number of others. When the distribution is approximately symmetric (see a description of the *Normal* distribution in texts) the preferred methods such as the t-test are based on stronger assumptions but are more powerful. Corresponding procedures are used to estimate confidence intervals (see next section).

For discrete dependent variables the distribution is summarized by the proportion of cases in each category. The responses to a five-category attitudinal question will be summarized by a set of five proportions that sum to one. The procedure which corresponds to comparing the means of a continuous dependent variable for two groups is to compare the two sets of proportions. Figure 5 shows the response to the statement of whether teamwork was an important component of the work for sisters and staff nurses.

We test whether or not the two distributions of proportions could be considered the same. Do both sisters and staff nurses give similar patterns of response or do sisters, for example, more strongly agree with the proposition about teamwork? Hypotheses of this kind can be tested using χ^2 *(chi-squared)* testing procedures for two-way tables. As for all tests, the result will be presented as a P-value which is interpreted as described earlier.

There remains the question of how strong the evidence must be before we can confidently rest on any test conclusion. There is no definitive answer to this question since it depends on the level of risk (the *significance level*) which the researcher is prepared to accept that the conclusion of a genuine difference in age, for example, is in fact wrong. Usual levels of risk are 1 per cent or 5 per cent. Thus for a 5 per cent risk (a 5 per cent significance level), if the P-value reported is less than 0.05 then we reject the null hypothesis in favour of the alternative. Many statisticians would argue that historically there has been far too much attention paid to testing hypotheses and a slavish adherence to the result of a 5 per cent or 1 per cent P-value. There is force in this argument but it is very important that differences observed in data are not over-interpreted and a measure of the statistical significance of observed differences is important.

One other caveat must be strongly emphasized. A test measures how likely it is that the observed difference could have resulted by chance fluctuation alone. If we reject the null hypothesis we say that the observed difference is statistically significant. The distinction between statistical significance and substantive significance is very important. Statistical significance helps us to conclude that a genuine difference exists. If the sample sizes are large enough even a small difference (say a difference in average age of 6 months between the sisters and staff nurses) will be identified as statistically significant. However, a small difference may be of little substantive interest. The differences worth reporting are those that are both statistically and substantively significant and the second of these is a social science judgment rather than a statistical one.

Estimating Confidence Intervals

In many situations the emphasis will not be on testing hypotheses but on making estimates of the difference between groups. For the example of nurses' ages it is no surprise that the average age of sisters is greater than that of staff nurses. A significance test of the hypothesis of equal average age may be of no real interest. We wish to estimate how large the difference is.

The estimated difference of 6.3 years is known as a *point estimate* of the age difference. It is a single value which is our best estimate of the true age difference between the two staff categories. A point estimate alone is of limited use because we cannot be sure how much reliance to place on the value.

Procedures exist to estimate a *confidence interval* for the age difference. Applying one such procedure (the t-interval) to the comparison of sisters and staff nurses we obtain a 95 per cent confidence interval of 4.35 to 8.15 years. The formal interpretation of this range is that with probability 0.95 the range of values from 4.35 to 8.15 years covers the true difference in average age between the two grades of nurse. The estimate of 6.3 years is the best point estimate for the difference but the confidence interval gives an indication of a range which is likely to cover the true value. The choice of a 95 per cent confidence interval is somewhat arbitrary. A higher confidence of 99 per cent could be achieved but at the expense of making the interval wider and therefore perhaps less useful. A lower confidence interval would be narrower but with an increased risk that it did not cover the true difference between the two groups.

The main ideas in this section have been to summarize the distribution of the variable of interest by using a small number of numerical values. Separation of the data into subgroups is a natural development and allows similar methods to be used on each subgroup. Before making too much of subgroup differences there is a need to check that the differences shown in the sample data represent real differences in the underlying populations and significance tests are a method of assessing this. Point estimates of population values or of differences between groups are of primary interest but the use of confidence intervals gives more information on the possible range of values.

Designed Experiments

The essential idea of a simple two-group *designed experiment* is that the researcher can allocate subjects to either the *control* or *treatment* group and by comparing the means of a dependent variable within each of the two groups infer the effect of the treatment (see Chapter 18). This idea may be extended to a comparison of several treatments or to a combination of treatments. Data from designed experiments may be analyzed in the same way as described above. For comparison of more than two treatment groups the techniques of Analysis of Variance, often abbreviated to ANOVA may be used.

For the simple two-group designed experiment the assumption is that the two groups differ only in respect of the treatment. Other important characteristics of the subjects which may affect the dependent variable are assumed not to differ systematically between the treatment and control groups. This assumption rests on the researcher allocating the subjects to the two groups at random.

Sometimes, despite random allocation of subjects to treatment groups, there will exist differences between the groups apart from the treatment. For example a designed experiment to assess a new method of teaching reading may assign children to a control group and an experimental group (new method). However, despite random allocation, the groups may still differ systematically with respect to scores on a reading test administered before the experiment. If this is not taken into account, observed differences in reading scores for a test administered at the end of the experiment may be attributed to the teaching method but may, in fact, be due to initial differences in reading ability between the groups. The techniques of ANOVA can be extended to take account of such prior measurements using the technique of Analysis of Covariance (ACOVA).

In the social sciences, often the researcher cannot allocate subjects to treatments. For example some schools may introduce the new teaching method and others keep the old method. The researcher cannot allocate children to the schools but must work within the usual school enrolment procedures. This is an observational study or quasi-experiment. The same methods of analysis are used but the basis for assigning causality to the conclusions is weakened (see Chapter 18).

When designing quasi-experiments, the researcher will select subjects that improve the validity of the comparison. For example, one school may use the new teaching method and another not. However the schools may also differ in terms of the proportion of boys and girls, or the social background of the children. Particular children may be chosen from each school so that they match on gender and social background and thus are similar except for the teaching method. The idea of representative samples from each school is abandoned in favour of samples that are as similar as possible except for the teaching method.

The choice of design of an experiment can have a considerable impact on what statistical conclusions can be drawn from the data generated by the experiment. Efficient designs can make even small samples effective. It is therefore advisable to seek the advice of a statistician if a design of any complexity is required.

The Analysis of Large-Scale Surveys

The disadvantage of small-scale surveys is that the data are not extensive enough to pursue the questions which arise from preliminary analyses. Consider a small-scale study of reconviction rates for released prisoners. We observe an apparent relationship between the reconviction rate and possession of a trade. However similar results are observed in relation to other explanatory variables. Each finding rests on a simple analysis of the dependent variable (reconviction) and one explanatory variable at a time. We would like a single analysis to identify which were the most important factors and whether these reinforced each other or acted independently. This is an example of *multivariate analysis*. Using small samples it is very difficult in practice to disentangle the effects of the various factors with any confidence.

For large-scale data analysis these problems are, to a large extent, overcome and a variety of factors can be integrated into a single analysis. The approach to this is known as *statistical model building* and the dependent variable is related to a set of explanatory variables through an algebraic expression. The most familiar form of statistical model building is *linear regression analysis*.

Figure 6: *Simple regression of Y on X*

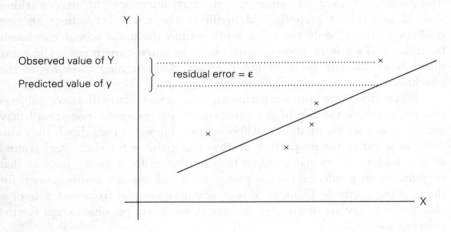

The simplest expression involves only one explanatory variable, X, and we summarize the relationship between the dependent variable, Y, and X by the equation

$$Y = a + bX + \varepsilon.$$

For the model defined by this equation the expected or average value of Y for a given value X of the explanatory variable is given by a + bX and this is represented by the straight line in Figure 6. The value a is known as the intercept and is the expected value for Y when X = 0. The value b is the slope and for every increase of one in X, the expected value for Y increases by b. If b is negative the expected value for Y decreases as X increases. The relationship between Y and X is not perfectly explained by the straight line and ε, the residual error, represents the amount by which each subject's Y value differs from that predicted by the straight line.

We may extend the idea and introduce additional explanatory variables. The statistical model becomes more complex, but is a better explanation of why the dependent variable varies from one subject to another. In algebraic terms further factors would be introduced as extra explanatory, X variables.

$$Y = a + b_1X_1 + b_2X_2 + b_3X_3 + \ldots + \varepsilon$$

The statistical modelling process seeks to identify as simple a model as possible while obtaining a good fit to the data. The procedure involves several stages:

1 The choice of potential explanatory variables to include in the model.
2 Adding and subtracting variables according to their effectiveness.
3 Examining the success of the model (goodness of fit) at each stage.
4 Examining the way in which each subject differs from the model to identify poor fit and to suggest refinements to the model.
5 Checking the distributional properties of the residual errors and adjusting the fitting procedure accordingly.
6 After arriving at a final expression for the model, interpreting the results.
7 Predicting the values of the dependent variable (Y) for particular values of the explanatory variables (X) if required.

A detailed description of these steps is beyond the scope of this chapter but it is important to understand the essential purpose. We seek to explain as much as possible of the variation between one subject and another by virtue of the values of the explanatory variables for each subject. The residual variation is the failure of the model to explain all the variation in the dependent variable between subjects by using the explanatory variables. We seek to minimize this. It is important to think about each explanatory variable and the way in which it affects the outcome of the dependent variable. This requires an understanding of the social process, the interrelationship between variables and the measurement process. It forces a mental discipline when thinking about explanation of social phenomena which can be very beneficial.

The above general discussion has been considered in terms of a continuous dependent variable and a linear regression model because this is the framework that is likely to be familiar to most readers. Indeed statistical methods such as the comparison of group means, the Analysis of Variance and the Analysis of Covariance can all be placed within the framework of regression analysis. However, the general approach is broader than this and can incorporate data of a wide variety of kinds. In particular discrete dependent variables and count data from cross-tabulations can all be modelled using advanced techniques. Cross-tabulations for example are perhaps the most common form of output from social research. Modelling techniques (under the general description of *loglinear* models for *contingency tables*) are widely used and computer software is widely available. This topic is not generally covered in introductory statistical texts but the reader is referred to Reynolds (1977) or Swafford (1980). When the dependent variable is discrete, and covariates may be a mixture of discrete and continuous variables, another modelling technique — known as *logistic* modelling — is available (see Anderson *et al.*, 1980). Like the use of loglinear models for contingency table, this is a more advanced technique for which specialist texts need to be consulted.

An important special class of analysis problems is becoming more dominant in social science research literature. These relate to life histories or event histories where the variable of interest is the duration of some event or condition. For example the length of time between a woman marrying or cohabiting and bearing a child, or the length of time between the first child's birth and a second. A second field of application is to the labour market where the duration between becoming unemployed and gaining new employment is of interest. From a social science perspective one would wish to investigate the factors that affect the duration. Special methods of analysis, known as *event history analysis* or *survival analysis* are required. An introduction to these methods is given in Allison (1989).

Further Reading

There are many introductions to statistical analysis available, but minor differences in terminology and notation between these texts and manuals for statistical computer packages can be confusing for students who lack confidence in statistics. Such students may prefer texts which present examples using specific packages. Introductions which cover the methods discussed above and give examples based on MINITAB are Kitchens (1987), Kvanli (1988), McGhee (1985) and Pagano (1986); a corresponding text with examples in SPSS is provided by Frude (1987). See Chapter 19 on survey methods for comments on the use of alternative statistical packages. Another useful text focusing on data description and display is Marsh (1989). The analysis of designed experiments using ANOVA and ACOVA is discussed in Keppel and Saufley (1980). For an introduction to regression and statistical modelling see Kleinbaum *et al.* (1988). Introductions to a variety of other more advanced methods are provided by the Sage Quantitative Social Science series of which Allison (1989) is an instance, although it is inadvisable to embark on the use of sophisticated procedures without appropriate statistical training.

References

ALLISON, P.D. (1989) *Event History Analysis: Regression for Longitudinal Event Data*, Newbury Park, Sage.
ANDERSON, S., AUQUIER, A., HAUCK, W., OAKES, D., VANDEALE, W. and WEISBERG, H. (1980) *Statistical Methods for Comparative Studies*, New York, Wiley.
FRUDE, N. (1987) *A Guide to SPSS/PC+*, London, Macmillan.
KEPPEL, G. and SAUFLEY, W.H. (1980) *Introduction to Design and Analysis*, New York, W.H. Freeman.
KITCHENS, L.J. (1987) *Exploring Statistics*, St. Paul, West.
KLEINBAUM, D.G., KUPPER, L.L. and MULLER, K.E. (1988) *Applied Regression Analysis and Other Multivariate Methods*, Boston, PWS-Kent.
KVANLI, A.H. (1988) *Statistics: A Computer Integrated Approach*, St. Paul, West.

MARSH, C. (1989) *Exploring Data*, Cambridge, Polity Press.

McGHEE, J.W. (1985) *Introductory Statistics*, St. Paul, West.

PAGANO, R.R. (1986) *Understanding Statistics in the Behavioural Sciences*, St. Paul, West.

REYNOLDS, H.T. (1977) *The Analysis of Cross-Tabulations*, Glencoe, Free Press.

SWAFFORD, M. (1980) 'Three parametric techniques for contingency table analysis: A nontechnical commentary', *American Journal of Sociology*, **45**, pp. 664–90.

Index

abbreviations, use of 100
Abramson, J.H. 218, 222
abstracts, use of
abstracting 69, 75
access
  to computers 65–6
  to data 128–9, 131–3, 182, 229, 248, 255
  to documents 118
  to facilities 12, 38, 48, 60, 62
  for interviews 209
  to research 158, 169–70, 173
  to samples 231
Adelman, C. 191, 201
adjustment to study 12, 18, 20, 39
age and interviews 211–12
agencies, negotiating with 3, 128–30, 173–4
  access to agency-generated data 132–3
  data analysis and reports 135–6
  data collection, establishing contact with agency users 134–5
  data collection, involving agency 133–4
  identification of data sources 132
  objectives of research, formulation of 130
  partnership and credibility 136–7
  presentation of formal proposal 130–1
  presentation and dissemination of findings 136
Alexander, P. 219

Allan, G. 177–88
Allison, P.D. 272
analysis
  computer data 244–5
  data 18–19, 32, 44, 61, 135–6, 143, 153, 163, 174–5, 177, 179, 181, 183, 192, 215–17, 220–1, 245–6, 268
  qualitative research 177–88
  statistical 169, 190, 251–4
  survey 243–6
Anderson, M. 249
Anderson, S. *et al.* 219, 271
androcentrism 37, 153–4, 156
anonymity 132–3, 135, 140, 148–9
ANOVA (analysis of variance) 268, 271
appeals 12
appendix, writing an 54, 96
apprentices, postgraduates as 15, 47
aptitude 226–7, 229, 250
Arber, S. 251, 252, 254, 256, 257
Arregui, Begoña 39–42
archives 61, 117–19, 198
  data 254, 256, 261
argument, intellectual 55–6, 105, 111, 185
assessment 9, 12
Atkinson, P. 187, 204, 206, 207, 208, 209, 210, 211, 212
Atkins, M. 14
attitude scales 226, 234–6, 266
audience and oral presentation 108–11, 113–15